WARREN PLEECE · SHAZLEEN KHAN · ROBIN JONES

# FREEDOM BOUND

Written and Drawn by **Warren Pleece**

Additional text and Story based on research by
**Simon P. Newman and Nelson Mundell**

Inks & Colours for Chapter 1 & 2 by **Shazleen Khan**

Lettering by **Robin Jones**

Publication design by Kirsty Hunter

Edited by Sha Nazir & Jack Lothian

All stories are based on research from the Runaway Slaves project by the University of Glasgow, Andrew Hook Centre for American Studies.

**For more information on the project visit Runaway Slaves in Britain project, www.runaways.gla.ac.uk**

First printing 2018. Published in Glasgow by BHP Comics Ltd.





Made in Scotland. Printed in Great Britain by Bell & Bain Ltd.

ISBN: 978-1-910775-12-7 (Hardback)
ISBN: 978-1-910775-13-4 (Softback)

A CIP catalogue reference for this book is available from the British Library Ask your local comic or book shop to stock BHP Comics.

**Visit BHPcomics.com for more info.**

---

Research for the 'Runaway Slaves in Britain' project was funded by the Leverhulme Trust. Freedom Bound was supported by an Impact Acceleration award by the Economic and Social Research Council, and a grant from the College of Arts of the University of Glasgow.

We are grateful to all of the following for their advice and support in the creation of this work: Ms. Morayo Akandé, Ms. Moyo Akandé, Prof. John W. Cairns, Dr. Roslyn Chapman, Dr. Stephen Mullen, and Mr. May Sumbwanyambe.

Any profits from Freedom Bound accruing to the University of Glasgow and its staff will go to the McCune Smith Fund. This fund is named in honour of James McCune Smith, who was born a slave in New York City, but gained his freedom and three degrees from the University of Glasgow, in the process becoming the first African American to receive a medical degree.

---

LEVERHULME TRUST

RUNAWAY SLAVES IN BRITAIN

E·S·R·C ECONOMIC & SOCIAL RESEARCH COUNCIL

University of Glasgow

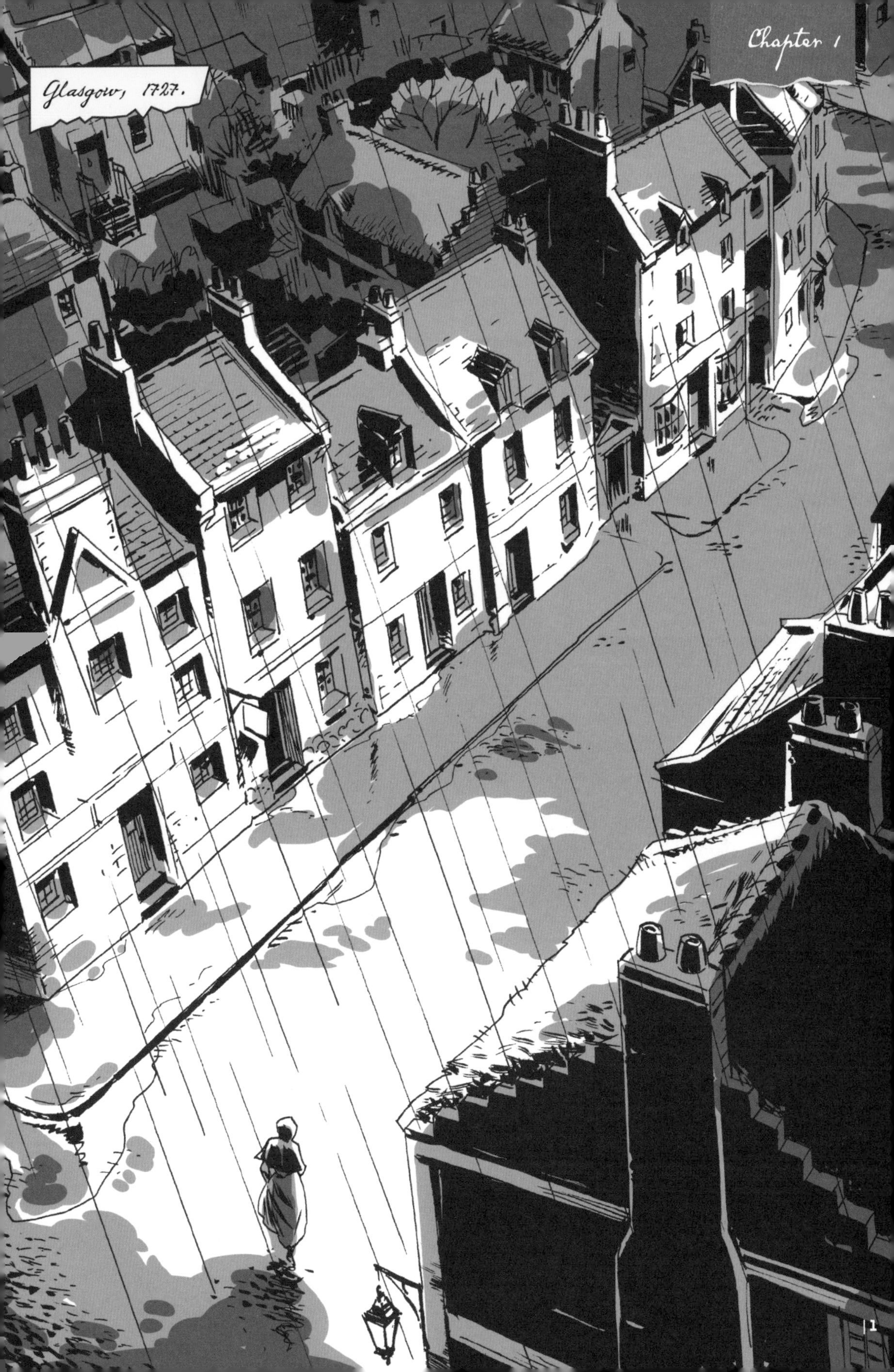
Chapter 1
Glasgow, 1727.

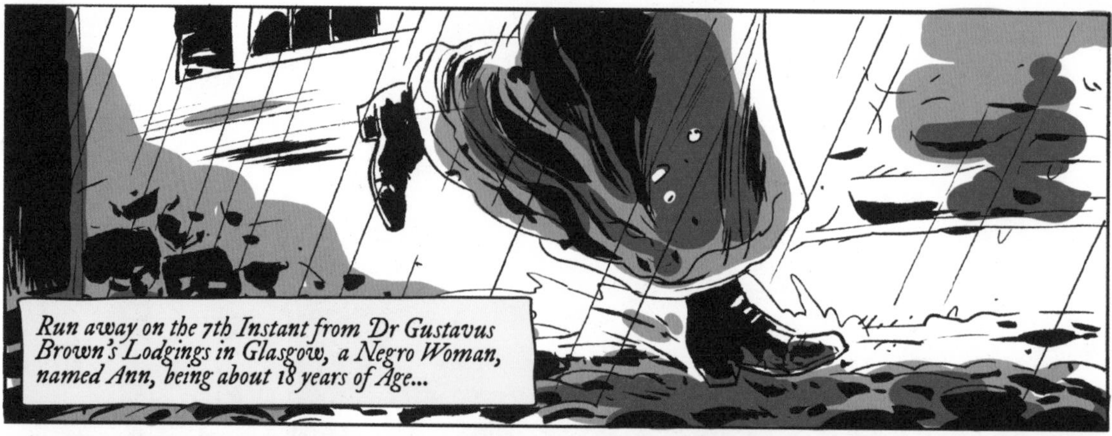
*Run away on the 7th Instant from Dr Gustavus Brown's Lodgings in Glasgow, a Negro Woman, named Ann, being about 18 years of Age...*

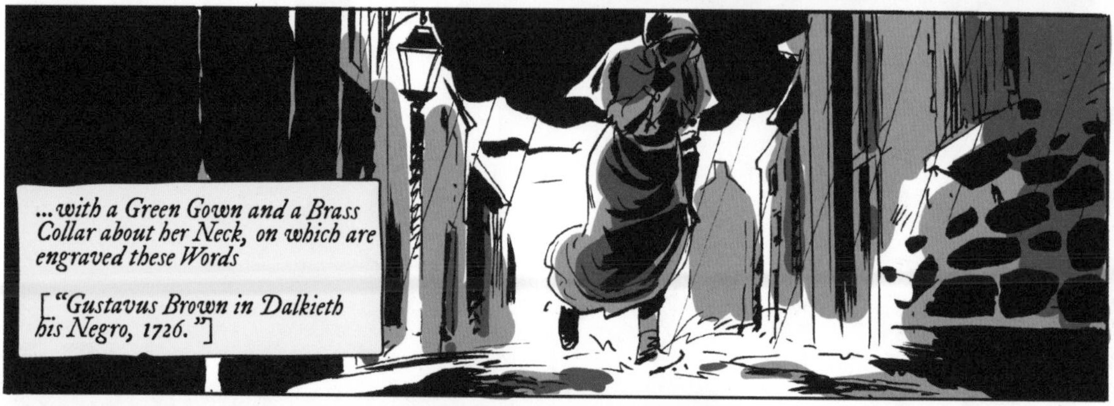
*...with a Green Gown and a Brass Collar about her Neck, on which are engraved these Words*
*["Gustavus Brown in Dalkieth his Negro, 1726."]*

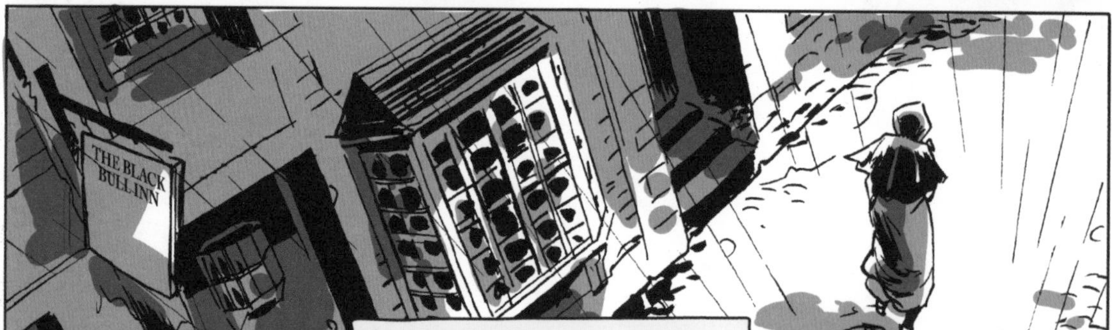
THE BLACK BULL·INN
*Whoever apprehends her, so as she may be recovered shall have Two Guineas Reward, and necessary Charges...*

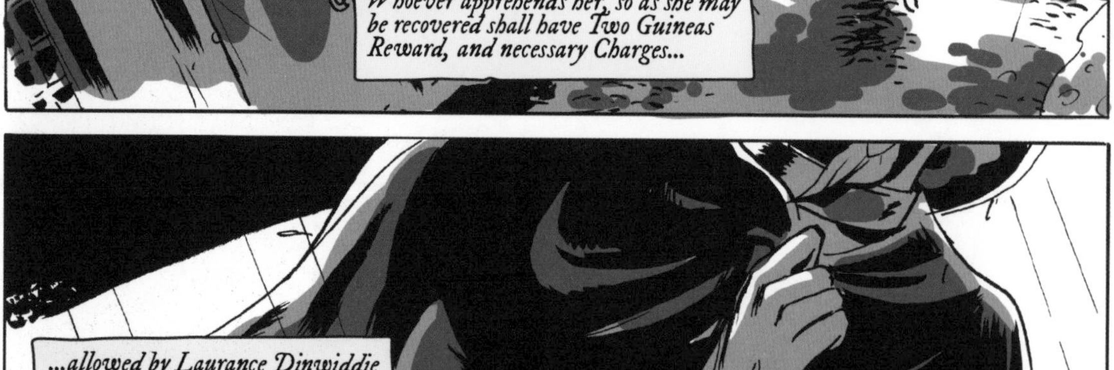
*...allowed by Laurance Dinwiddie Junior Merchant in Glasgow, or by James Mitchellson, Jeweller in Edinburgh.*

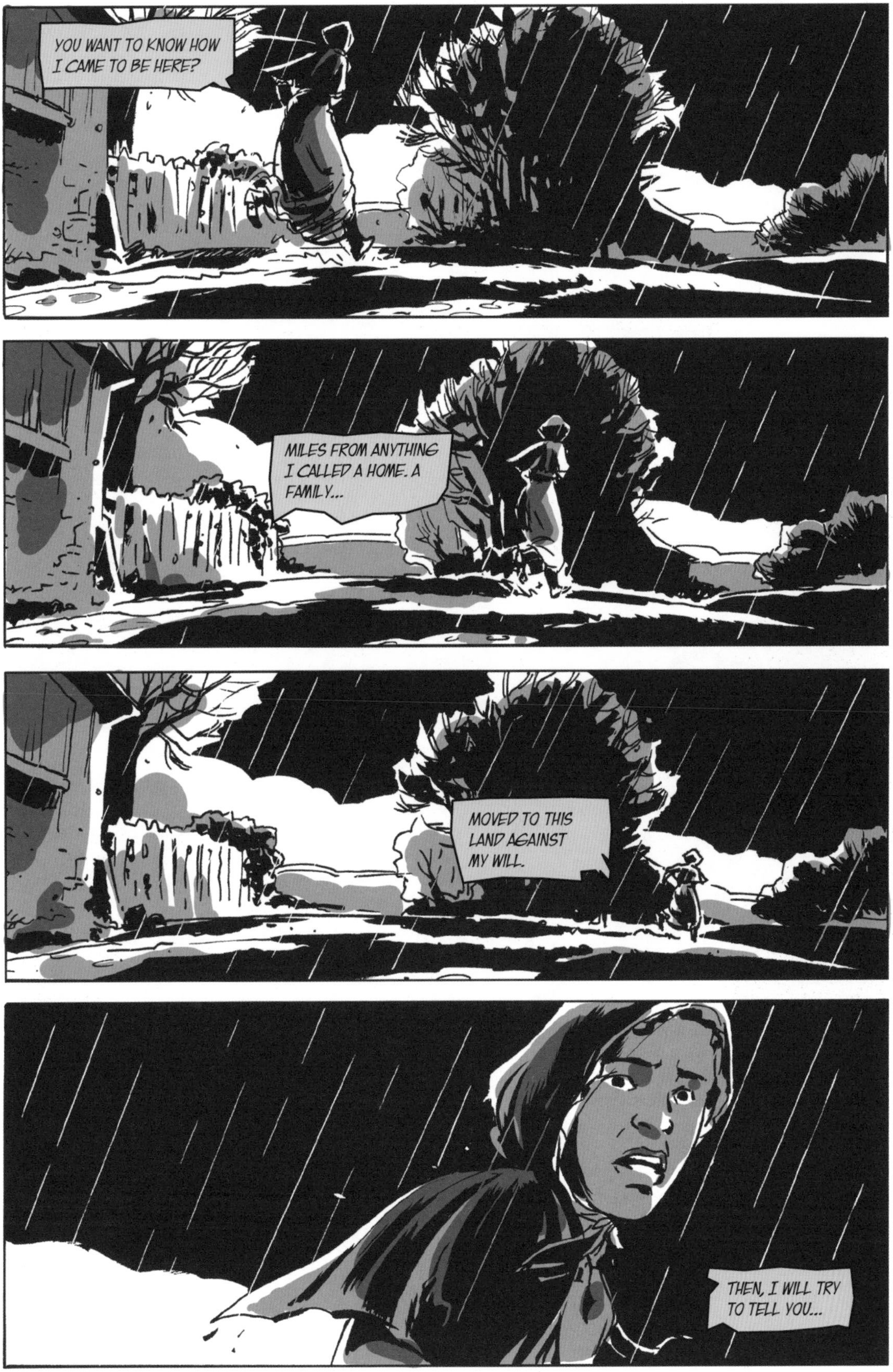
YOU WANT TO KNOW HOW I CAME TO BE HERE?
MILES FROM ANYTHING I CALLED A HOME. A FAMILY...
MOVED TO THIS LAND AGAINST MY WILL.
THEN, I WILL TRY TO TELL YOU...

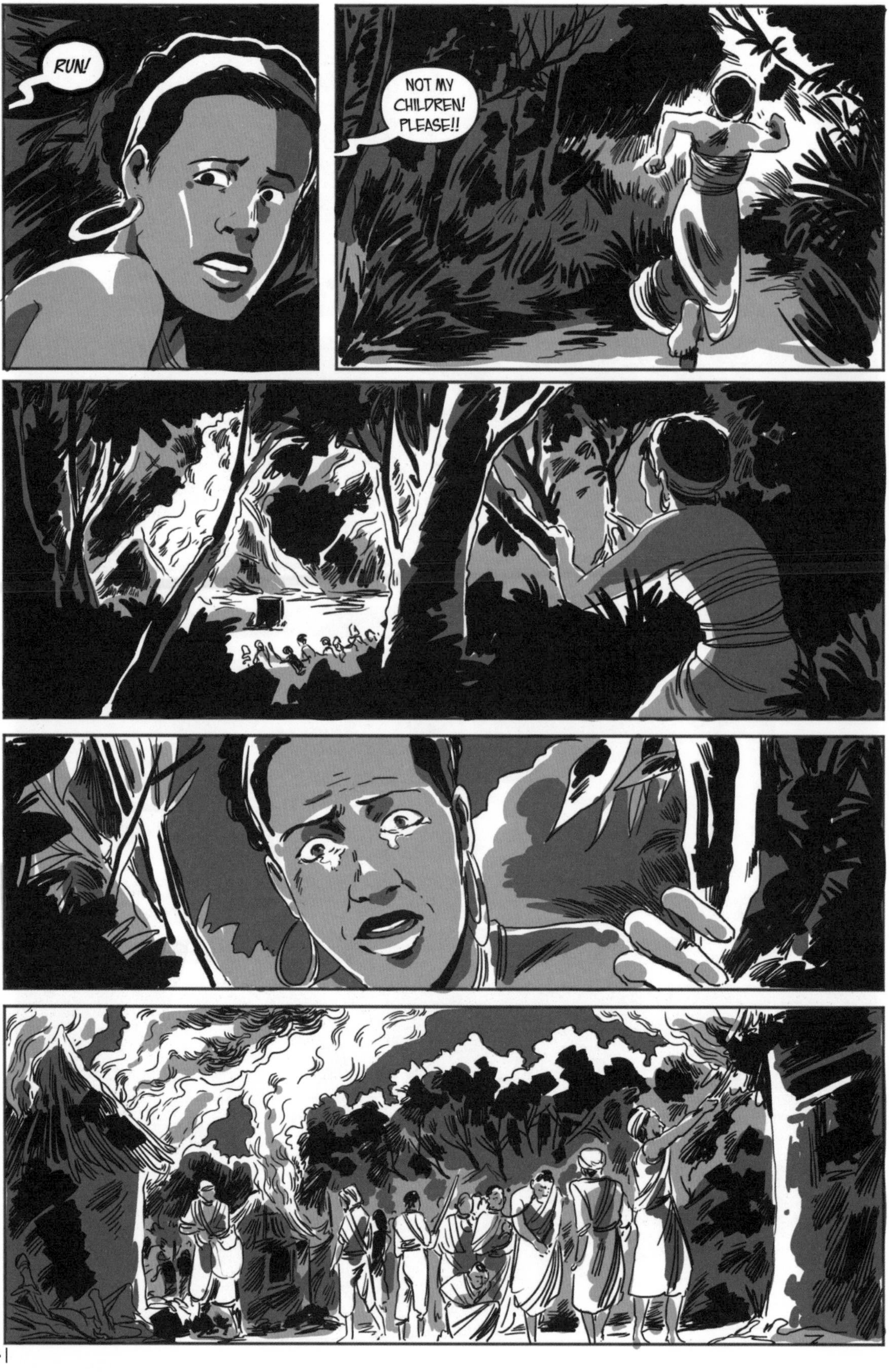
RUN!
NOT MY CHILDREN! PLEASE!!

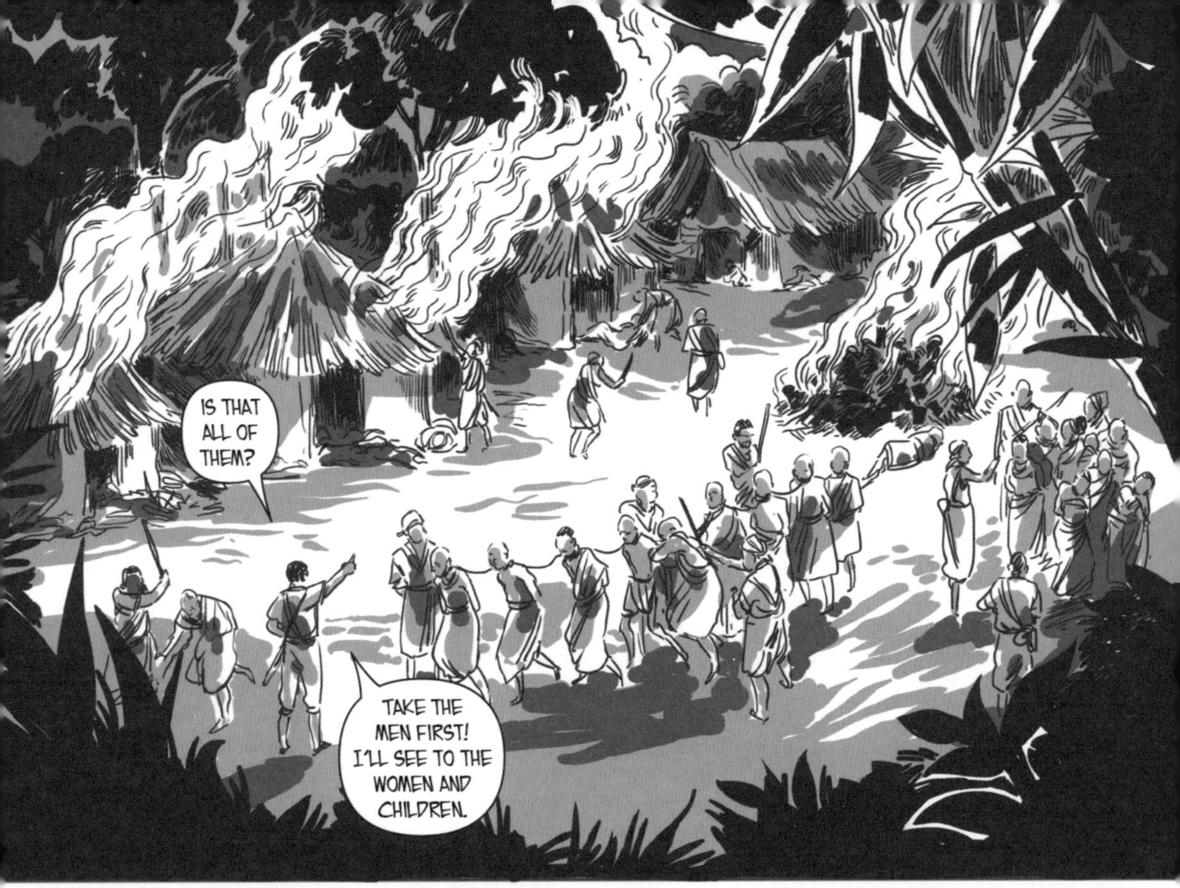
IS THAT ALL OF THEM?
TAKE THE MEN FIRST! I'LL SEE TO THE WOMEN AND CHILDREN.

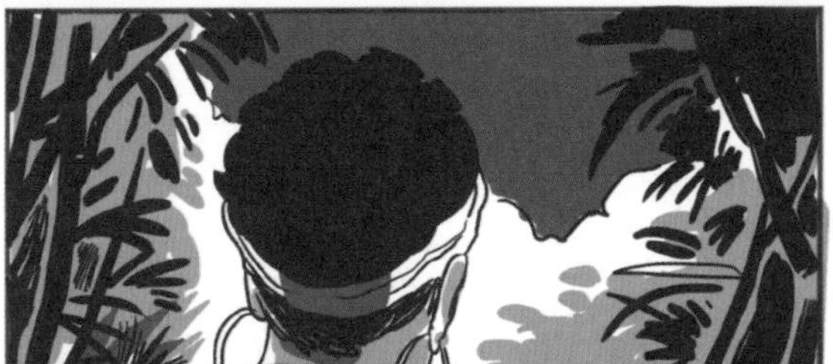

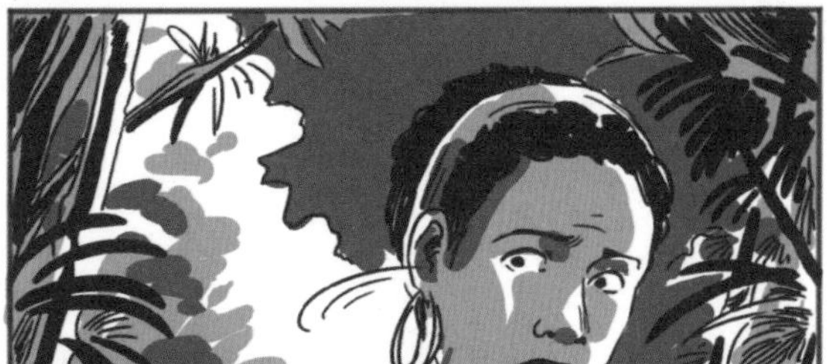

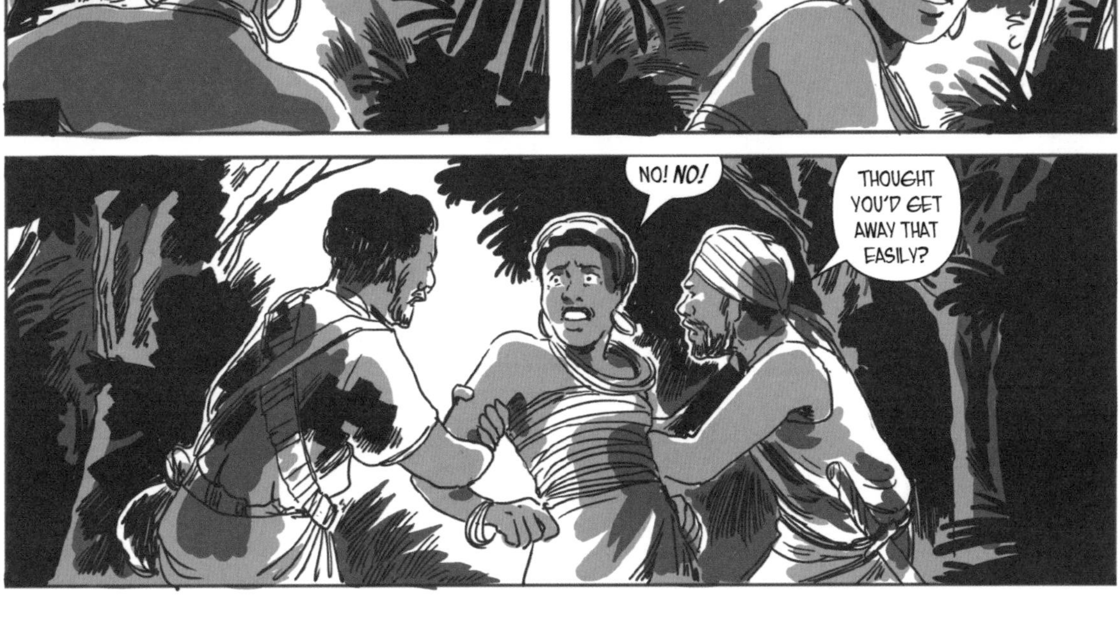
NO! NO!
THOUGHT YOU'D GET AWAY THAT EASILY?

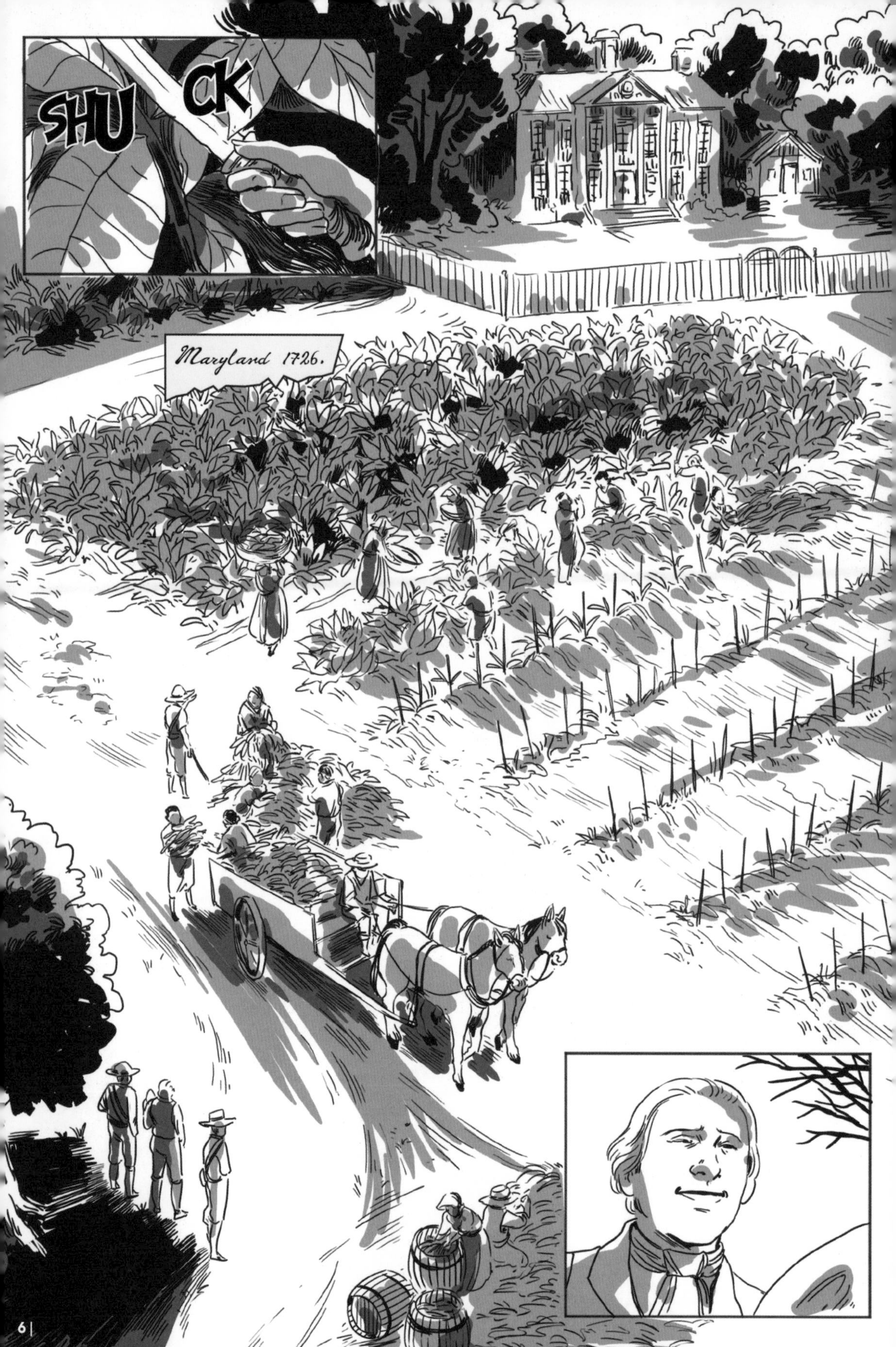
SHU CK
Maryland 1726.

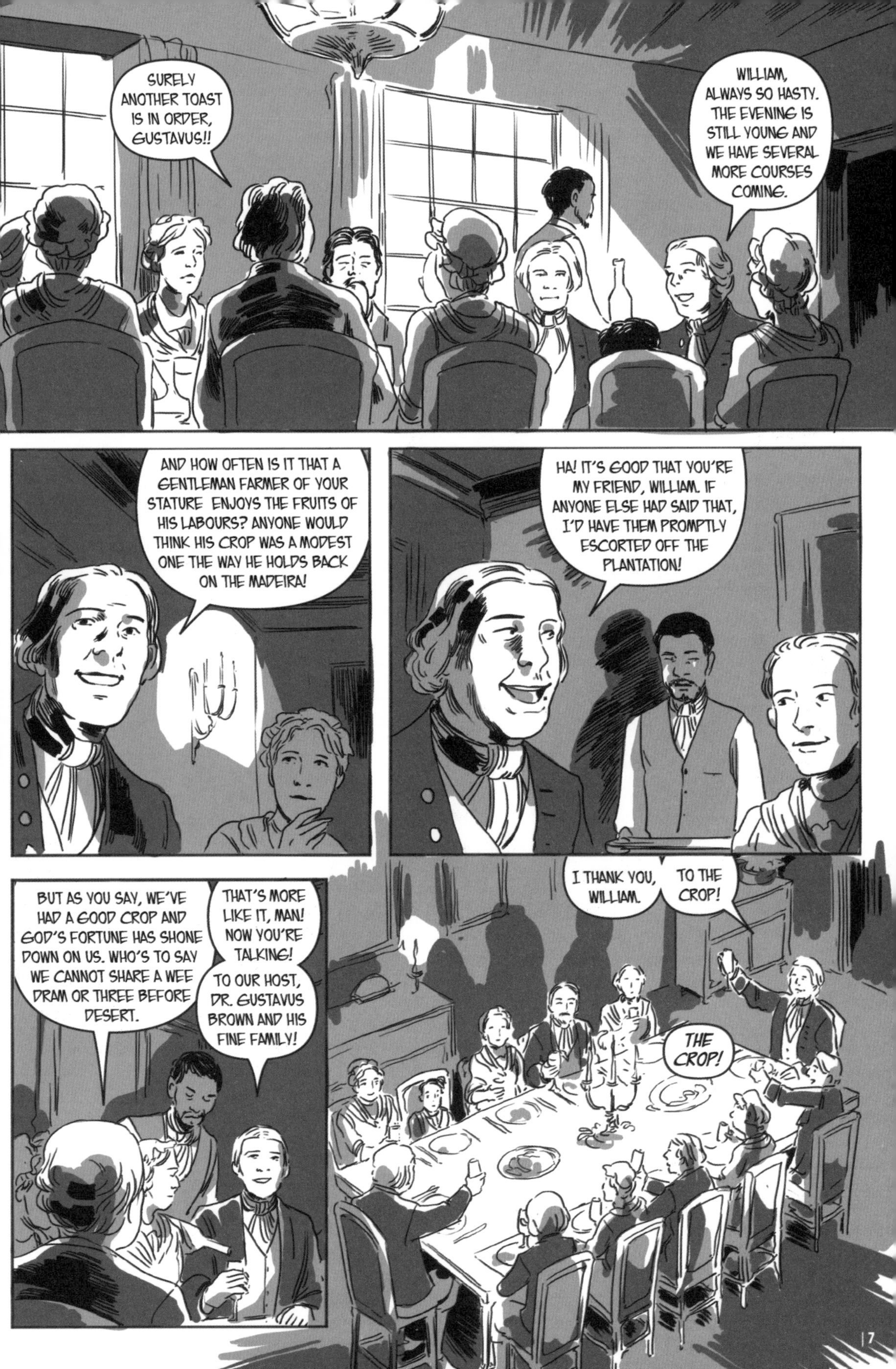
SURELY ANOTHER TOAST IS IN ORDER, GUSTAVUS!!
WILLIAM, ALWAYS SO HASTY. THE EVENING IS STILL YOUNG AND WE HAVE SEVERAL MORE COURSES COMING.
AND HOW OFTEN IS IT THAT A GENTLEMAN FARMER OF YOUR STATURE ENJOYS THE FRUITS OF HIS LABOURS? ANYONE WOULD THINK HIS CROP WAS A MODEST ONE THE WAY HE HOLDS BACK ON THE MADEIRA!
HA! IT'S GOOD THAT YOU'RE MY FRIEND, WILLIAM. IF ANYONE ELSE HAD SAID THAT, I'D HAVE THEM PROMPTLY ESCORTED OFF THE PLANTATION!
BUT AS YOU SAY, WE'VE HAD A GOOD CROP AND GOD'S FORTUNE HAS SHONE DOWN ON US. WHO'S TO SAY WE CANNOT SHARE A WEE DRAM OR THREE BEFORE DESERT.
THAT'S MORE LIKE IT, MAN! NOW YOU'RE TALKING!
TO OUR HOST, DR. GUSTAVUS BROWN AND HIS FINE FAMILY!
I THANK YOU, WILLIAM.
TO THE CROP!
THE CROP!

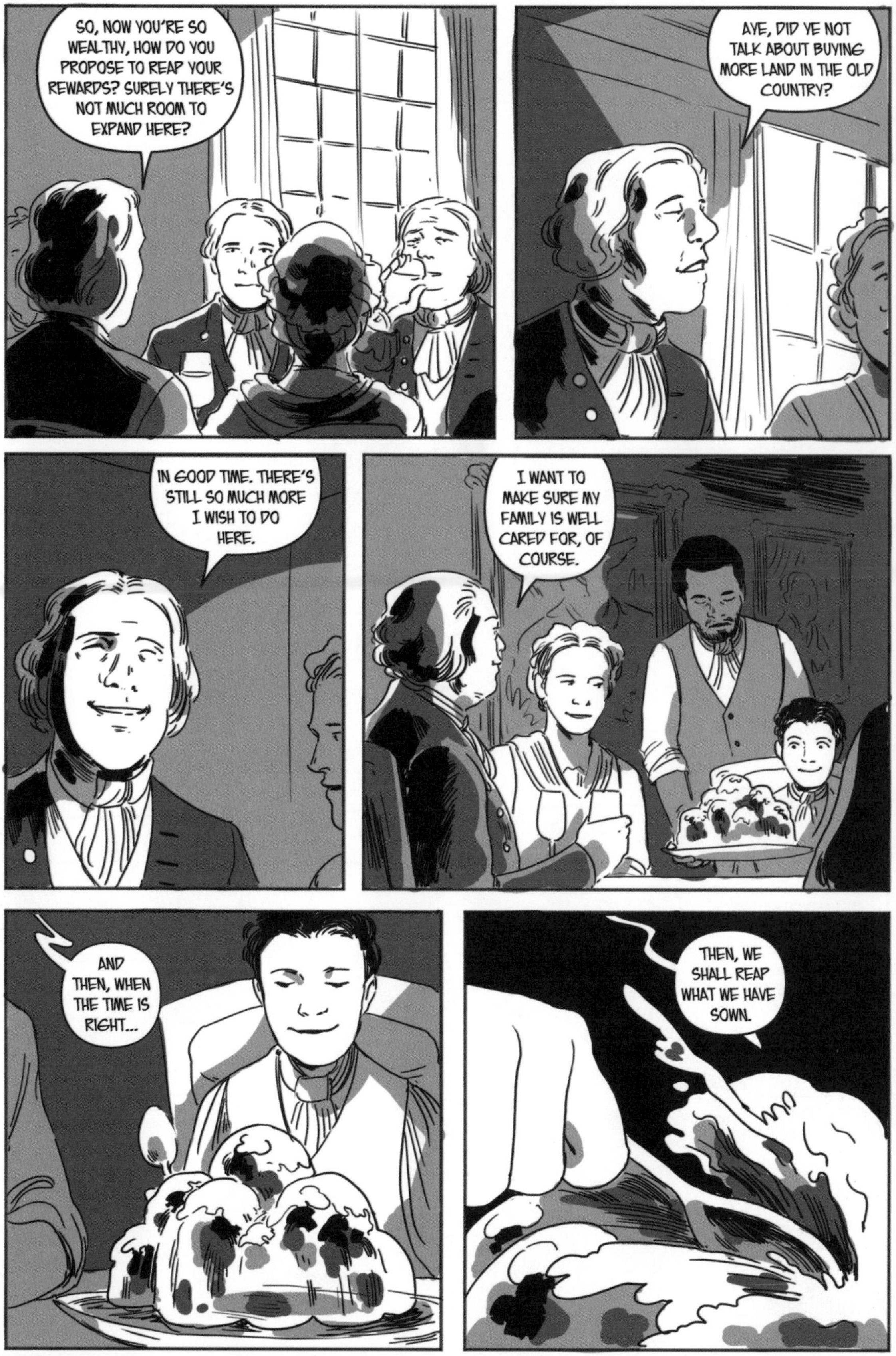
SO, NOW YOU'RE SO WEALTHY, HOW DO YOU PROPOSE TO REAP YOUR REWARDS? SURELY THERE'S NOT MUCH ROOM TO EXPAND HERE?
AYE, DID YE NOT TALK ABOUT BUYING MORE LAND IN THE OLD COUNTRY?
IN GOOD TIME. THERE'S STILL SO MUCH MORE I WISH TO DO HERE.
I WANT TO MAKE SURE MY FAMILY IS WELL CARED FOR, OF COURSE.
AND THEN, WHEN THE TIME IS RIGHT...
THEN, WE SHALL REAP WHAT WE HAVE SOWN.

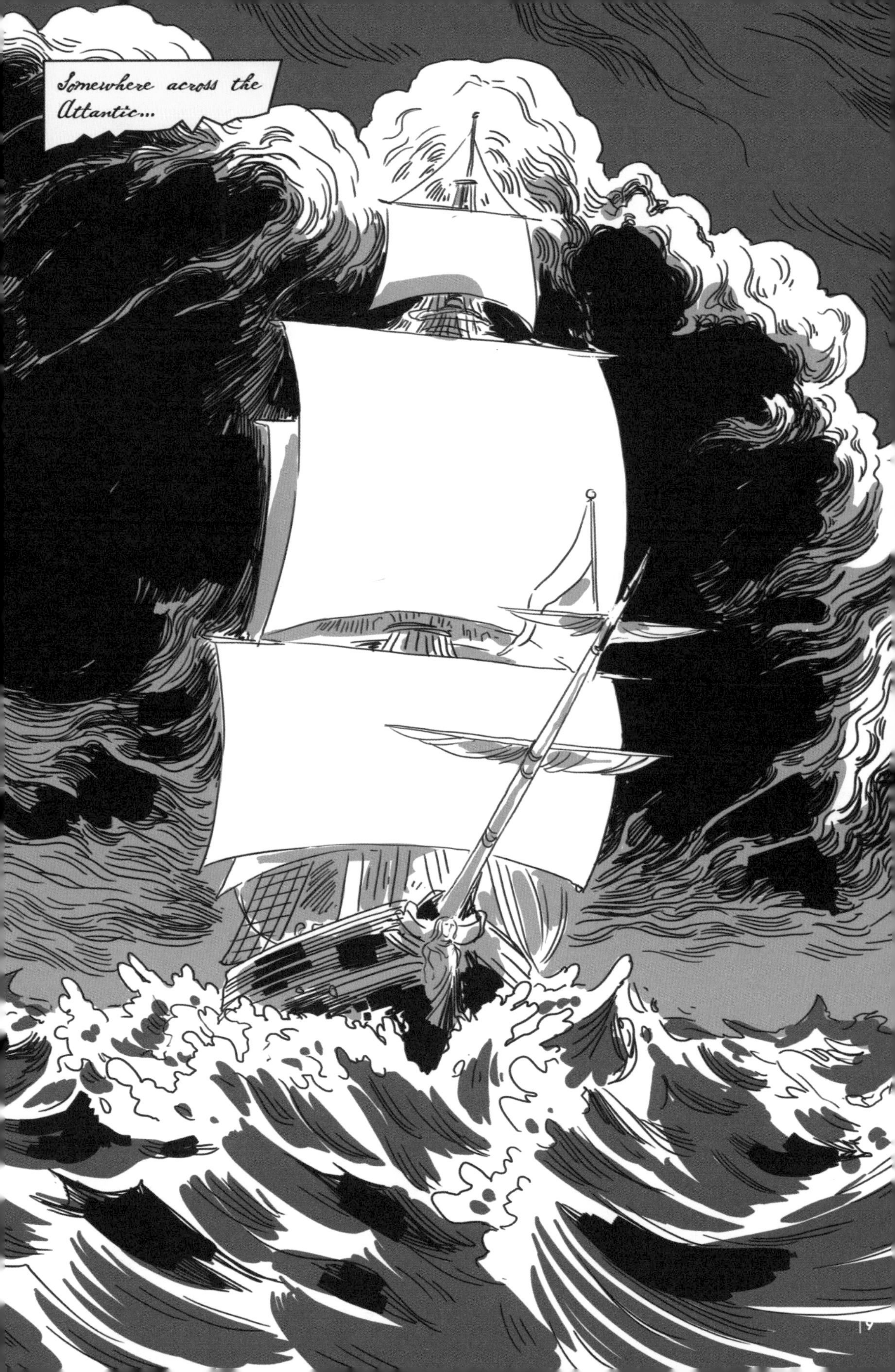
Somewhere across the Atlantic...

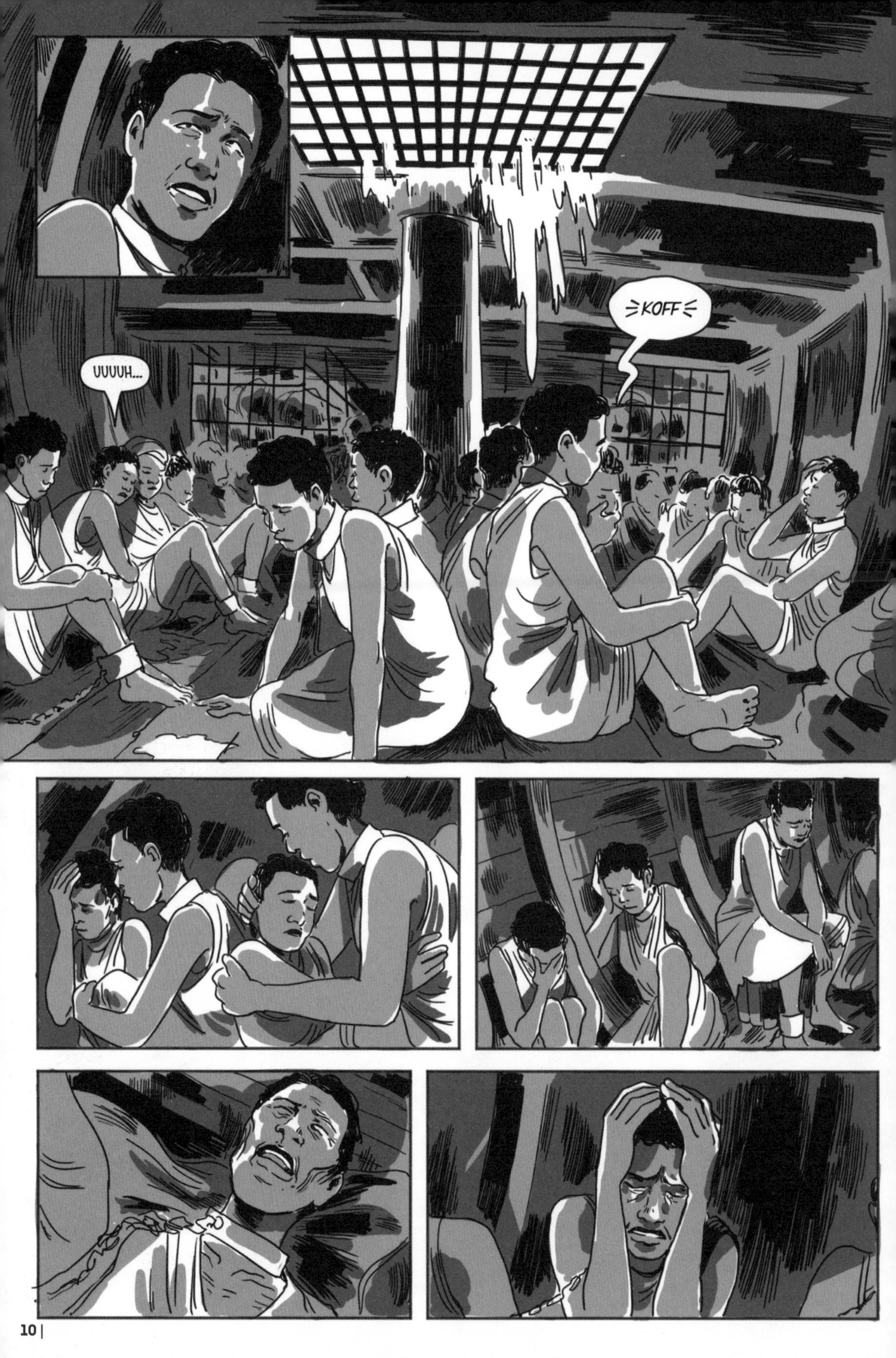
UUUUH...
KOFF

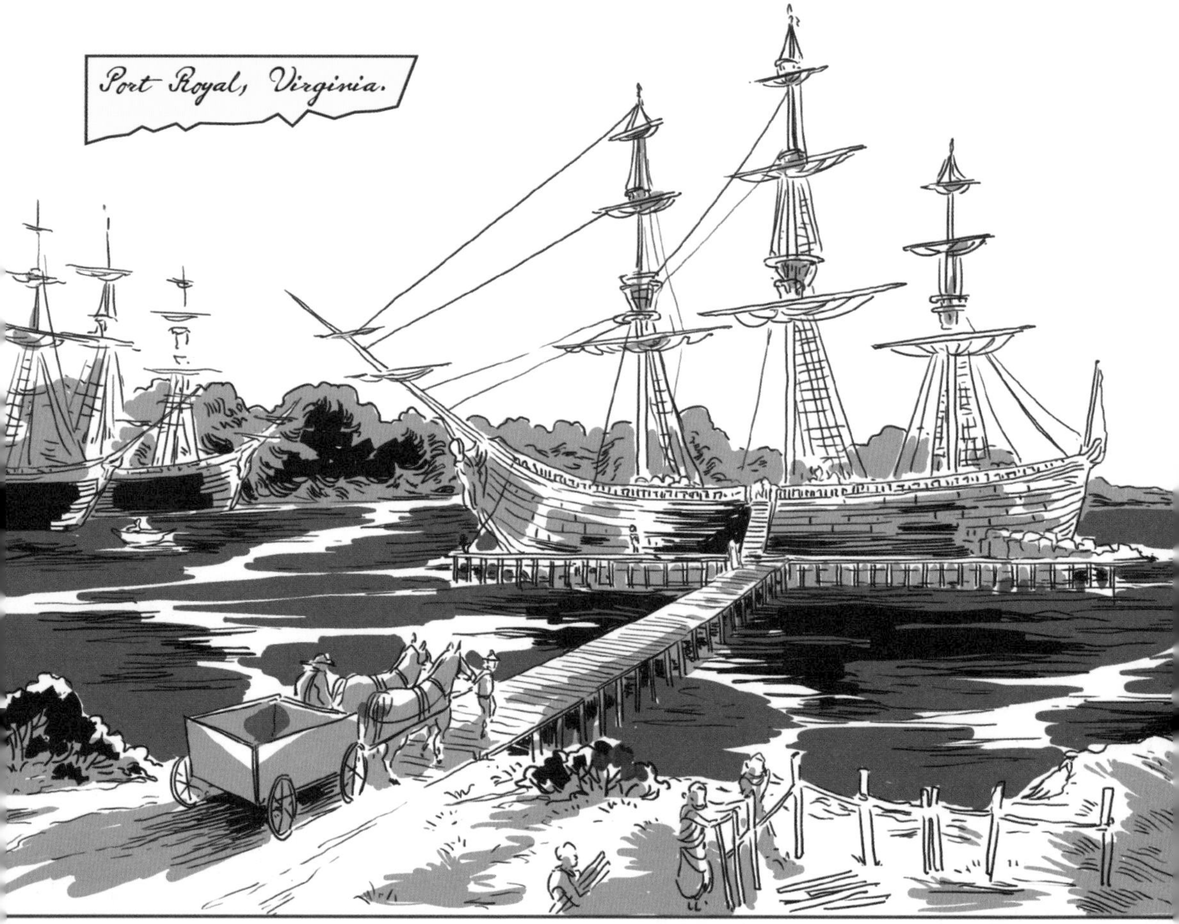
Port Royal, Virginia.

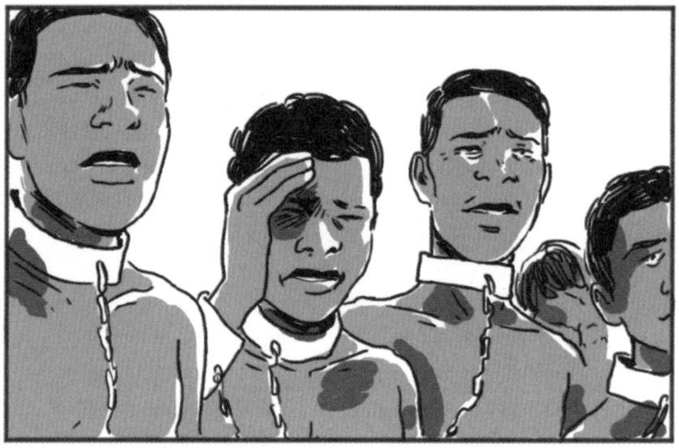

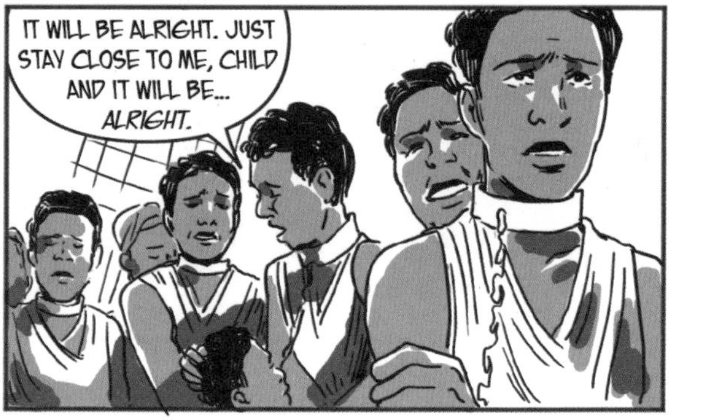
IT WILL BE ALRIGHT. JUST STAY CLOSE TO ME, CHILD AND IT WILL BE... ALRIGHT.

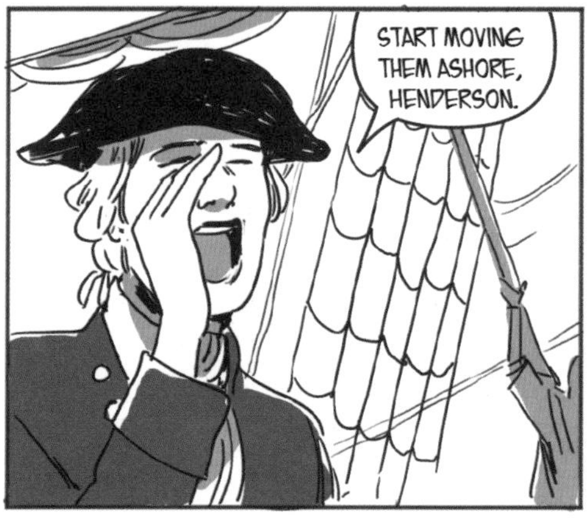
START MOVING THEM ASHORE, HENDERSON.

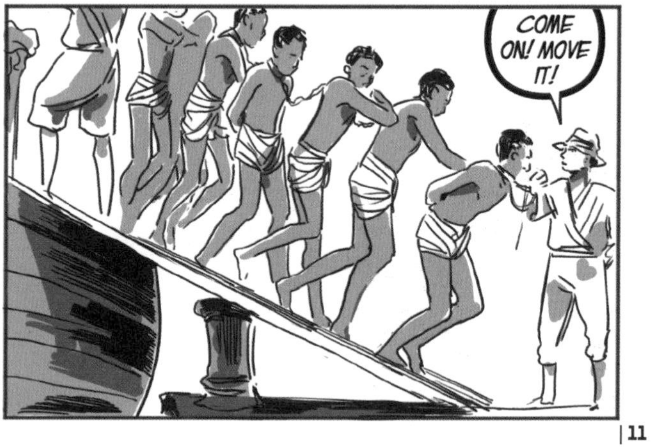
COME ON! MOVE IT!

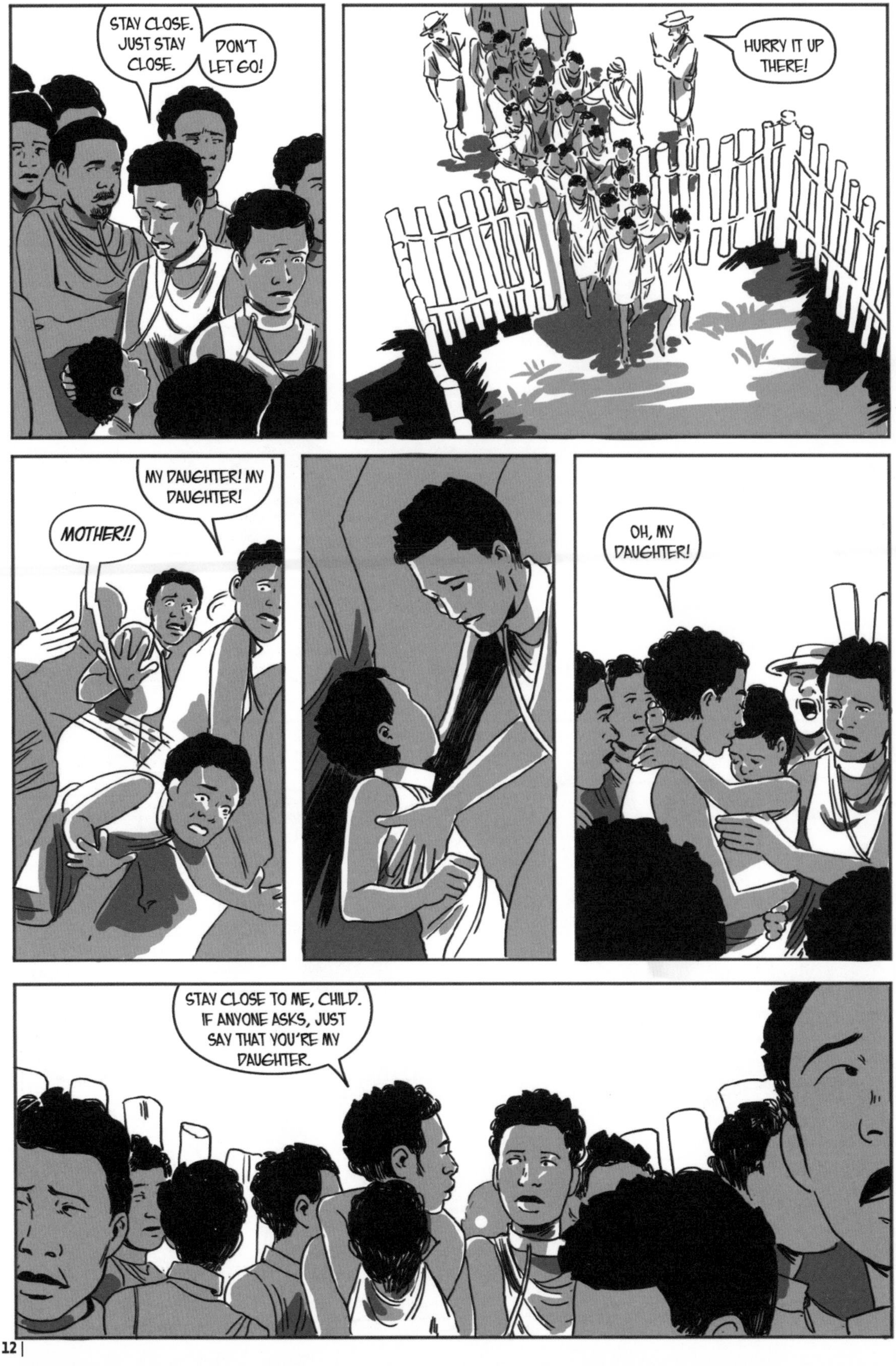
STAY CLOSE. JUST STAY CLOSE.
DON'T LET GO!
HURRY IT UP THERE!
MY DAUGHTER! MY DAUGHTER!
MOTHER!!
OH, MY DAUGHTER!
STAY CLOSE TO ME, CHILD. IF ANYONE ASKS, JUST SAY THAT YOU'RE MY DAUGHTER.

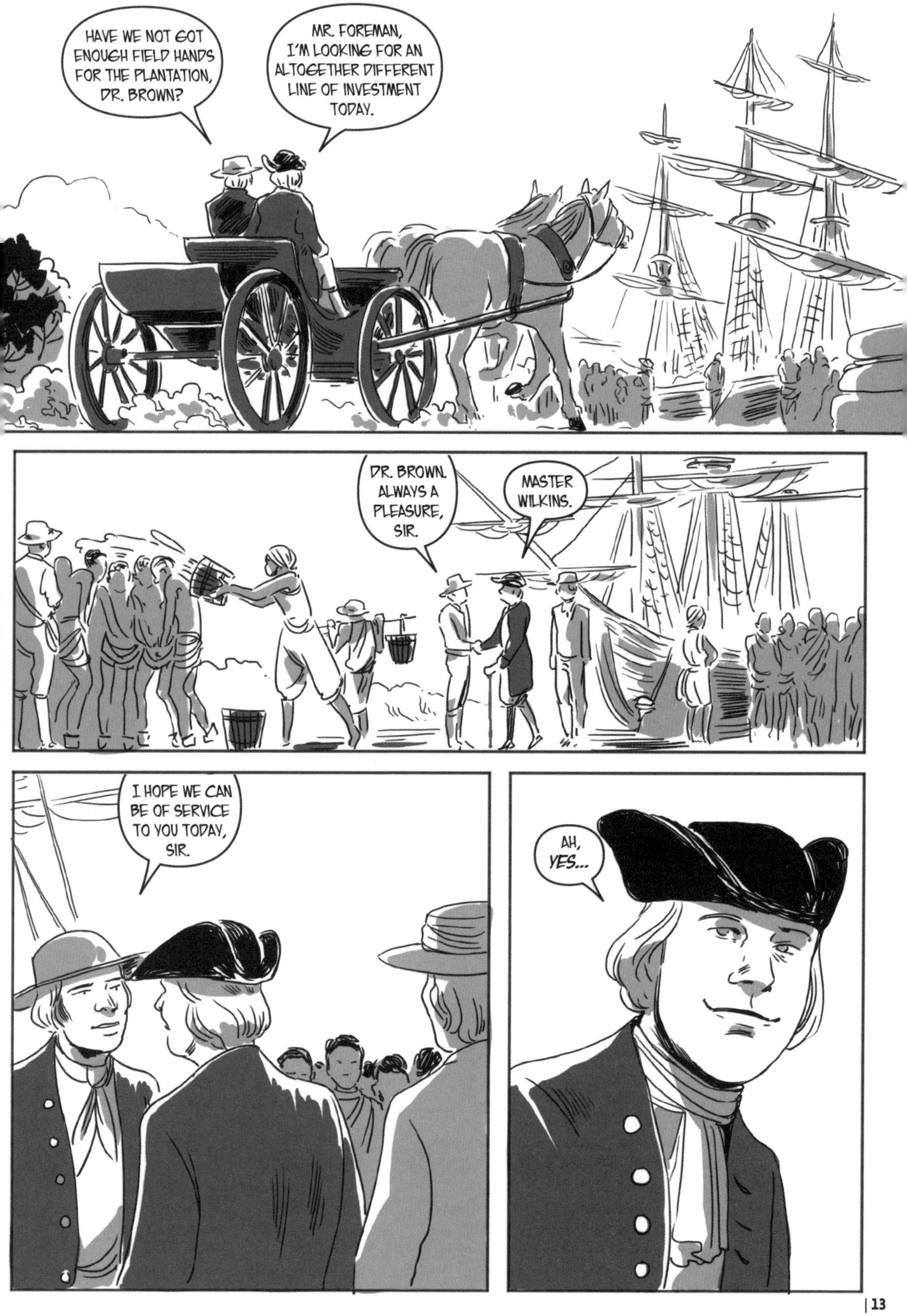
HAVE WE NOT GOT ENOUGH FIELD HANDS FOR THE PLANTATION, DR. BROWN?
MR. FOREMAN, I'M LOOKING FOR AN ALTOGETHER DIFFERENT LINE OF INVESTMENT TODAY.
DR. BROWN. ALWAYS A PLEASURE, SIR.
MASTER WILKINS.
I HOPE WE CAN BE OF SERVICE TO YOU TODAY, SIR.
AH, *YES...*

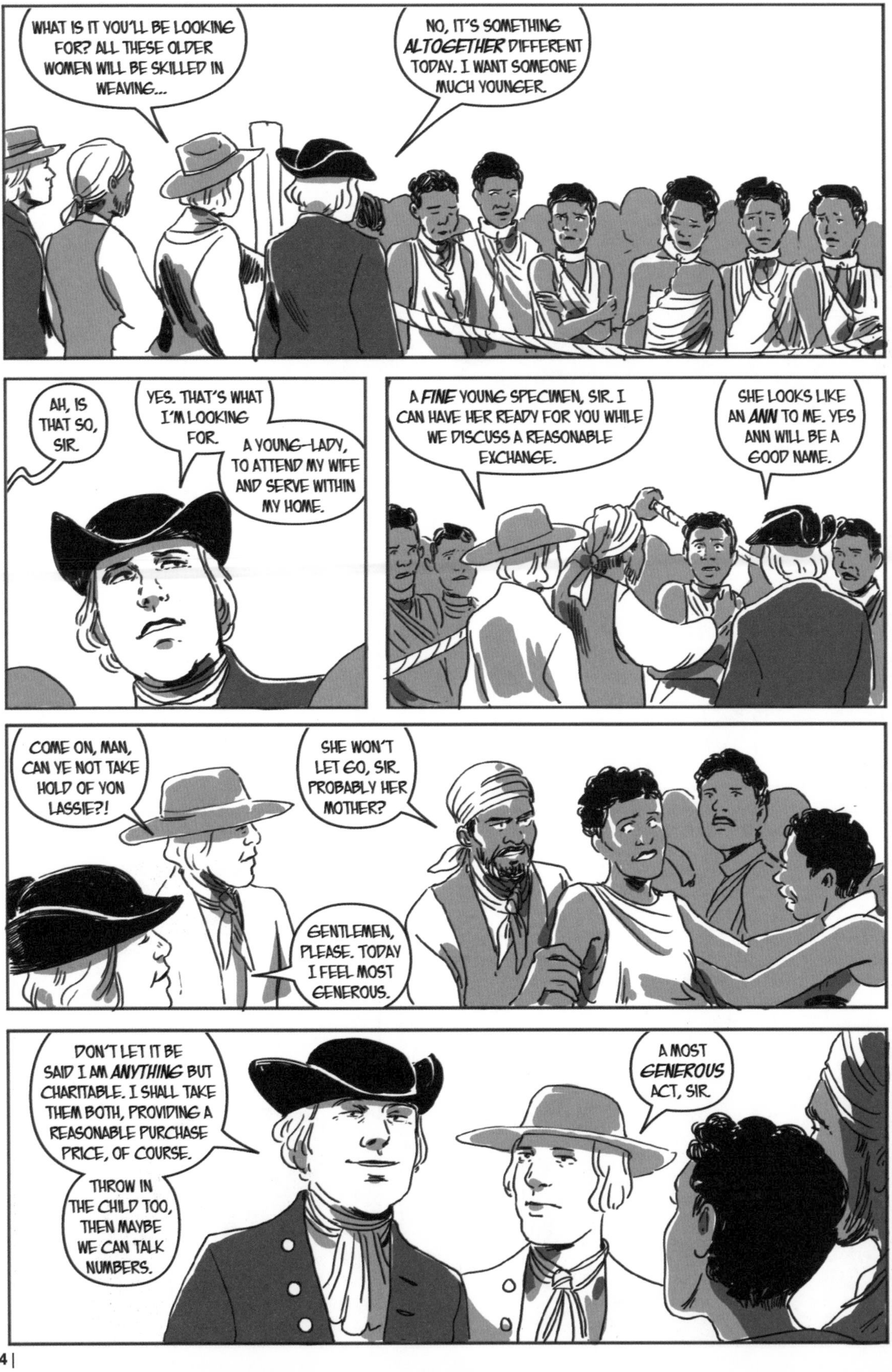
WHAT IS IT YOU'LL BE LOOKING FOR? ALL THESE OLDER WOMEN WILL BE SKILLED IN WEAVING...
NO, IT'S SOMETHING *ALTOGETHER* DIFFERENT TODAY. I WANT SOMEONE MUCH YOUNGER.
AH, IS THAT SO, SIR.
YES. THAT'S WHAT I'M LOOKING FOR.
A YOUNG-LADY, TO ATTEND MY WIFE AND SERVE WITHIN MY HOME.
A *FINE* YOUNG SPECIMEN, SIR. I CAN HAVE HER READY FOR YOU WHILE WE DISCUSS A REASONABLE EXCHANGE.
SHE LOOKS LIKE AN *ANN* TO ME. YES ANN WILL BE A GOOD NAME.
COME ON, MAN, CAN YE NOT TAKE HOLD OF YON LASSIE?!
SHE WON'T LET GO, SIR. PROBABLY HER MOTHER?
GENTLEMEN, PLEASE. TODAY I FEEL MOST GENEROUS.
DON'T LET IT BE SAID I AM *ANYTHING* BUT CHARITABLE. I SHALL TAKE THEM BOTH, PROVIDING A REASONABLE PURCHASE PRICE, OF COURSE.
THROW IN THE CHILD TOO, THEN MAYBE WE CAN TALK NUMBERS.
A MOST *GENEROUS* ACT, SIR.

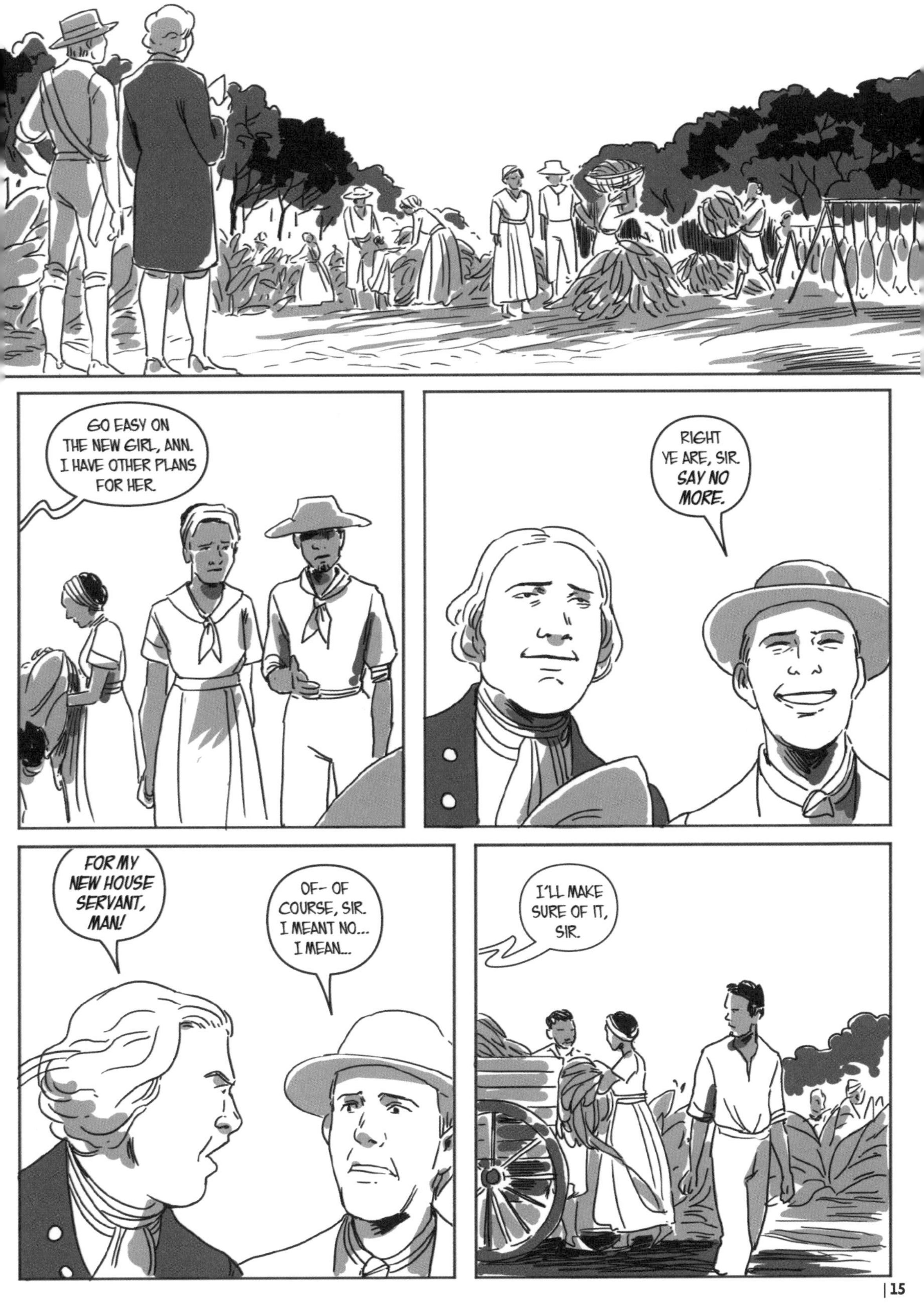
GO EASY ON THE NEW GIRL, ANN. I HAVE OTHER PLANS FOR HER.
RIGHT YE ARE, SIR. SAY NO MORE.
FOR MY NEW HOUSE SERVANT, MAN!
OF- OF COURSE, SIR. I MEANT NO... I MEAN...
I'LL MAKE SURE OF IT, SIR.

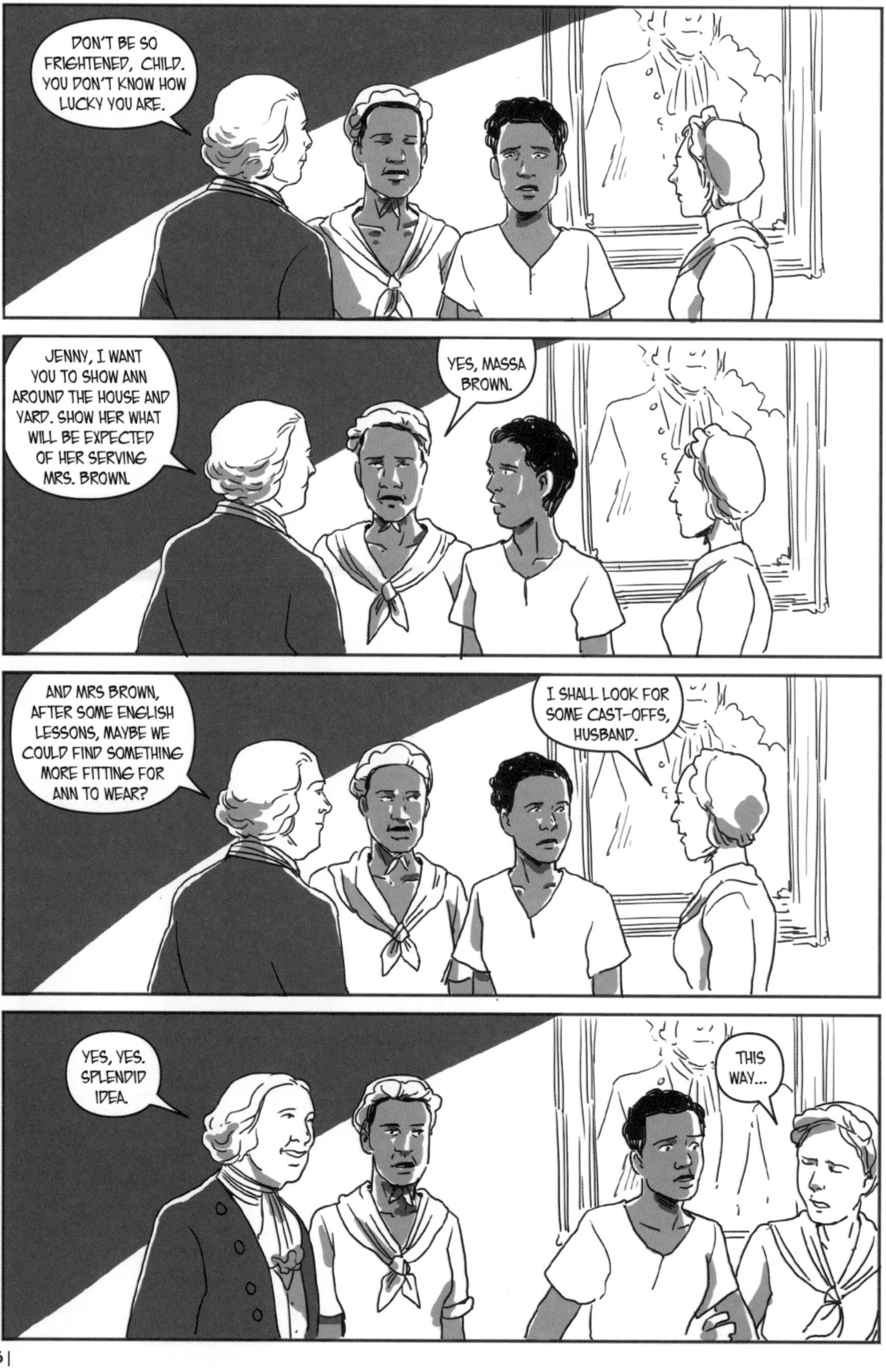
DON'T BE SO FRIGHTENED, CHILD. YOU DON'T KNOW HOW LUCKY YOU ARE.
JENNY, I WANT YOU TO SHOW ANN AROUND THE HOUSE AND YARD. SHOW HER WHAT WILL BE EXPECTED OF HER SERVING MRS. BROWN.
YES, MASSA BROWN.
AND MRS BROWN, AFTER SOME ENGLISH LESSONS, MAYBE WE COULD FIND SOMETHING MORE FITTING FOR ANN TO WEAR?
I SHALL LOOK FOR SOME CAST-OFFS, HUSBAND.
YES, YES. SPLENDID IDEA.
THIS WAY...

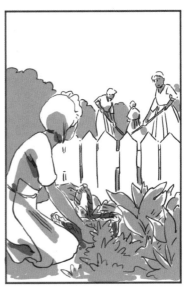

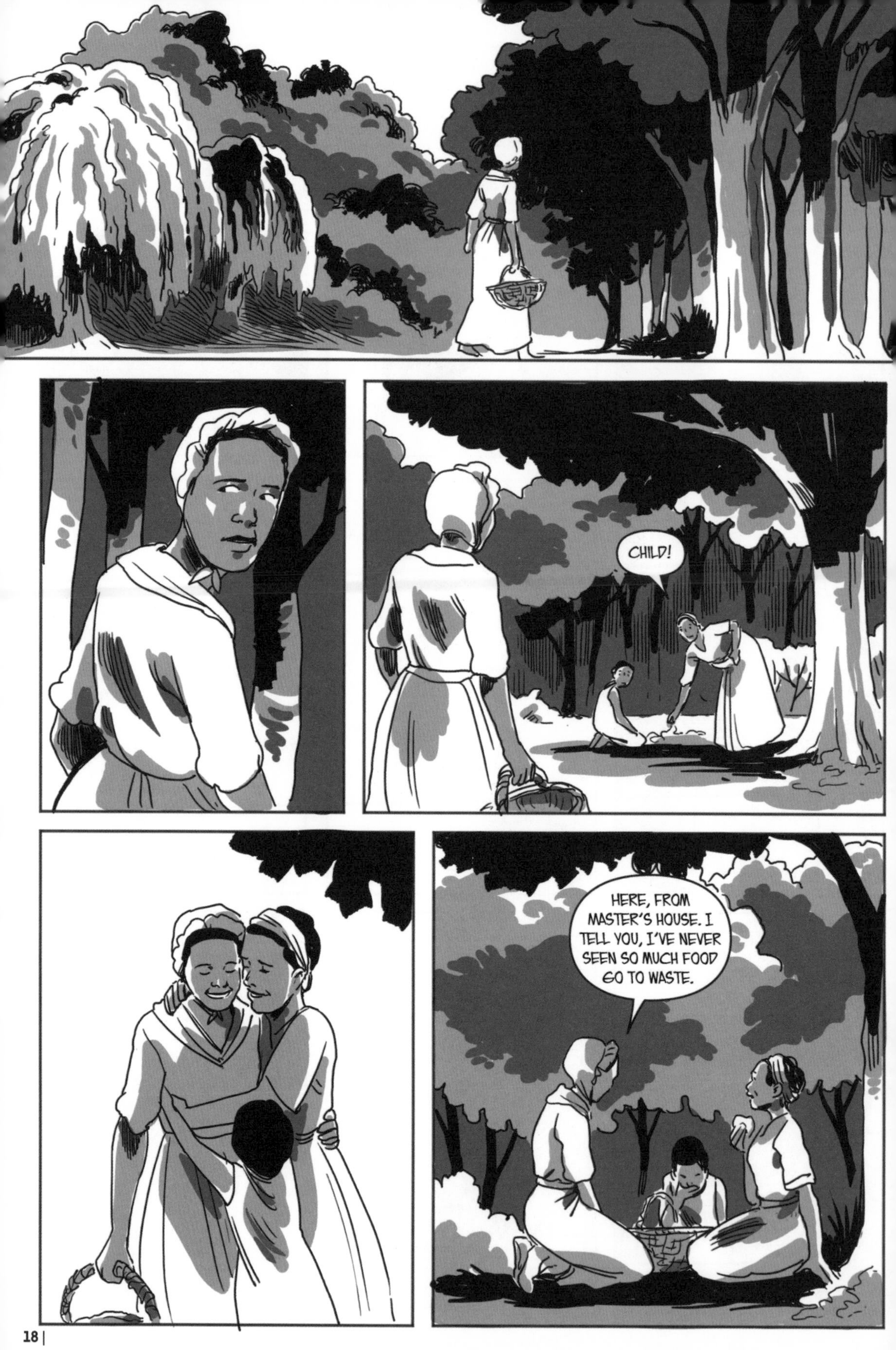
CHILD!
HERE, FROM MASTER'S HOUSE. I TELL YOU, I'VE NEVER SEEN SO MUCH FOOD GO TO WASTE.

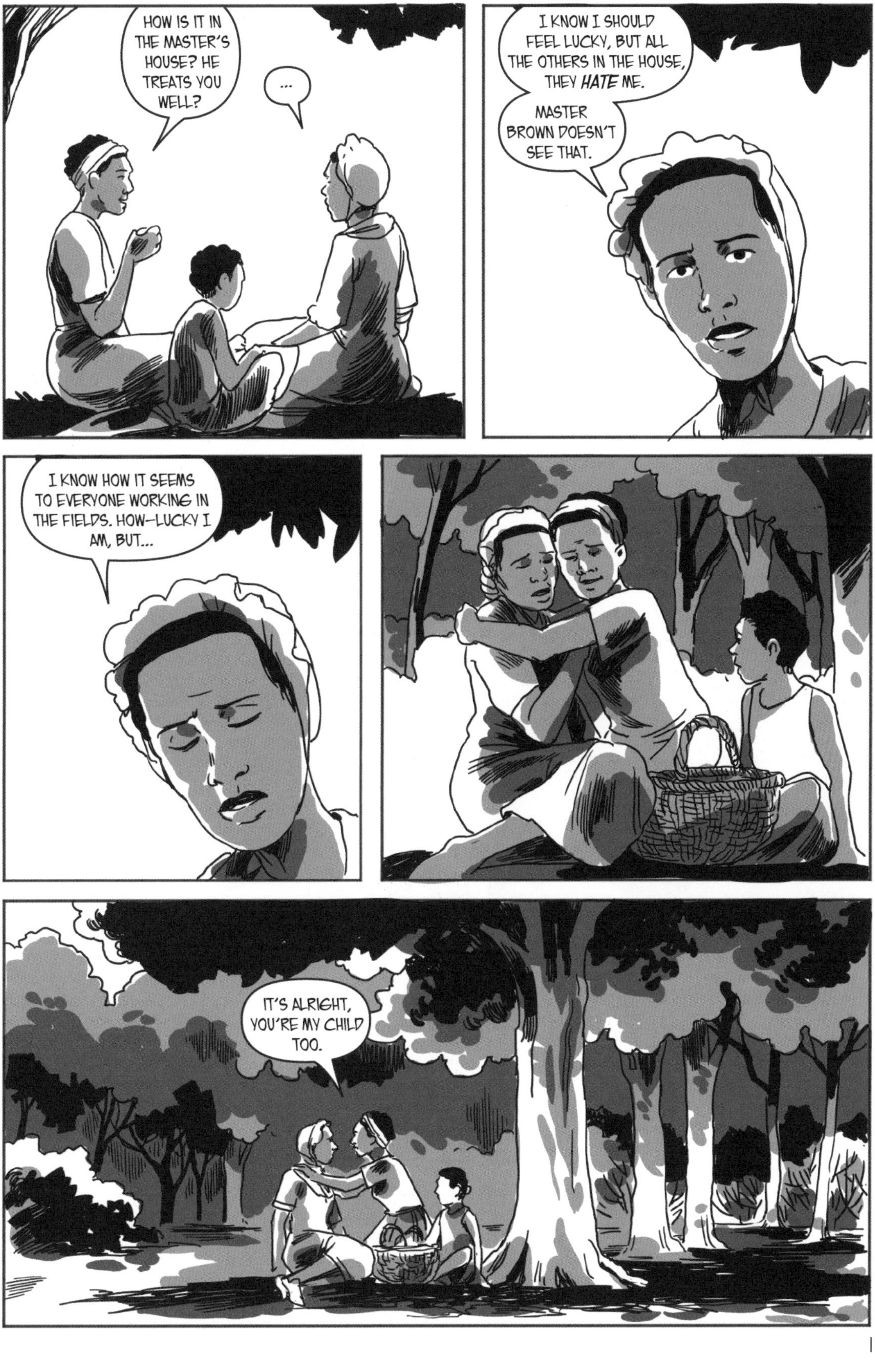
HOW IS IT IN THE MASTER'S HOUSE? HE TREATS YOU WELL?
...
I KNOW I SHOULD FEEL LUCKY, BUT ALL THE OTHERS IN THE HOUSE, THEY *HATE* ME.
MASTER BROWN DOESN'T SEE THAT.
I KNOW HOW IT SEEMS TO EVERYONE WORKING IN THE FIELDS. HOW-LUCKY I AM, BUT...
IT'S ALRIGHT, YOU'RE MY CHILD TOO.

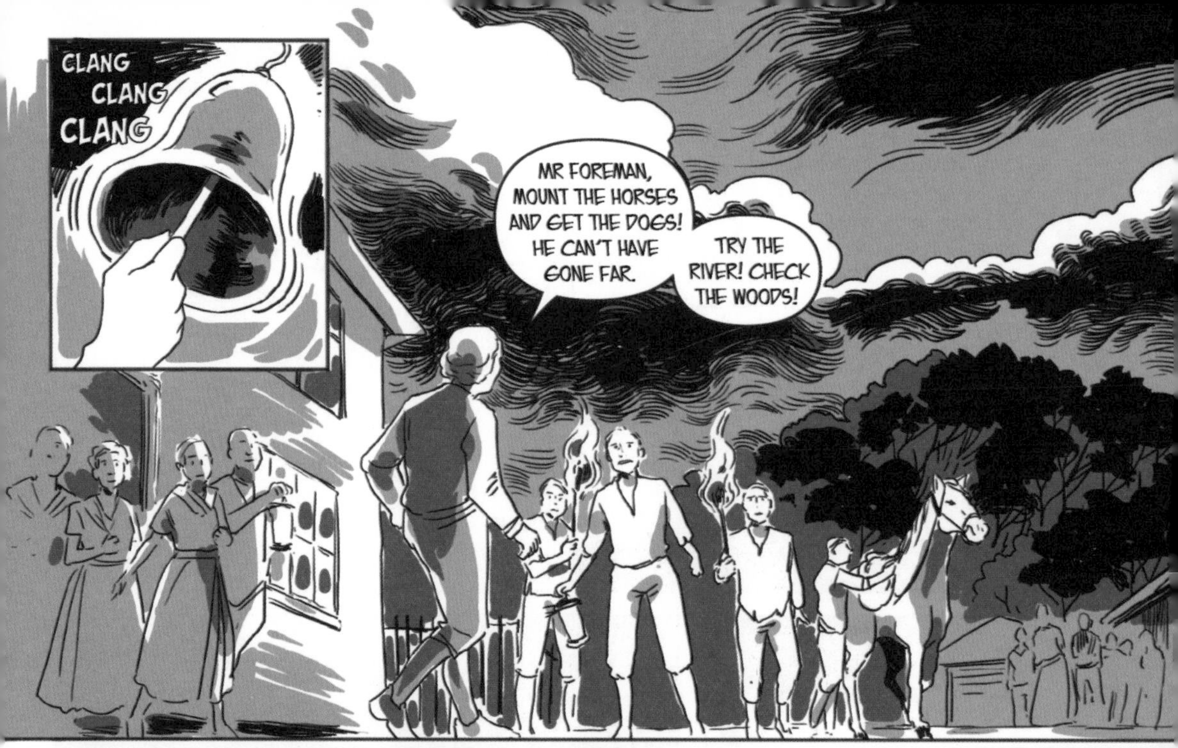
CLANG
CLANG
CLANG
MR FOREMAN, MOUNT THE HORSES AND GET THE DOGS! HE CAN'T HAVE GONE FAR.
TRY THE RIVER! CHECK THE WOODS!

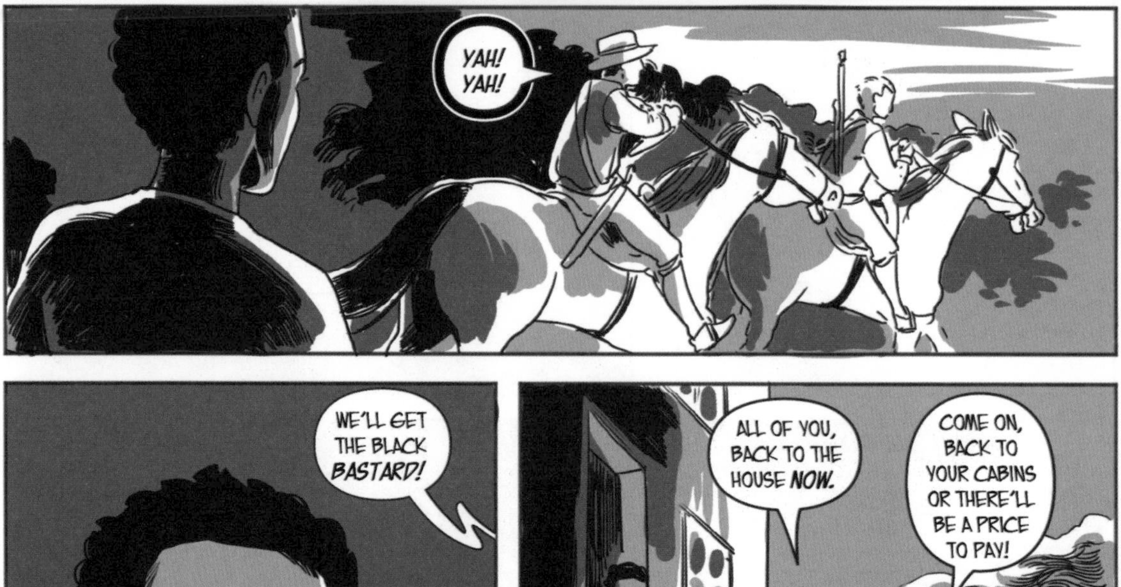
YAH! YAH!

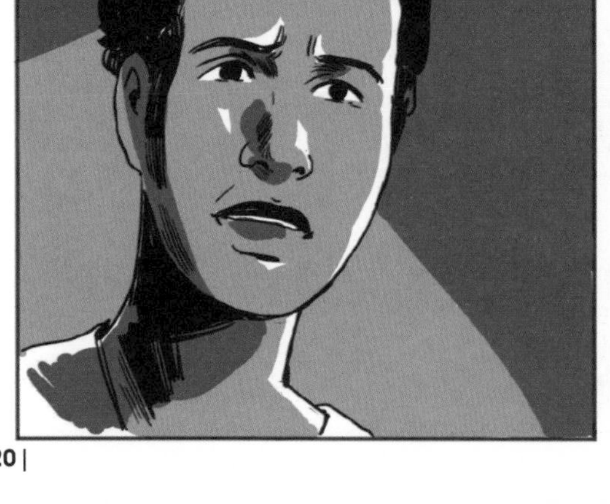
WE'LL GET THE BLACK *BASTARD!*

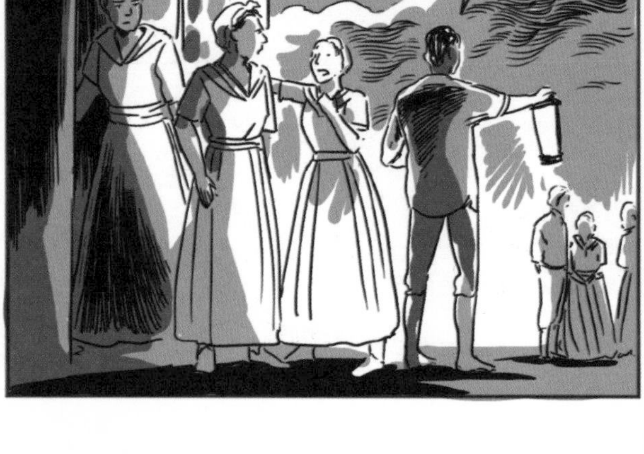
ALL OF YOU, BACK TO THE HOUSE **NOW.**
COME ON, BACK TO YOUR CABINS OR THERE'LL BE A PRICE TO PAY!

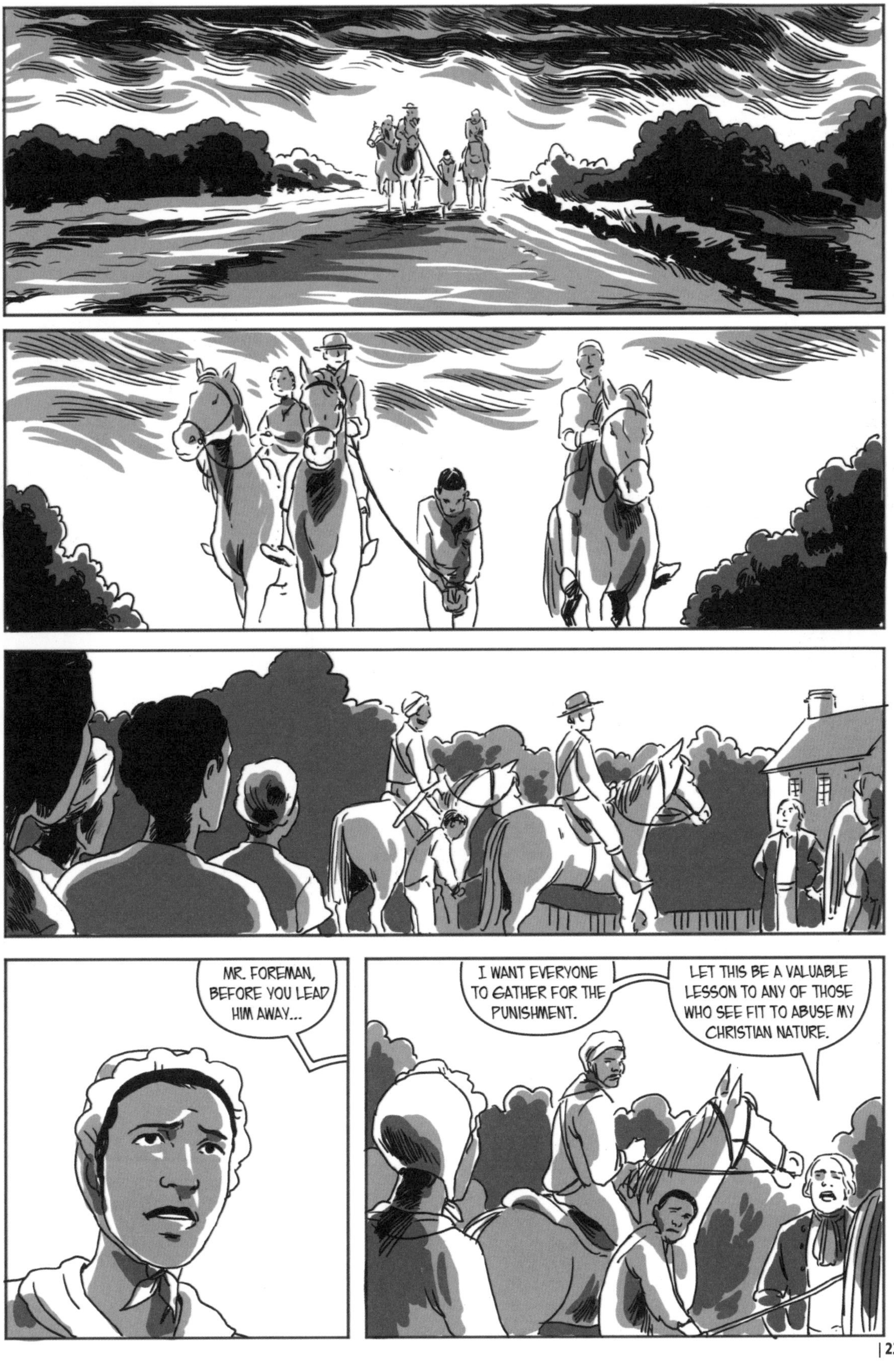
MR. FOREMAN, BEFORE YOU LEAD HIM AWAY...
I WANT EVERYONE TO GATHER FOR THE PUNISHMENT.
LET THIS BE A VALUABLE LESSON TO ANY OF THOSE WHO SEE FIT TO ABUSE MY CHRISTIAN NATURE.

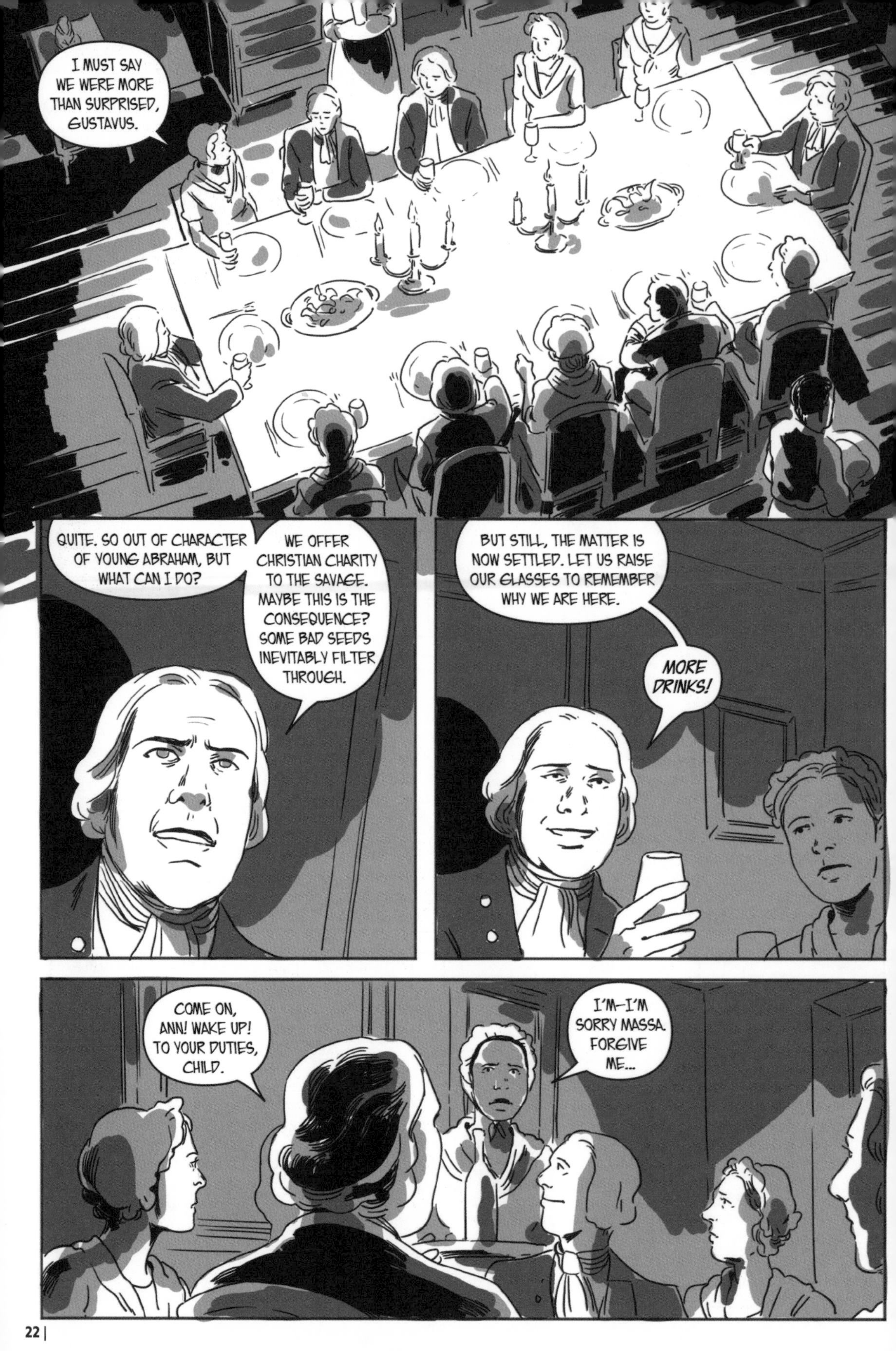

I MUST SAY WE WERE MORE THAN SURPRISED, GUSTAVUS.
QUITE. SO OUT OF CHARACTER OF YOUNG ABRAHAM, BUT WHAT CAN I DO?
WE OFFER CHRISTIAN CHARITY TO THE SAVAGE. MAYBE THIS IS THE CONSEQUENCE? SOME BAD SEEDS INEVITABLY FILTER THROUGH.
BUT STILL, THE MATTER IS NOW SETTLED. LET US RAISE OUR GLASSES TO REMEMBER WHY WE ARE HERE.
*MORE DRINKS!*
COME ON, ANN! WAKE UP! TO YOUR DUTIES, CHILD.
I'M—I'M SORRY MASSA. FORGIVE ME...

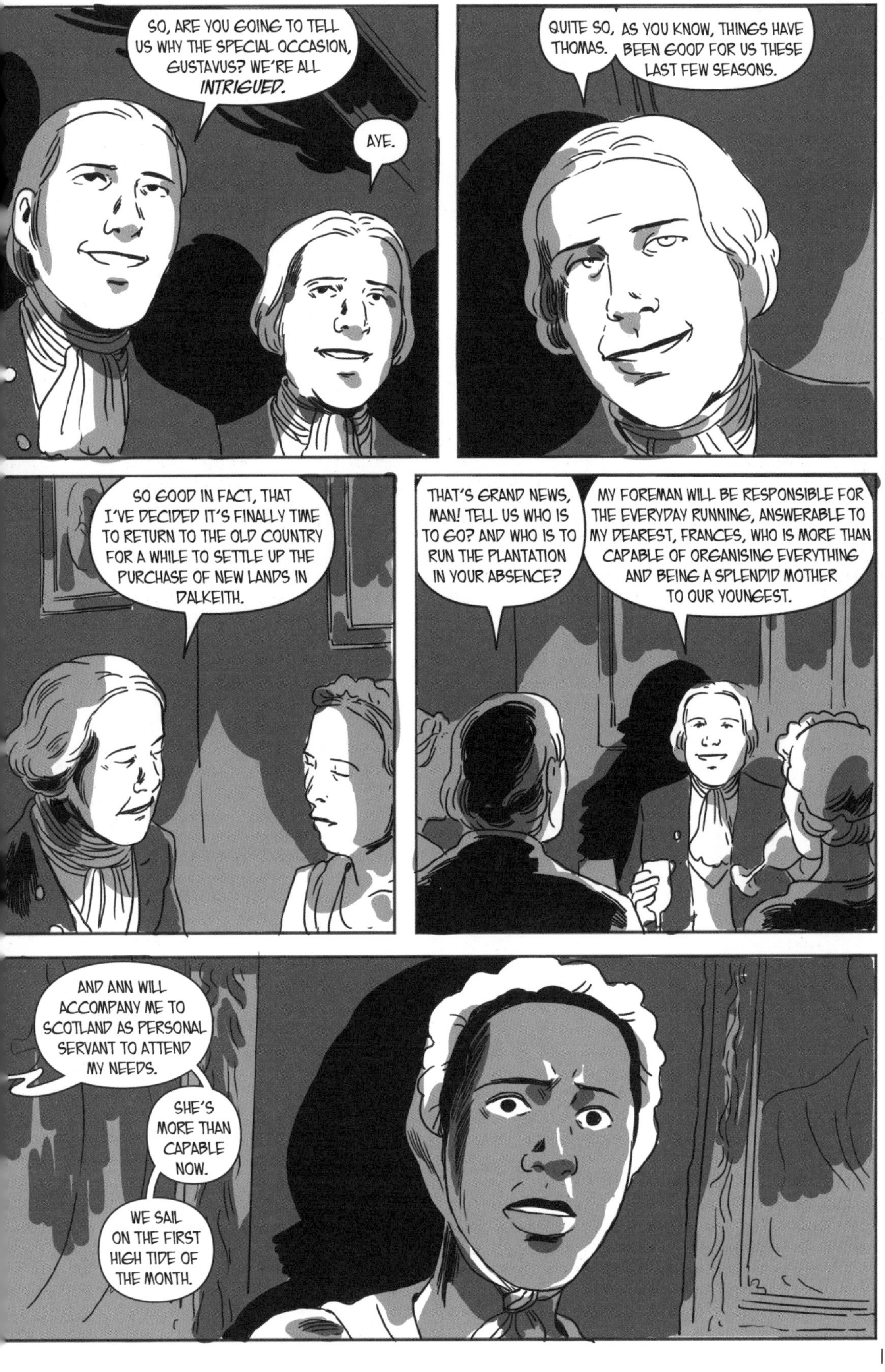
SO, ARE YOU GOING TO TELL US WHY THE SPECIAL OCCASION, GUSTAVUS? WE'RE ALL *INTRIGUED.*
AYE.
QUITE SO, THOMAS.
AS YOU KNOW, THINGS HAVE BEEN GOOD FOR US THESE LAST FEW SEASONS.
SO GOOD IN FACT, THAT I'VE DECIDED IT'S FINALLY TIME TO RETURN TO THE OLD COUNTRY FOR A WHILE TO SETTLE UP THE PURCHASE OF NEW LANDS IN DALKEITH.
THAT'S GRAND NEWS, MAN! TELL US WHO IS TO GO? AND WHO IS TO RUN THE PLANTATION IN YOUR ABSENCE?
MY FOREMAN WILL BE RESPONSIBLE FOR THE EVERYDAY RUNNING, ANSWERABLE TO MY DEAREST, FRANCES, WHO IS MORE THAN CAPABLE OF ORGANISING EVERYTHING AND BEING A SPLENDID MOTHER TO OUR YOUNGEST.
AND ANN WILL ACCOMPANY ME TO SCOTLAND AS PERSONAL SERVANT TO ATTEND MY NEEDS.
SHE'S MORE THAN CAPABLE NOW.
WE SAIL ON THE FIRST HIGH TIDE OF THE MONTH.

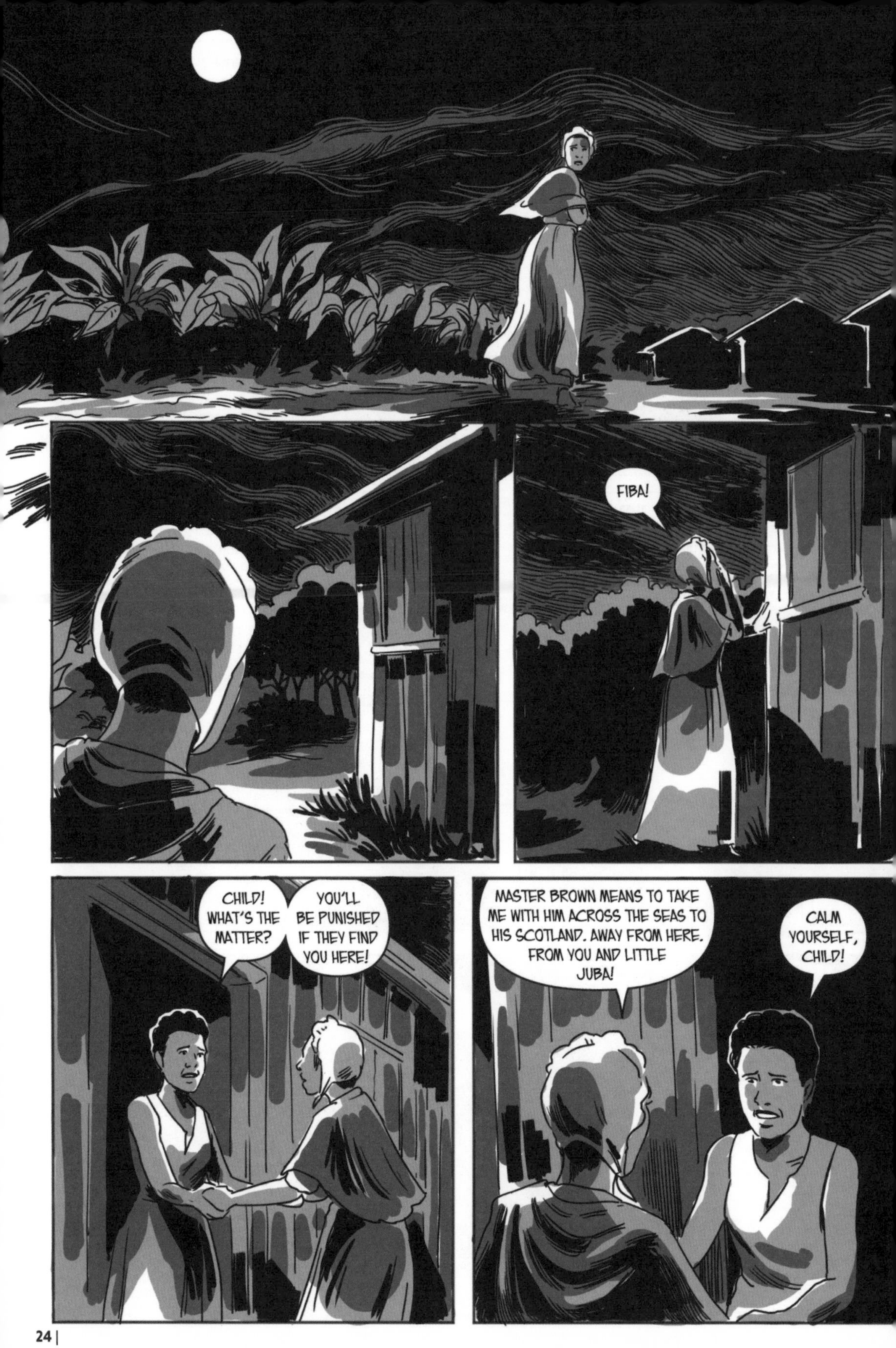
FIBA!
CHILD! WHAT'S THE MATTER?
YOU'LL BE PUNISHED IF THEY FIND YOU HERE!
MASTER BROWN MEANS TO TAKE ME WITH HIM ACROSS THE SEAS TO HIS SCOTLAND. AWAY FROM HERE. FROM YOU AND LITTLE JUBA!
CALM YOURSELF, CHILD!

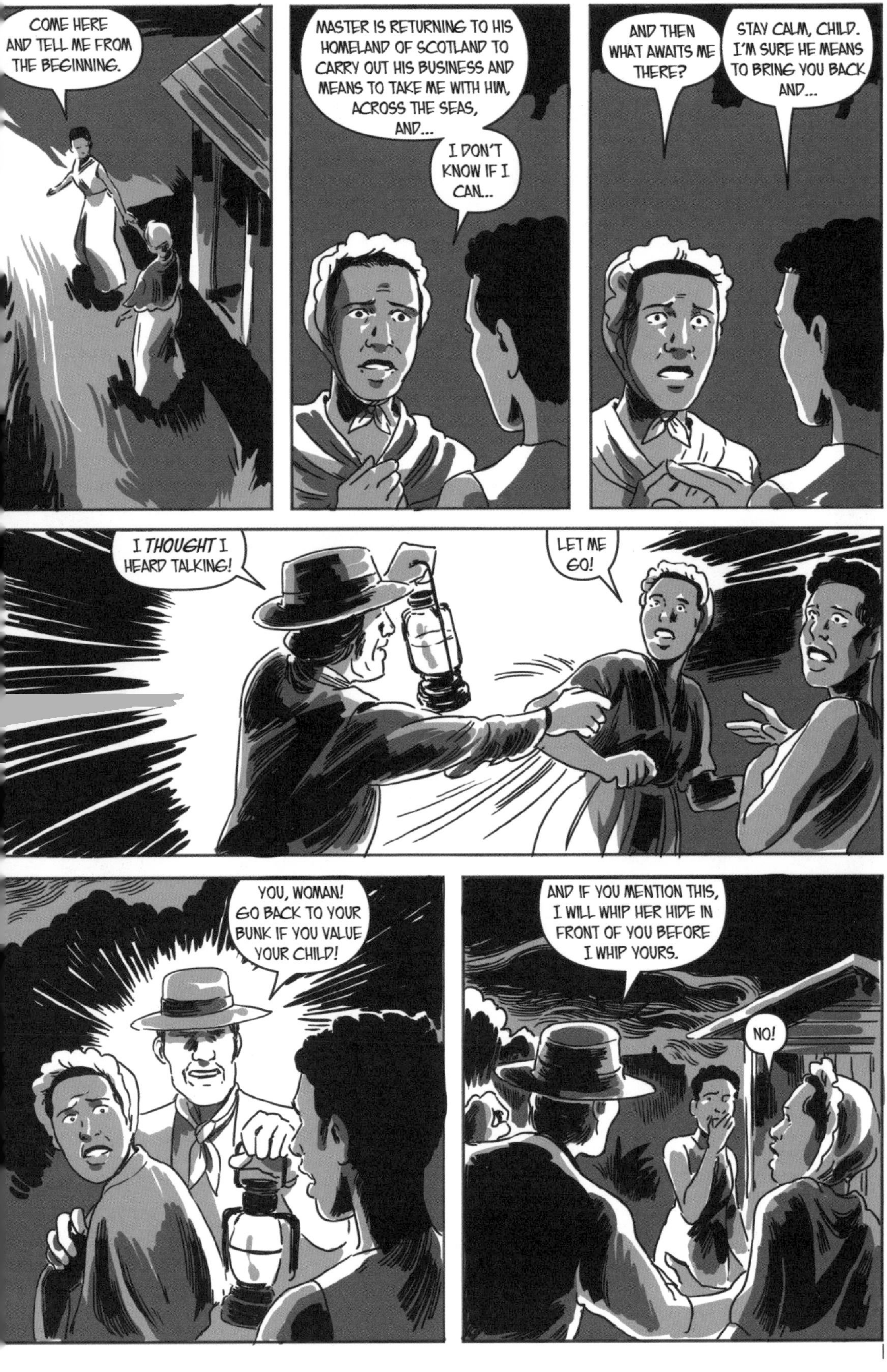
COME HERE AND TELL ME FROM THE BEGINNING.
MASTER IS RETURNING TO HIS HOMELAND OF SCOTLAND TO CARRY OUT HIS BUSINESS AND MEANS TO TAKE ME WITH HIM, ACROSS THE SEAS, AND...
I DON'T KNOW IF I CAN...
AND THEN WHAT AWAITS ME THERE?
STAY CALM, CHILD. I'M SURE HE MEANS TO BRING YOU BACK AND...
I *THOUGHT* I HEARD TALKING!
LET ME GO!
YOU, WOMAN! GO BACK TO YOUR BUNK IF YOU VALUE YOUR CHILD!
AND IF YOU MENTION THIS, I WILL WHIP HER HIDE IN FRONT OF YOU BEFORE I WHIP YOURS.
NO!

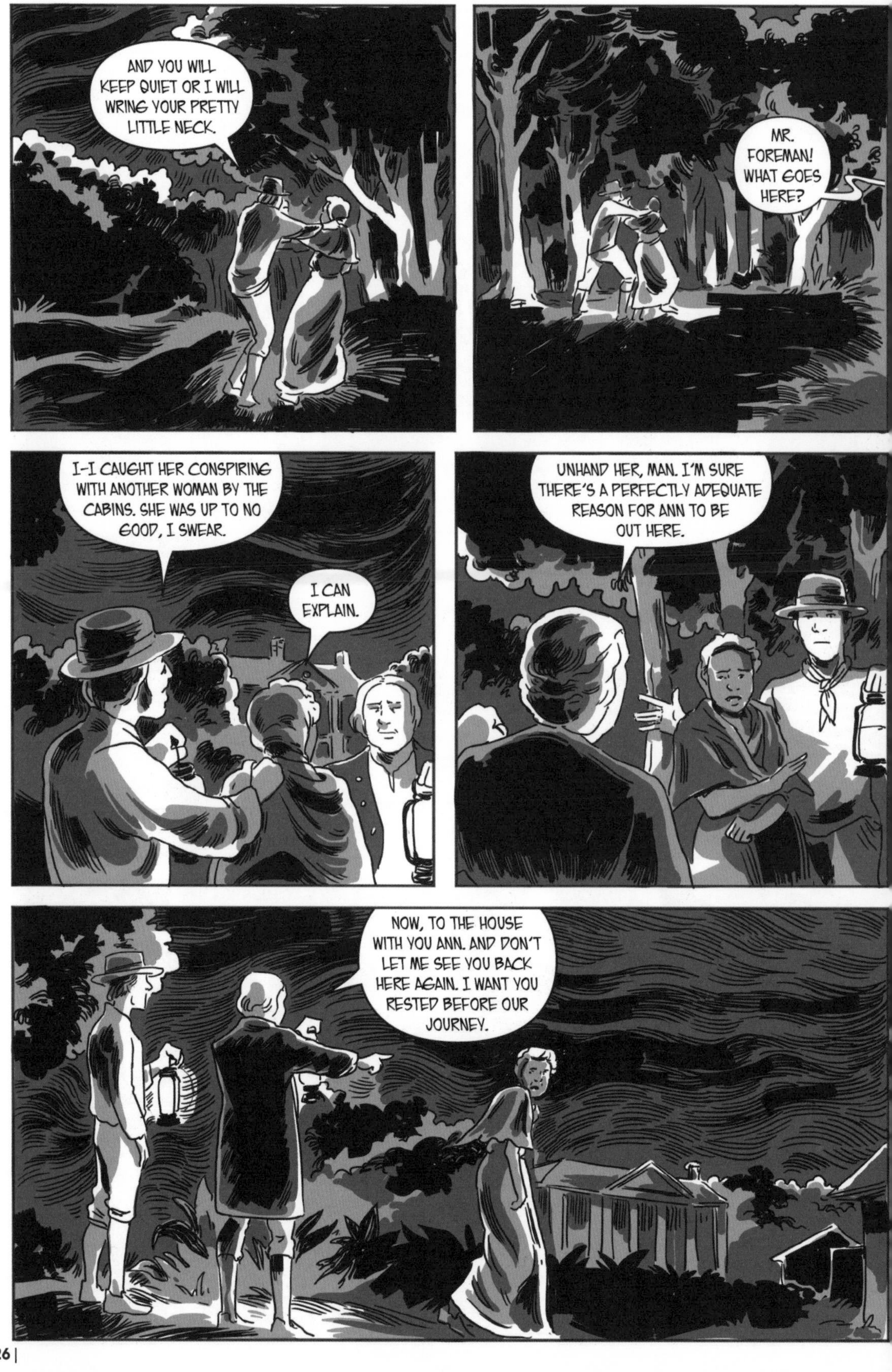
AND YOU WILL KEEP QUIET OR I WILL WRING YOUR PRETTY LITTLE NECK.
MR. FOREMAN! WHAT GOES HERE?
I–I CAUGHT HER CONSPIRING WITH ANOTHER WOMAN BY THE CABINS. SHE WAS UP TO NO GOOD, I SWEAR.
I CAN EXPLAIN.
UNHAND HER, MAN. I'M SURE THERE'S A PERFECTLY ADEQUATE REASON FOR ANN TO BE OUT HERE.
NOW, TO THE HOUSE WITH YOU ANN. AND DON'T LET ME SEE YOU BACK HERE AGAIN. I WANT YOU RESTED BEFORE OUR JOURNEY.

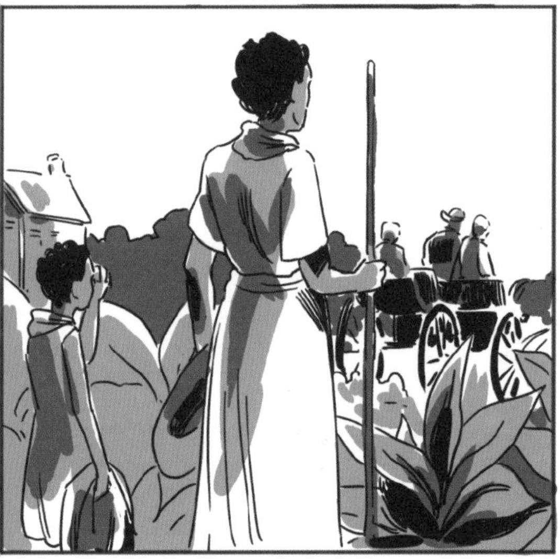

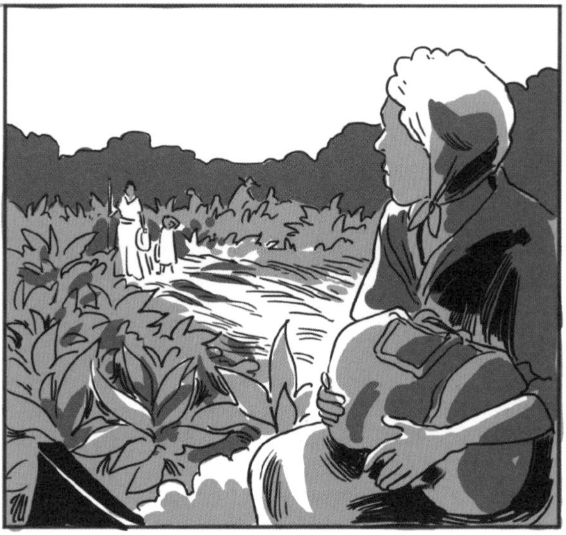

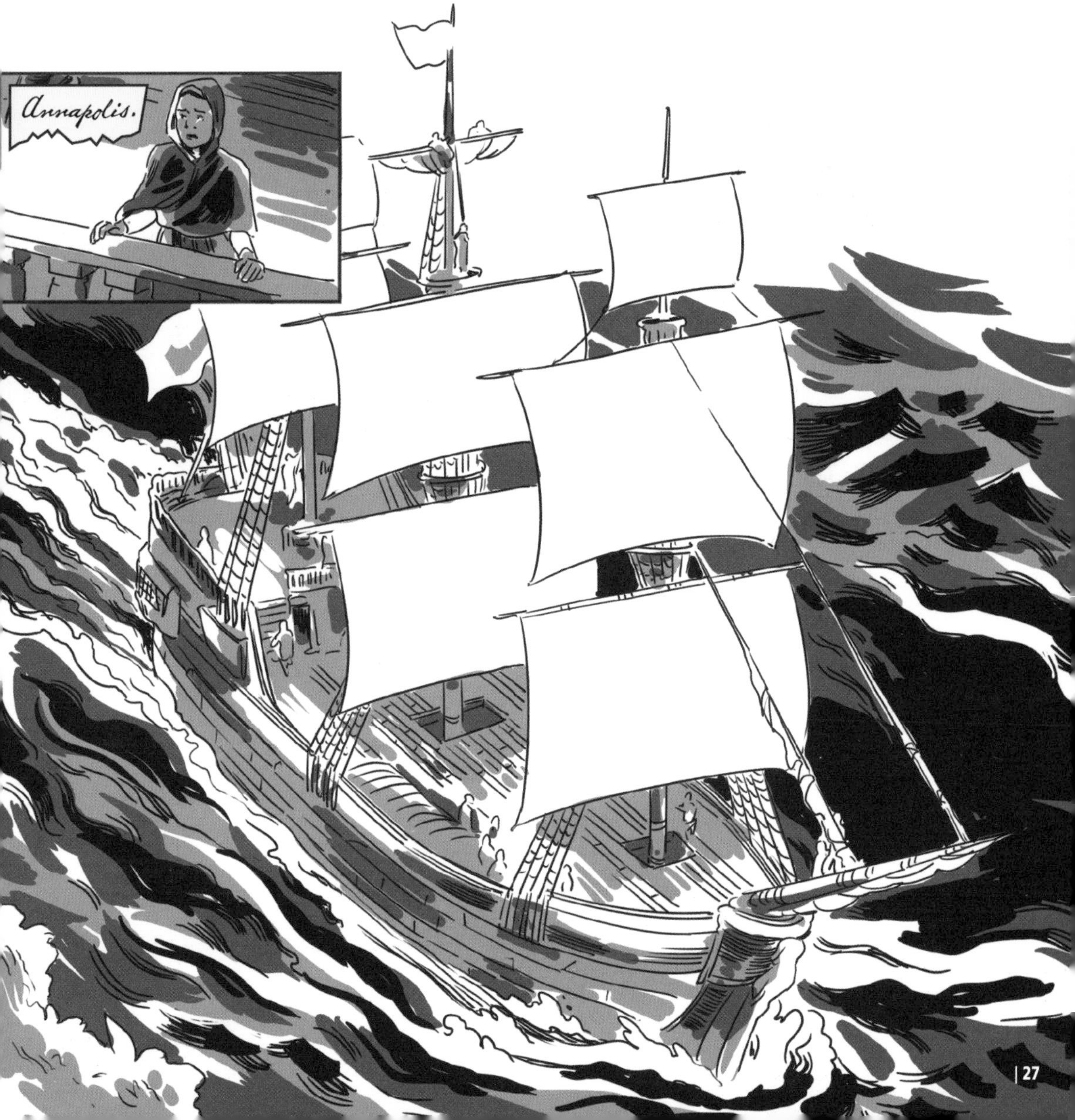
Annapolis.

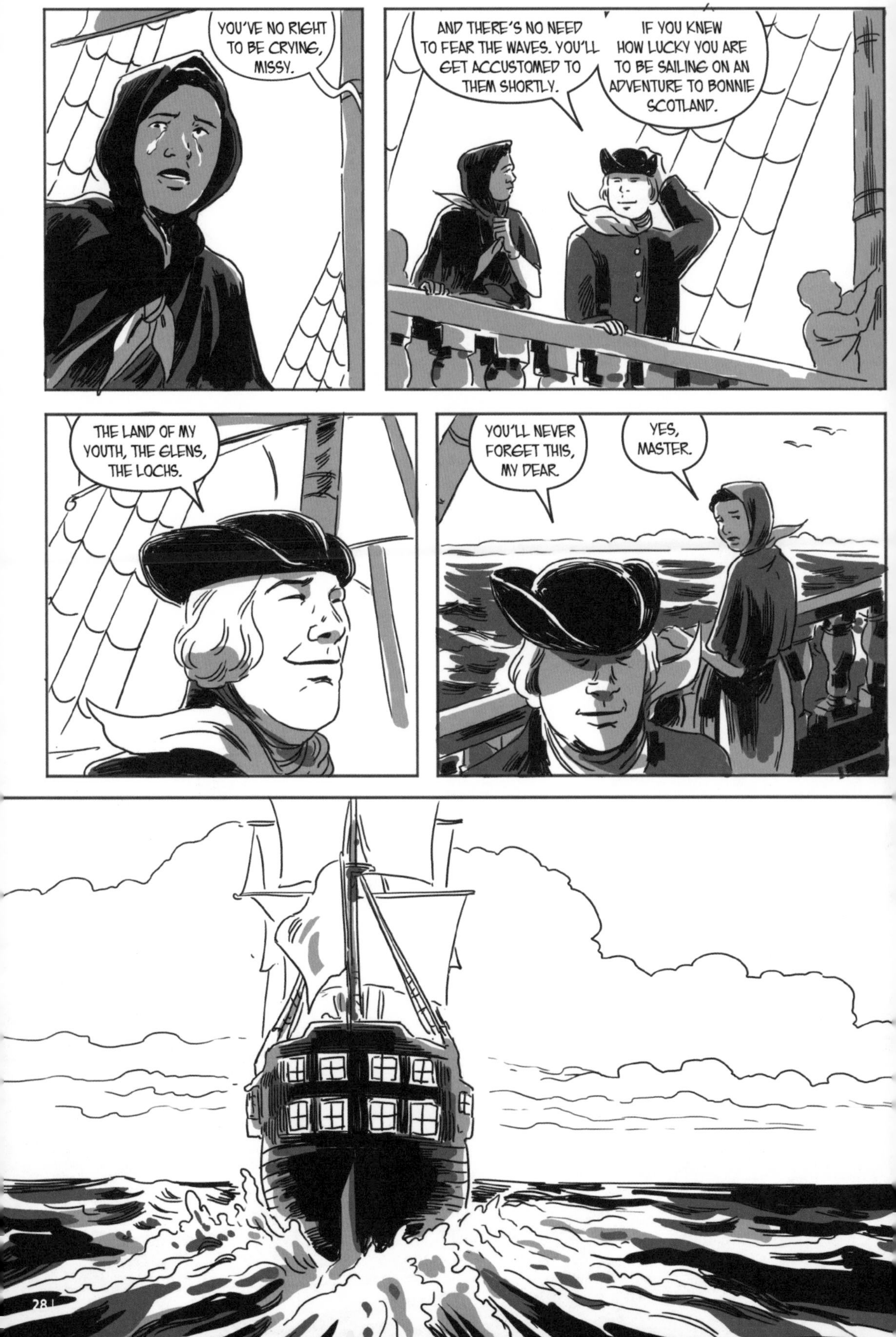
YOU'VE NO RIGHT TO BE CRYING, MISSY.
AND THERE'S NO NEED TO FEAR THE WAVES. YOU'LL GET ACCUSTOMED TO THEM SHORTLY.
IF YOU KNEW HOW LUCKY YOU ARE TO BE SAILING ON AN ADVENTURE TO BONNIE SCOTLAND.
THE LAND OF MY YOUTH, THE GLENS, THE LOCHS.
YOU'LL NEVER FORGET THIS, MY DEAR.
YES, MASTER.

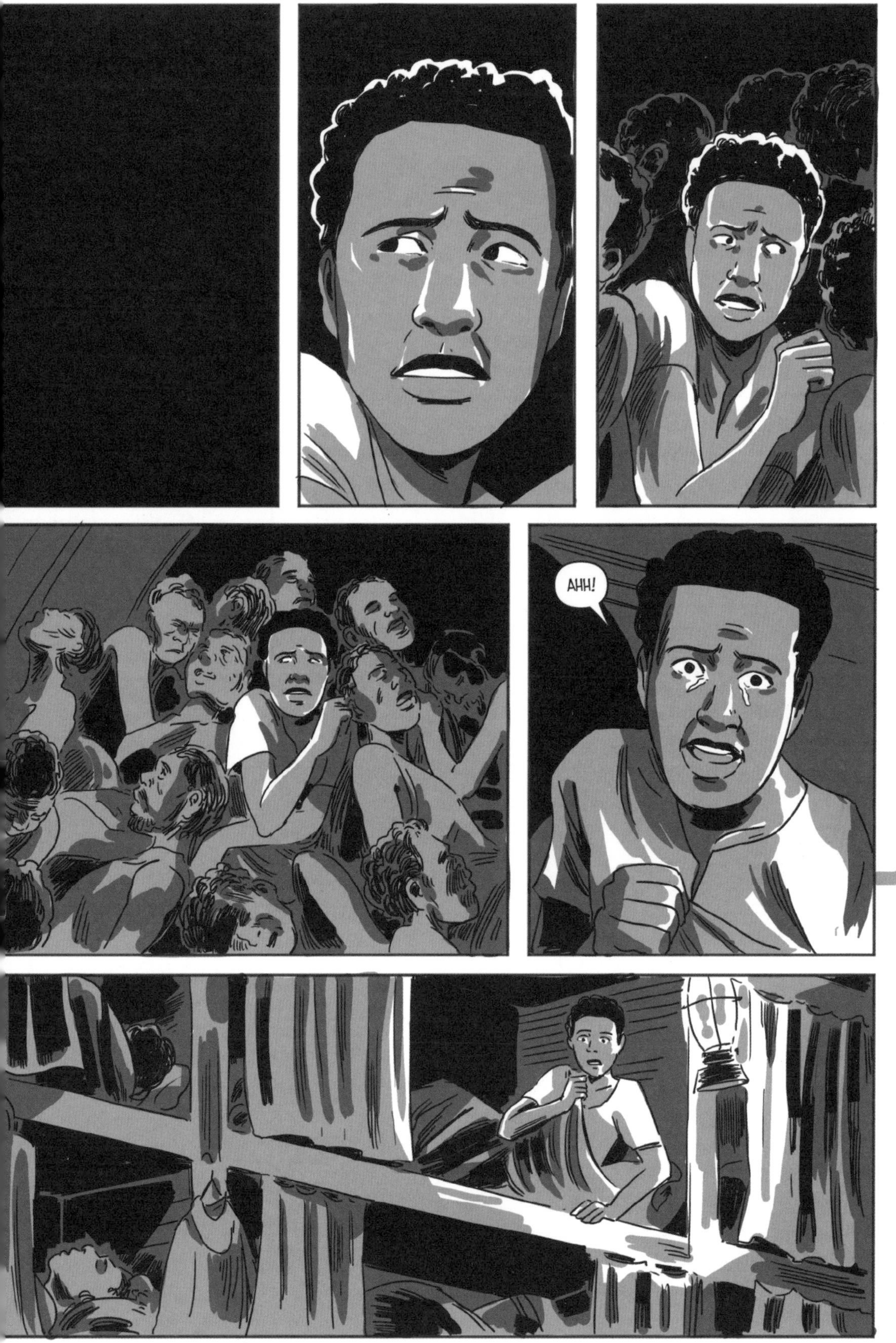
AHH!

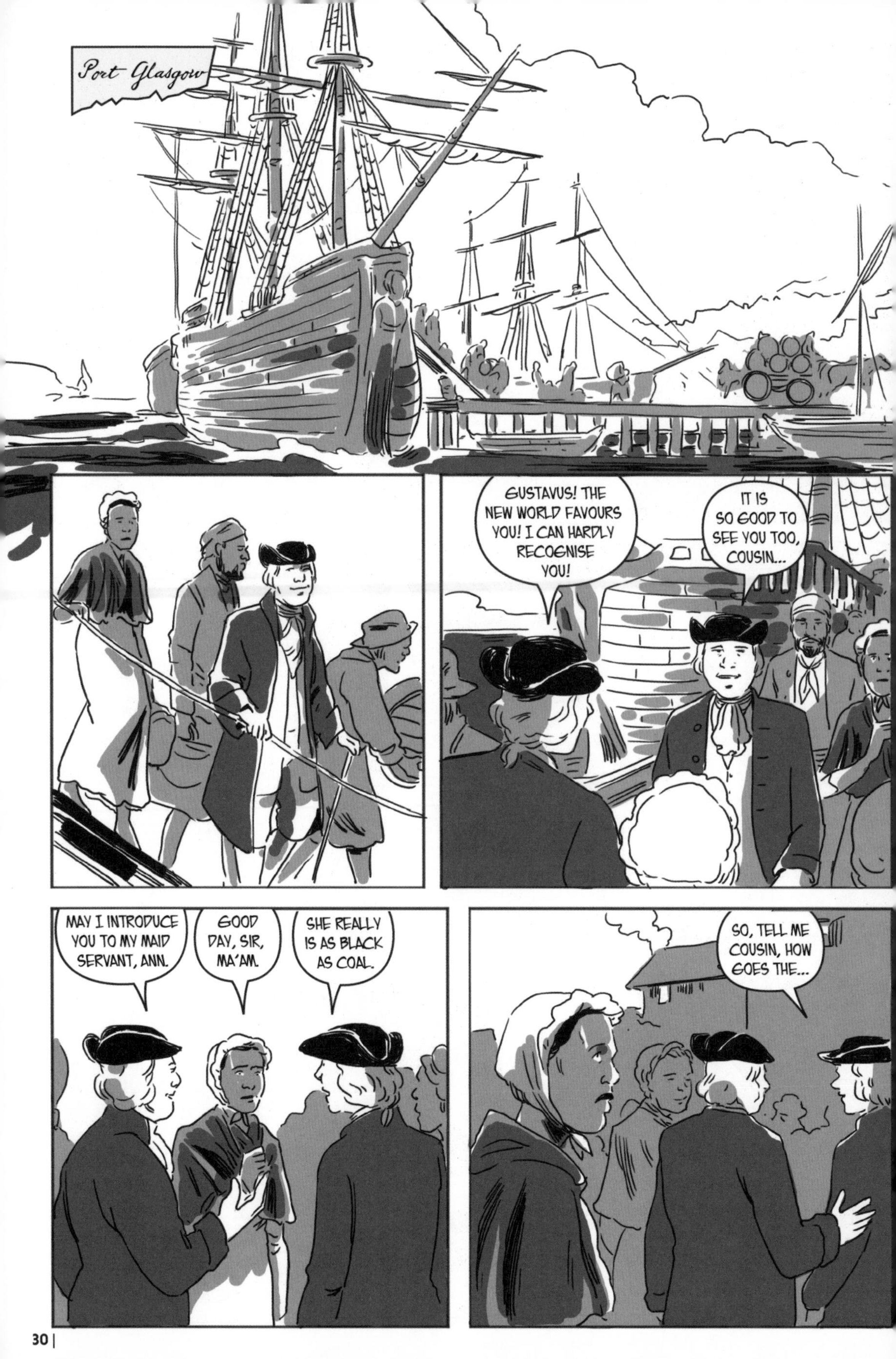
Port Glasgow
GUSTAVUS! THE NEW WORLD FAVOURS YOU! I CAN HARDLY RECOGNISE YOU!
IT IS SO GOOD TO SEE YOU TOO, COUSIN...
MAY I INTRODUCE YOU TO MY MAID SERVANT, ANN.
GOOD DAY, SIR, MA'AM.
SHE REALLY IS AS BLACK AS COAL.
SO, TELL ME COUSIN, HOW GOES THE...

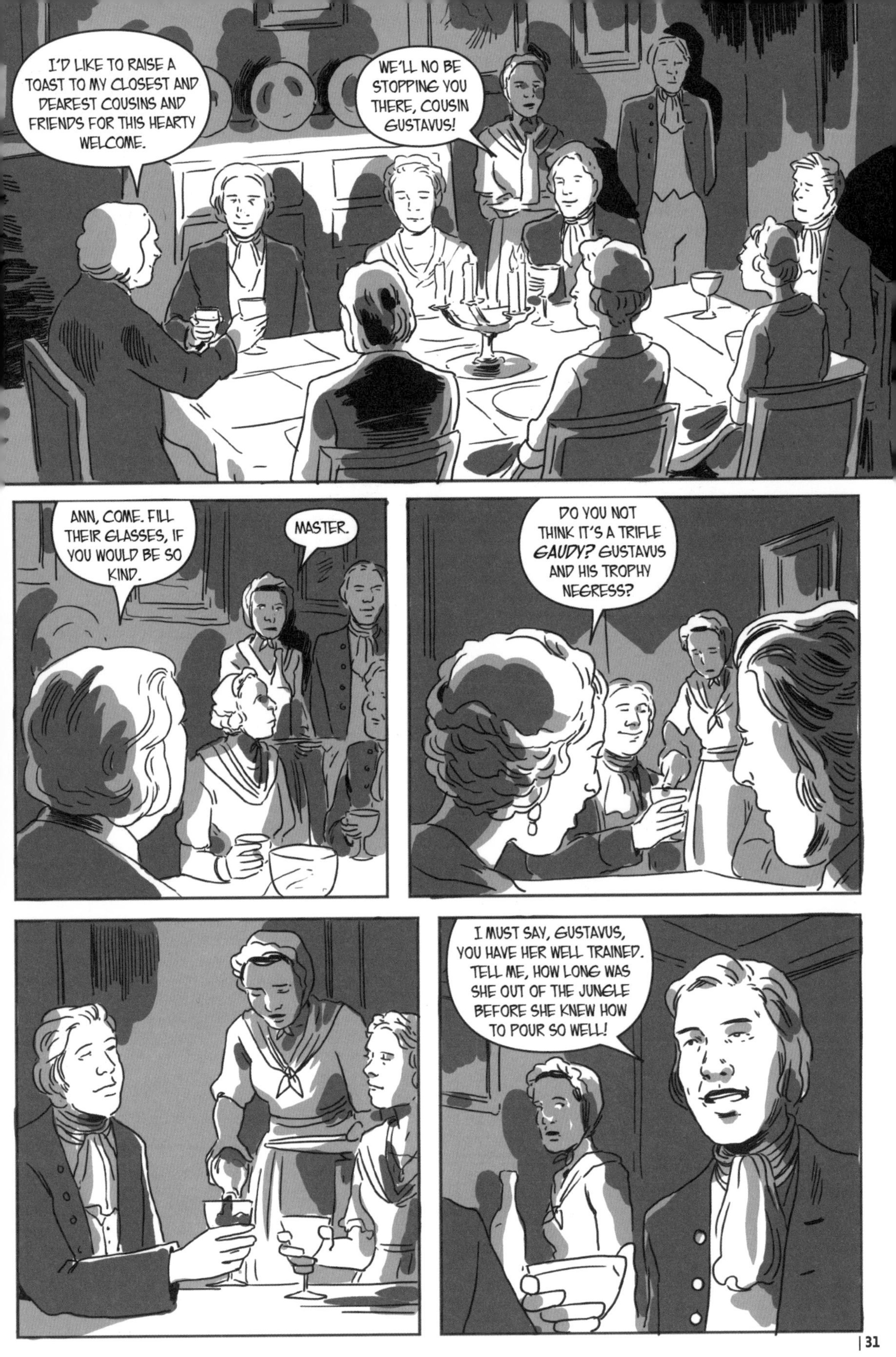
I'D LIKE TO RAISE A TOAST TO MY CLOSEST AND DEAREST COUSINS AND FRIENDS FOR THIS HEARTY WELCOME.
WE'LL NO BE STOPPING YOU THERE, COUSIN GUSTAVUS!
ANN, COME. FILL THEIR GLASSES, IF YOU WOULD BE SO KIND.
MASTER.
DO YOU NOT THINK IT'S A TRIFLE *GAUDY?* GUSTAVUS AND HIS TROPHY NEGRESS?
I MUST SAY, GUSTAVUS, YOU HAVE HER WELL TRAINED. TELL ME, HOW LONG WAS SHE OUT OF THE JUNGLE BEFORE SHE KNEW HOW TO POUR SO WELL!

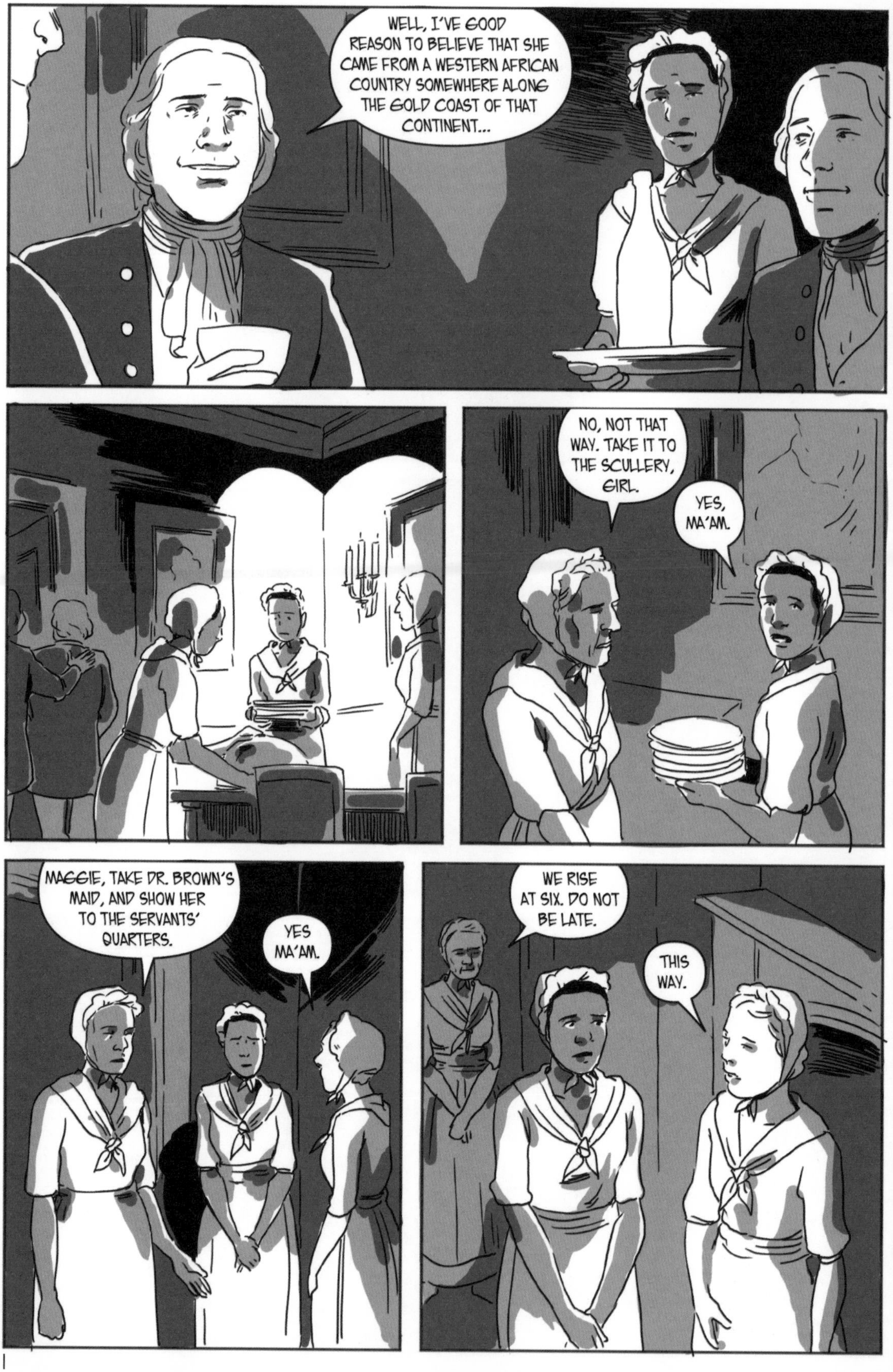
WELL, I'VE GOOD REASON TO BELIEVE THAT SHE CAME FROM A WESTERN AFRICAN COUNTRY SOMEWHERE ALONG THE GOLD COAST OF THAT CONTINENT...
NO, NOT THAT WAY. TAKE IT TO THE SCULLERY, GIRL.
YES, MA'AM.
MAGGIE, TAKE DR. BROWN'S MAID, AND SHOW HER TO THE SERVANTS' QUARTERS.
YES MA'AM.
WE RISE AT SIX. DO NOT BE LATE.
THIS WAY.

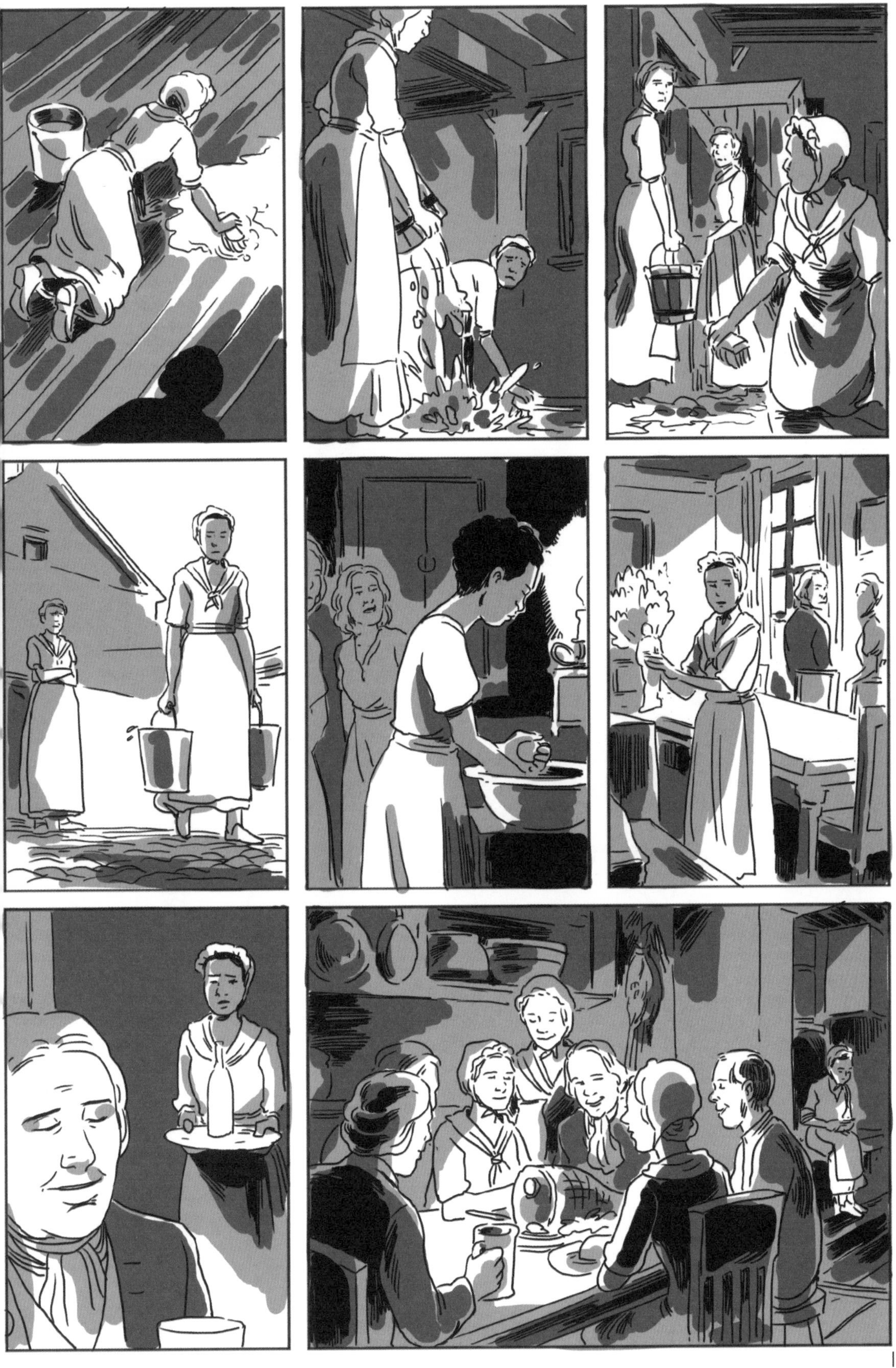

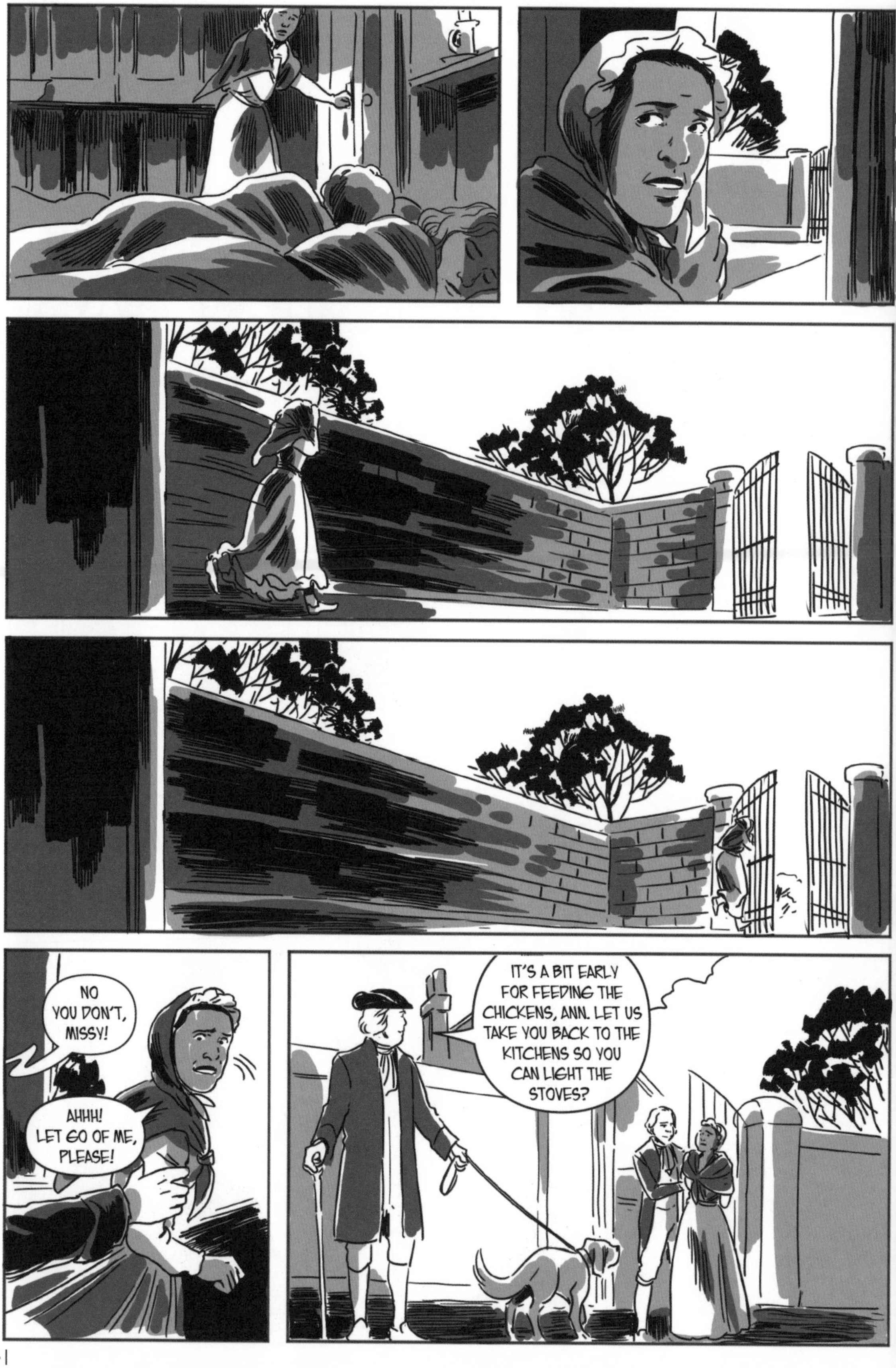
NO YOU DON'T, MISSY!
AHHH! LET GO OF ME, PLEASE!
IT'S A BIT EARLY FOR FEEDING THE CHICKENS, ANN. LET US TAKE YOU BACK TO THE KITCHENS SO YOU CAN LIGHT THE STOVES?

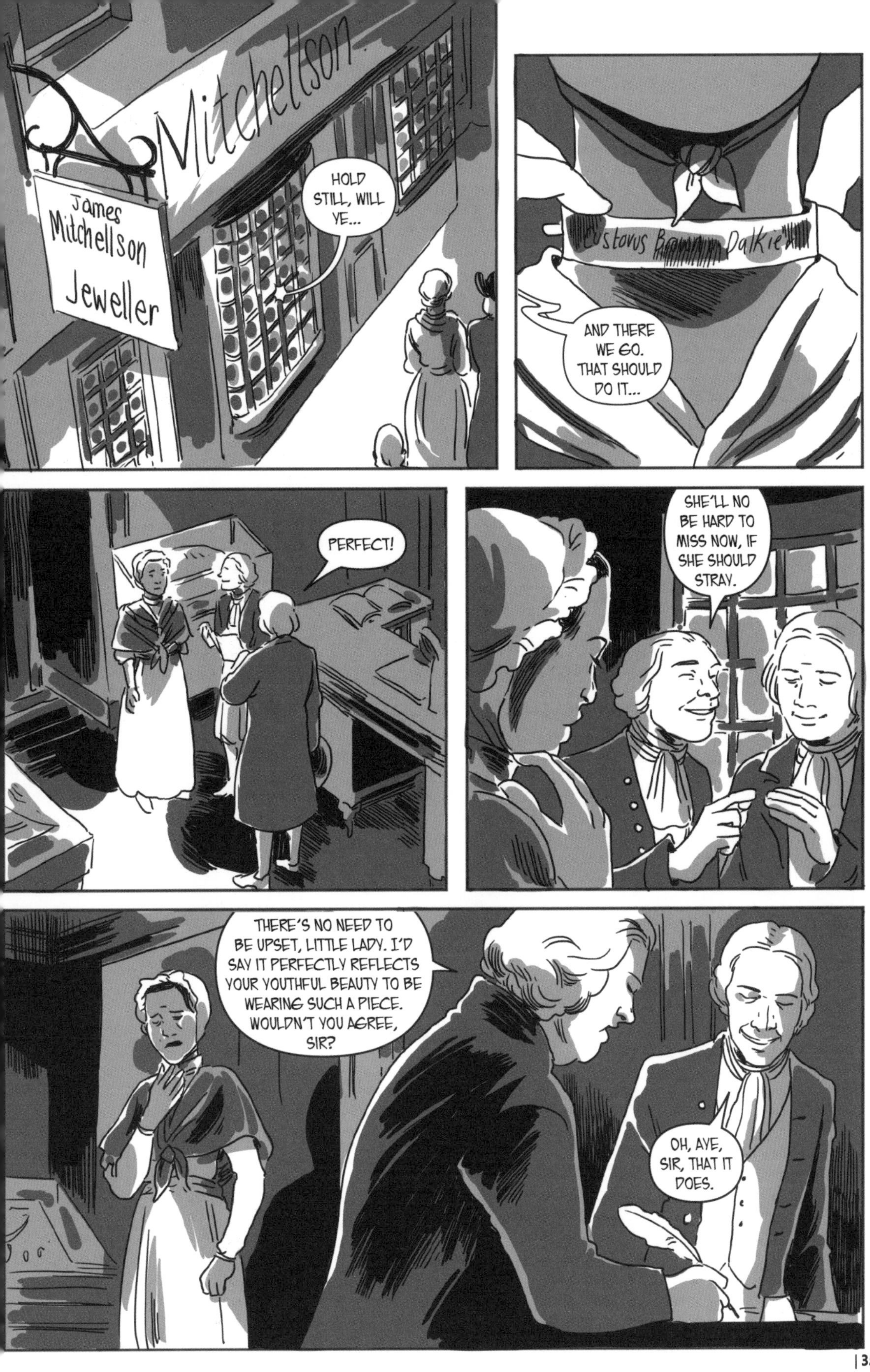
Mitchellson
James Mitchellson Jeweller
HOLD STILL, WILL YE...
AND THERE WE GO. THAT SHOULD DO IT...
PERFECT!
SHE'LL NO BE HARD TO MISS NOW, IF SHE SHOULD STRAY.
THERE'S NO NEED TO BE UPSET, LITTLE LADY. I'D SAY IT PERFECTLY REFLECTS YOUR YOUTHFUL BEAUTY TO BE WEARING SUCH A PIECE. WOULDN'T YOU AGREE, SIR?
OH, AYE, SIR, THAT IT DOES.

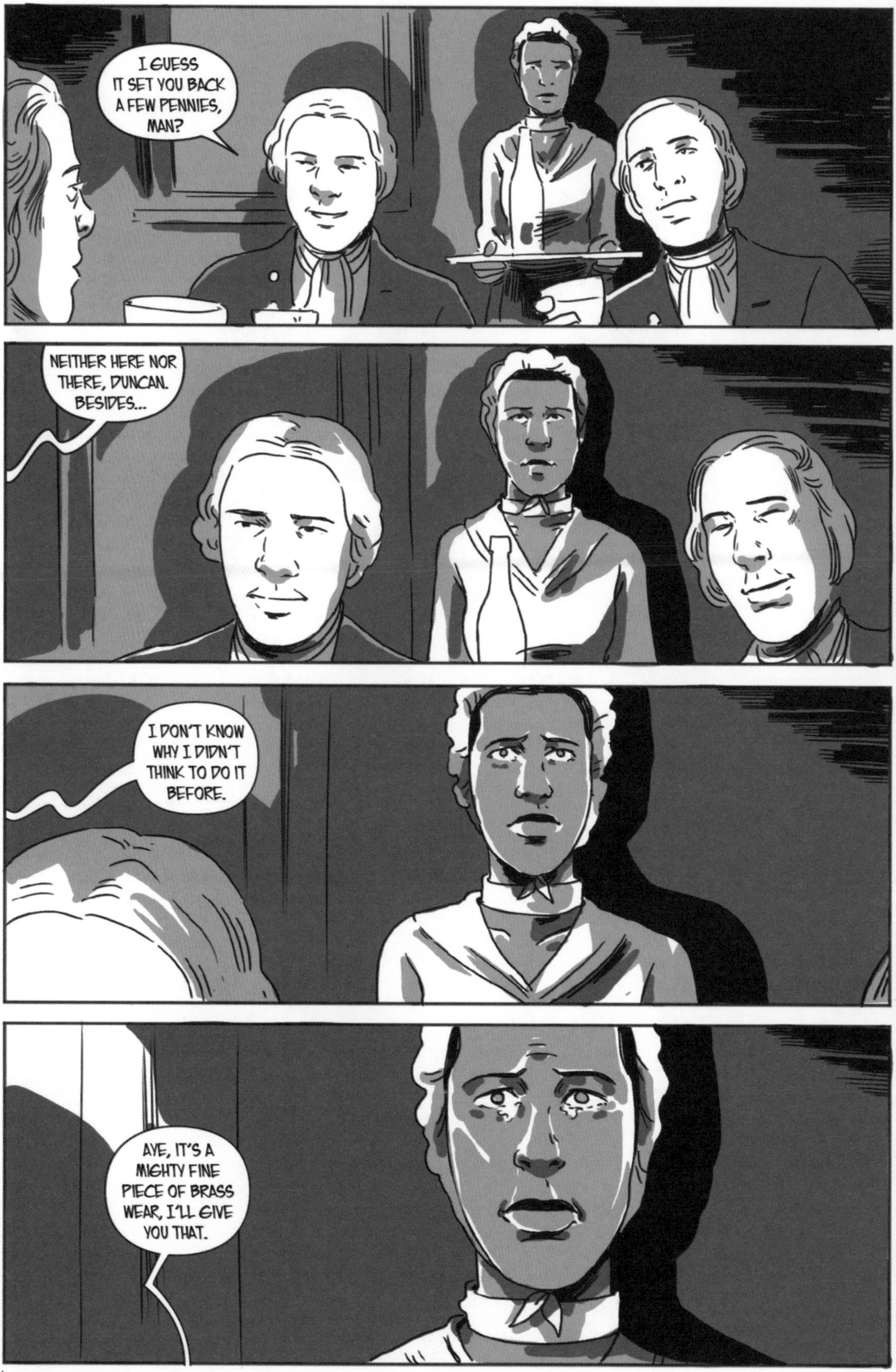
I GUESS IT SET YOU BACK A FEW PENNIES, MAN?
NEITHER HERE NOR THERE, DUNCAN. BESIDES...
I DON'T KNOW WHY I DIDN'T THINK TO DO IT BEFORE.
AYE, IT'S A MIGHTY FINE PIECE OF BRASS WEAR, I'LL GIVE YOU THAT.

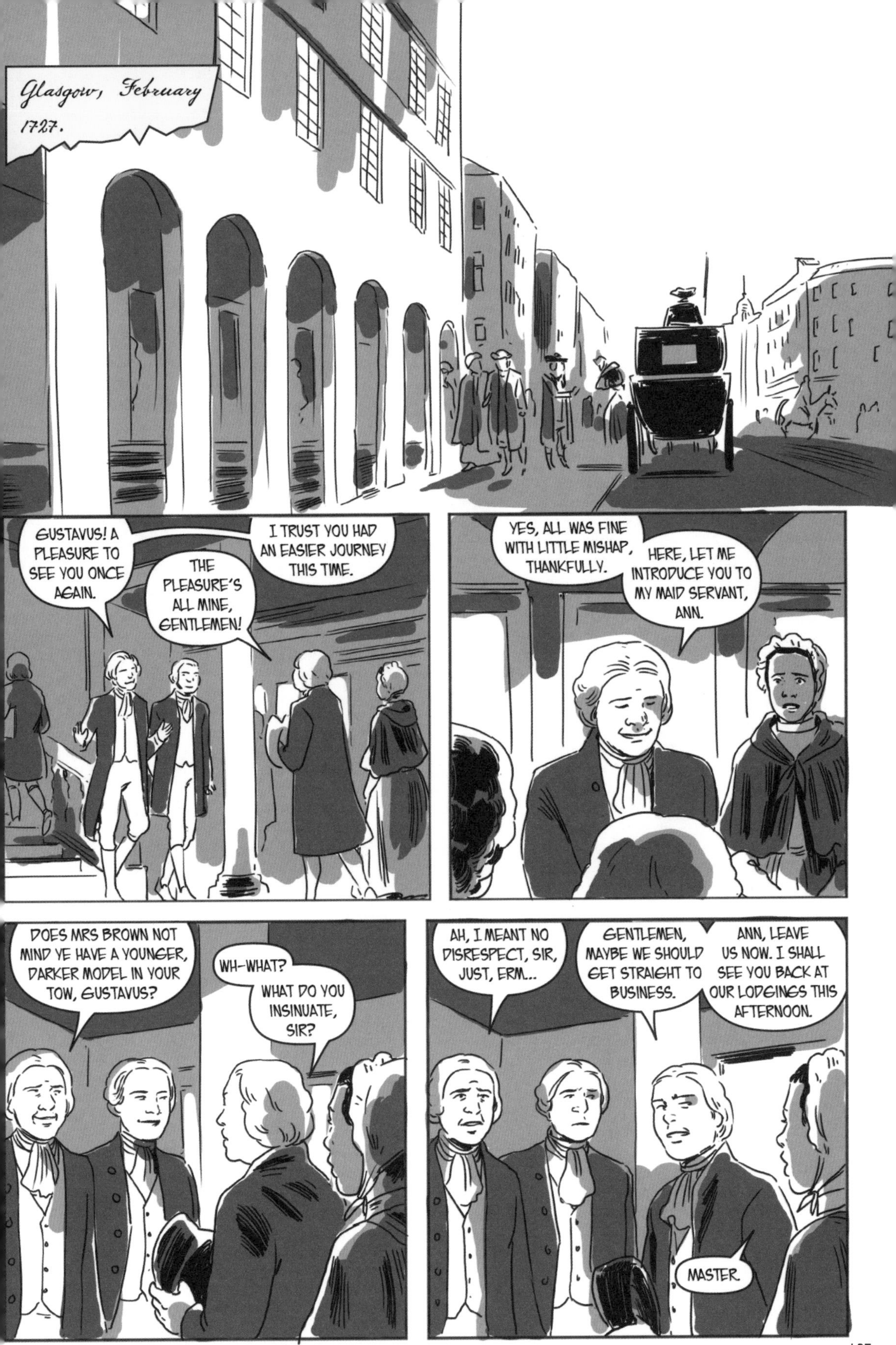
Glasgow, February 1727.
GUSTAVUS! A PLEASURE TO SEE YOU ONCE AGAIN.
THE PLEASURE'S ALL MINE, GENTLEMEN!
I TRUST YOU HAD AN EASIER JOURNEY THIS TIME.
YES, ALL WAS FINE WITH LITTLE MISHAP, THANKFULLY.
HERE, LET ME INTRODUCE YOU TO MY MAID SERVANT, ANN.
DOES MRS BROWN NOT MIND YE HAVE A YOUNGER, DARKER MODEL IN YOUR TOW, GUSTAVUS?
WH-WHAT?
WHAT DO YOU INSINUATE, SIR?
AH, I MEANT NO DISRESPECT, SIR, JUST, ERM...
GENTLEMEN, MAYBE WE SHOULD GET STRAIGHT TO BUSINESS.
ANN, LEAVE US NOW. I SHALL SEE YOU BACK AT OUR LODGINGS THIS AFTERNOON.
MASTER.

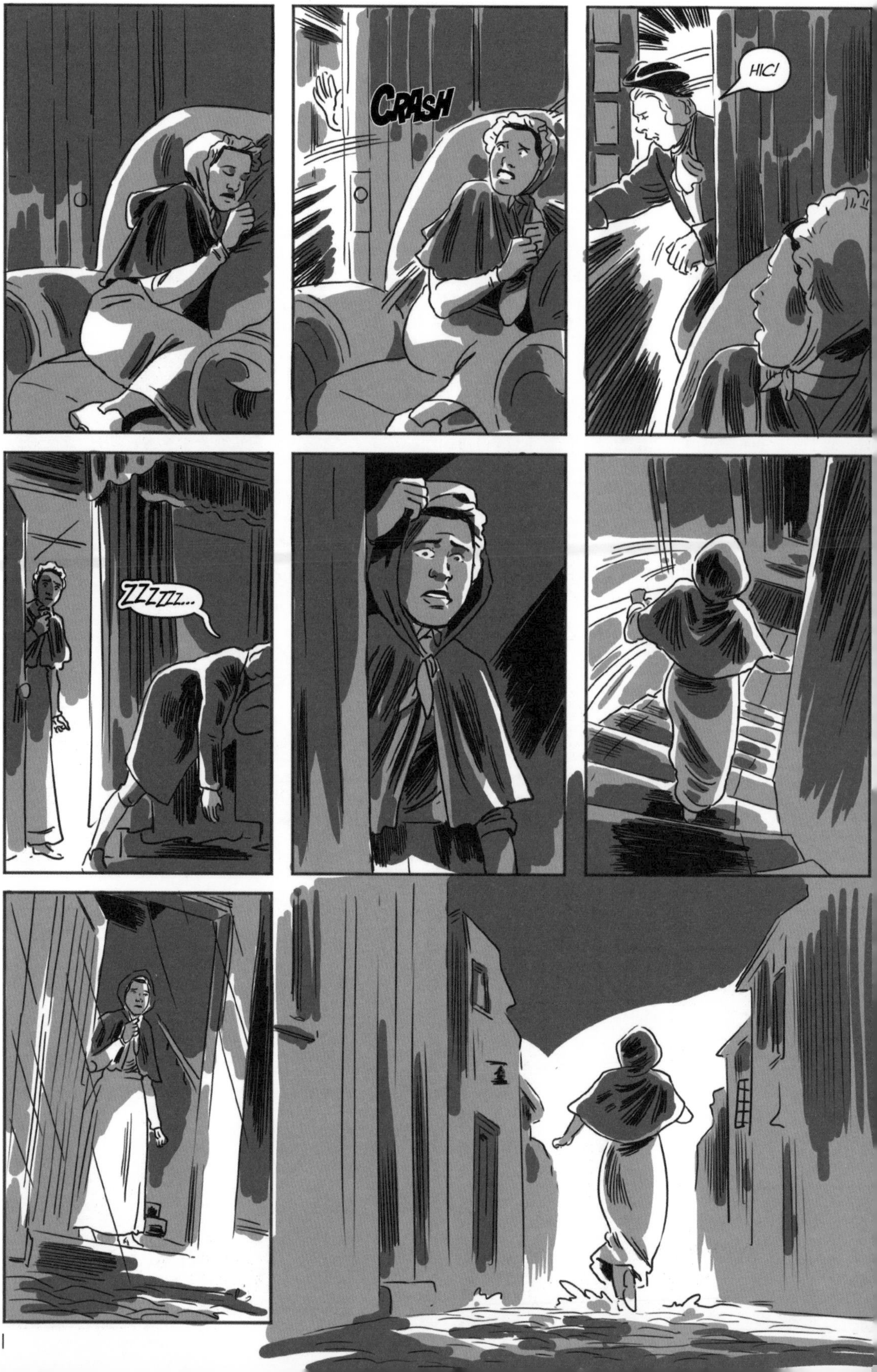
CRASH
HIC!
ZZZZZ...

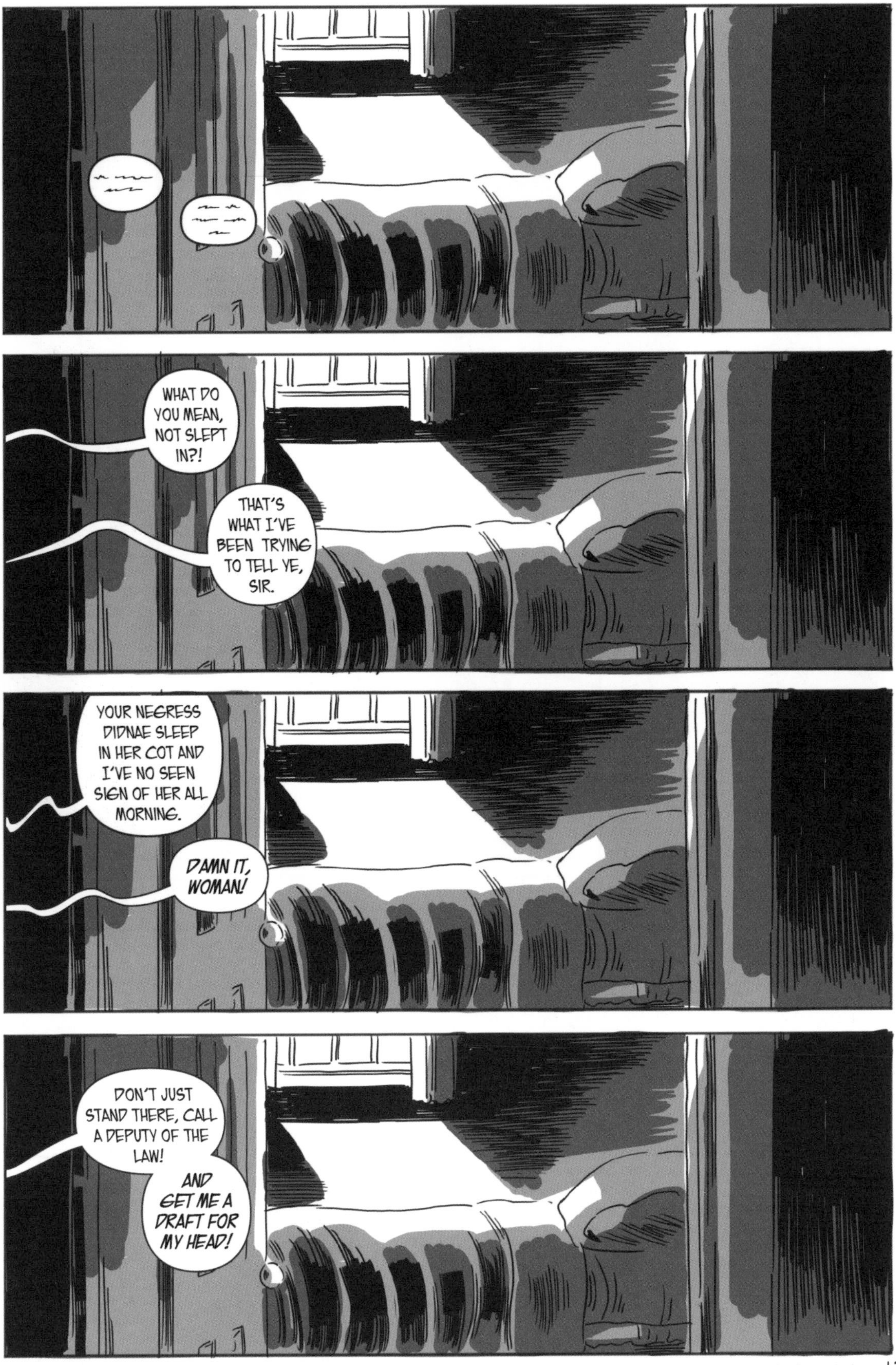
WHAT DO YOU MEAN, NOT SLEPT IN?!
THAT'S WHAT I'VE BEEN TRYING TO TELL YE, SIR.
YOUR NEGRESS DIDNAE SLEEP IN HER COT AND I'VE NO SEEN SIGN OF HER ALL MORNING.
DAMN IT, WOMAN!
DON'T JUST STAND THERE, CALL A DEPUTY OF THE LAW!
AND GET ME A DRAFT FOR MY HEAD!

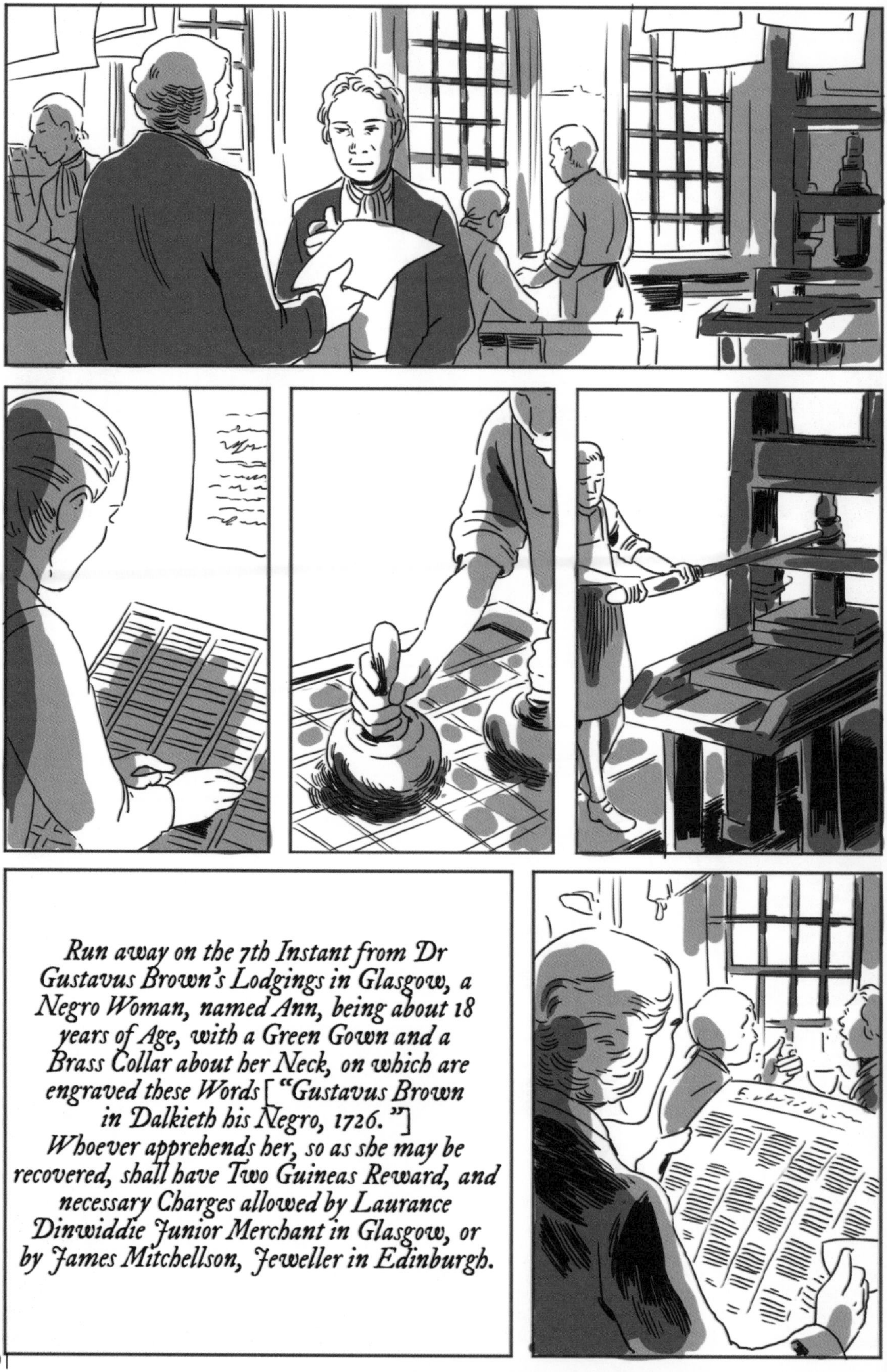
Run away on the 7th Instant from Dr Gustavus Brown's Lodgings in Glasgow, a Negro Woman, named Ann, being about 18 years of Age, with a Green Gown and a Brass Collar about her Neck, on which are engraved these Words ["Gustavus Brown in Dalkieth his Negro, 1726."] Whoever apprehends her, so as she may be recovered, shall have Two Guineas Reward, and necessary Charges allowed by Laurance Dinwiddie Junior Merchant in Glasgow, or by James Mitchellson, Jeweller in Edinburgh.

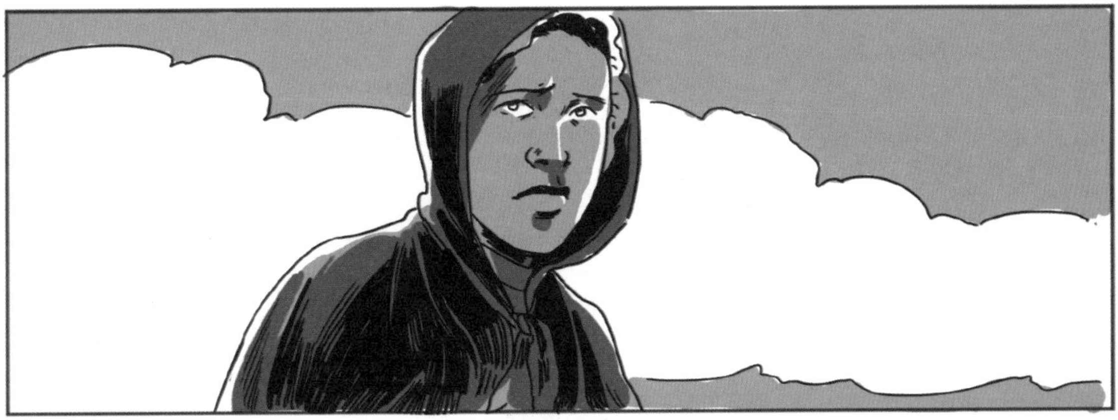

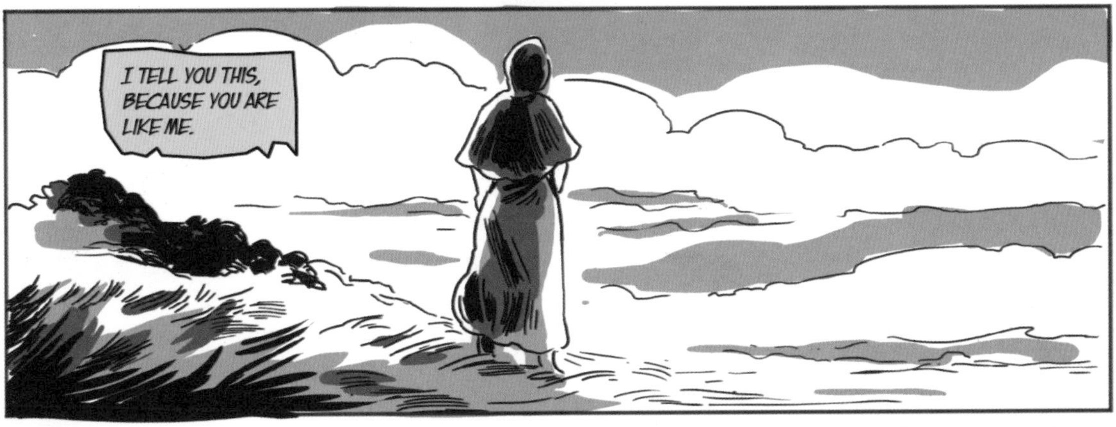
I TELL YOU THIS, BECAUSE YOU ARE LIKE ME.

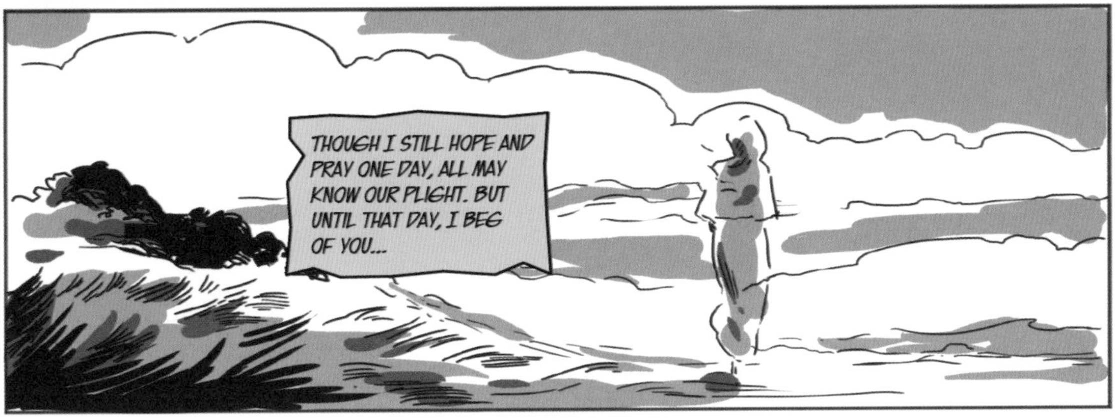
THOUGH I STILL HOPE AND PRAY ONE DAY, ALL MAY KNOW OUR PLIGHT. BUT UNTIL THAT DAY, I BEG OF YOU...

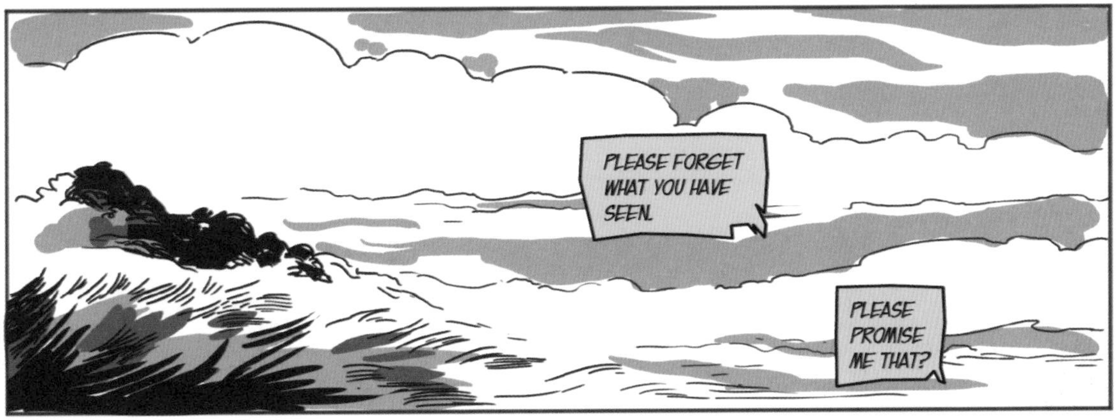
PLEASE FORGET WHAT YOU HAVE SEEN.
PLEASE PROMISE ME THAT?

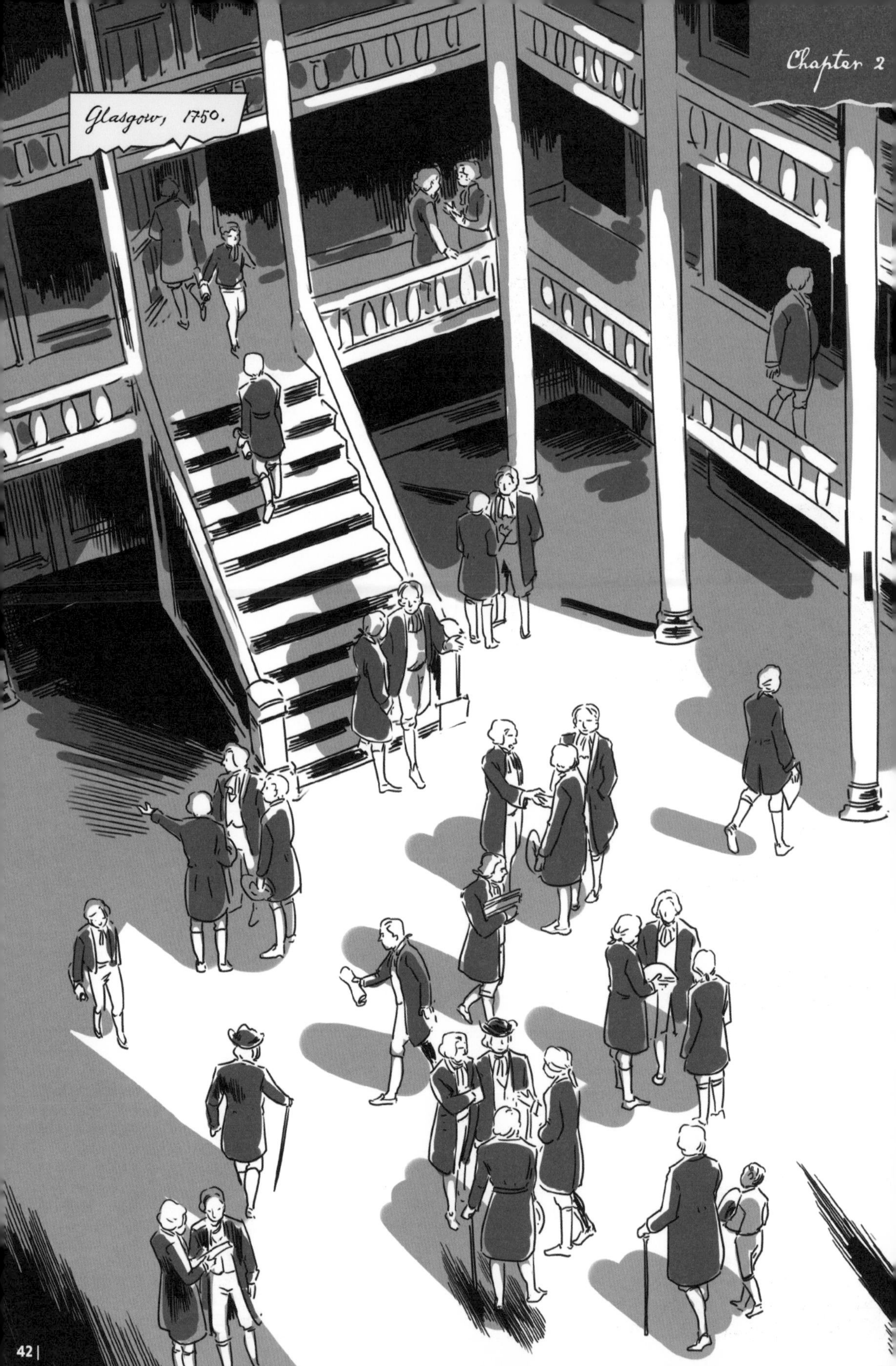
Chapter 2
Glasgow, 1750.

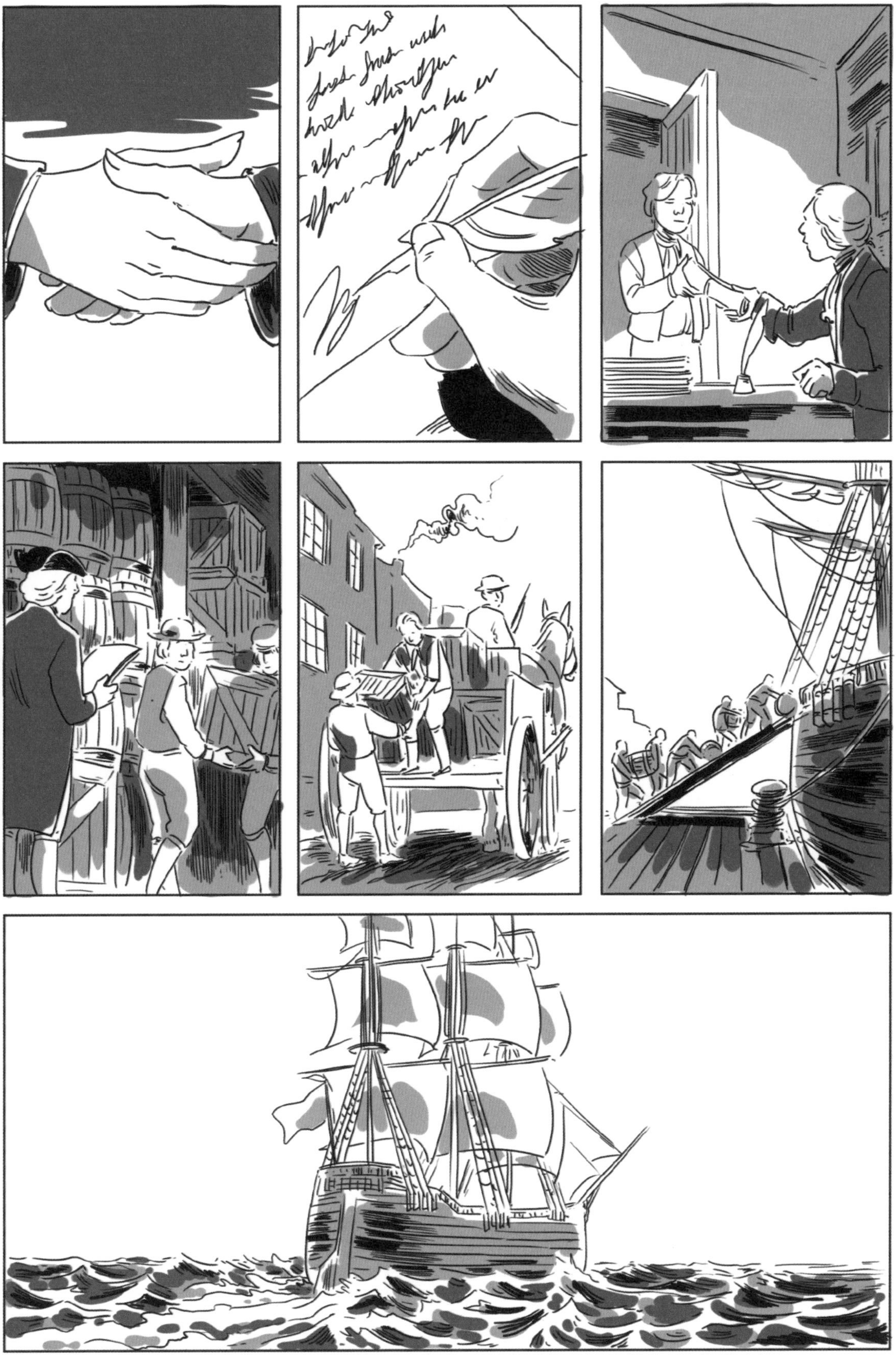

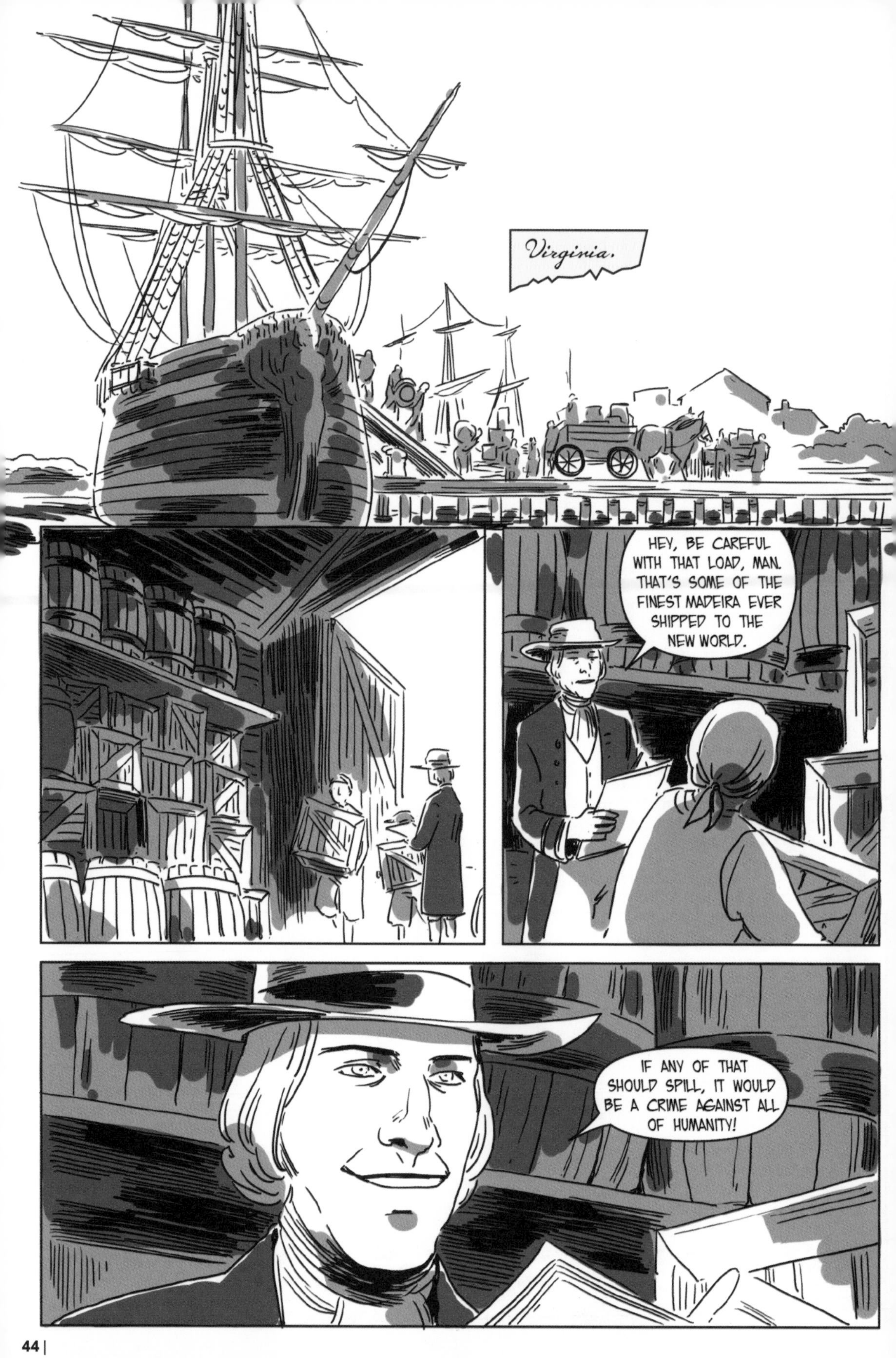
Virginia.
HEY, BE CAREFUL WITH THAT LOAD, MAN. THAT'S SOME OF THE FINEST MADEIRA EVER SHIPPED TO THE NEW WORLD.
IF ANY OF THAT SHOULD SPILL, IT WOULD BE A CRIME AGAINST ALL OF HUMANITY!

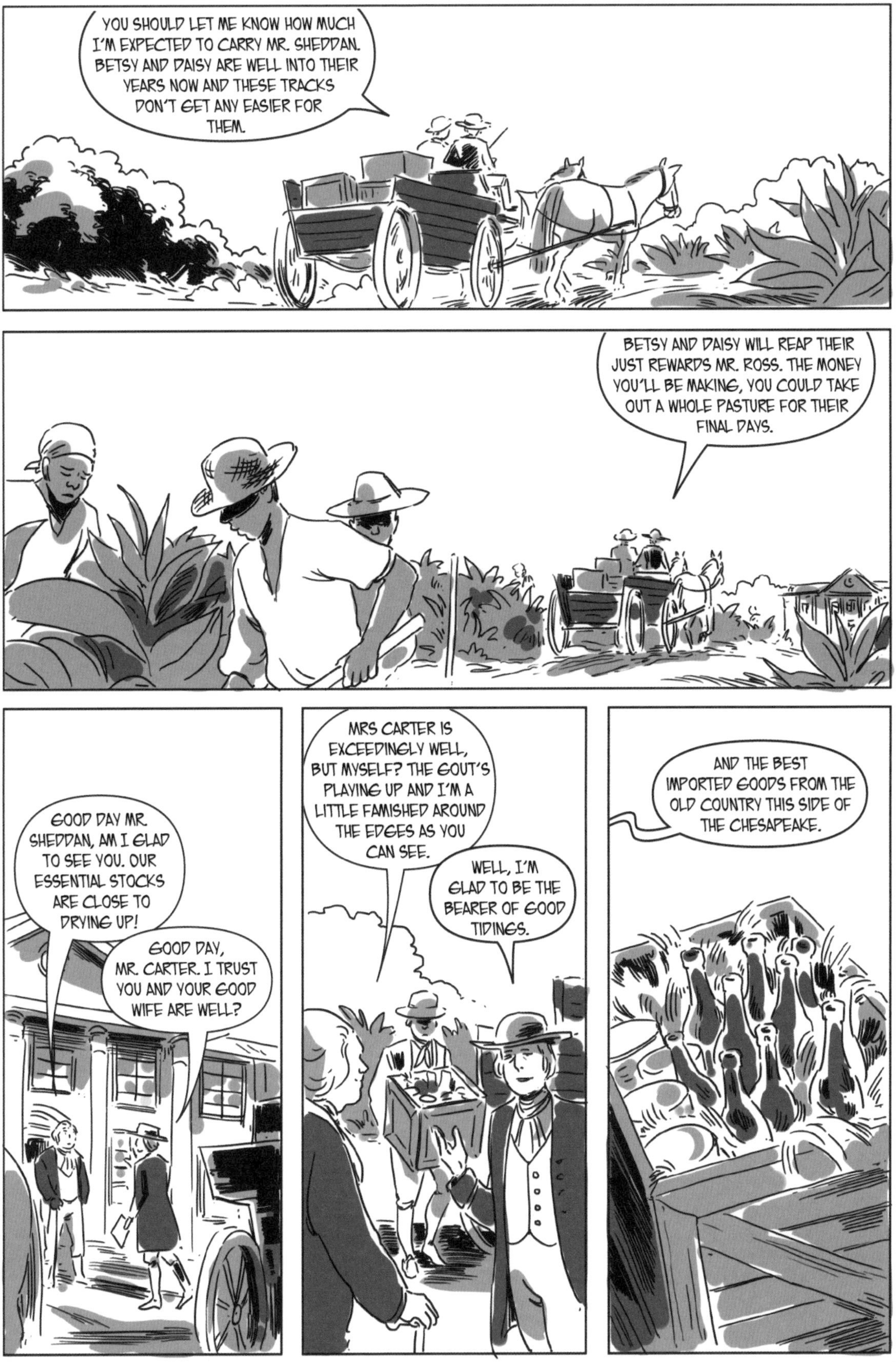
YOU SHOULD LET ME KNOW HOW MUCH I'M EXPECTED TO CARRY MR. SHEDDAN. BETSY AND DAISY ARE WELL INTO THEIR YEARS NOW AND THESE TRACKS DON'T GET ANY EASIER FOR THEM.
BETSY AND DAISY WILL REAP THEIR JUST REWARDS MR. ROSS. THE MONEY YOU'LL BE MAKING, YOU COULD TAKE OUT A WHOLE PASTURE FOR THEIR FINAL DAYS.
GOOD DAY MR. SHEDDAN, AM I GLAD TO SEE YOU. OUR ESSENTIAL STOCKS ARE CLOSE TO DRYING UP!
GOOD DAY, MR. CARTER. I TRUST YOU AND YOUR GOOD WIFE ARE WELL?
MRS CARTER IS EXCEEDINGLY WELL, BUT MYSELF? THE GOUT'S PLAYING UP AND I'M A LITTLE FAMISHED AROUND THE EDGES AS YOU CAN SEE.
WELL, I'M GLAD TO BE THE BEARER OF GOOD TIDINGS.
AND THE BEST IMPORTED GOODS FROM THE OLD COUNTRY THIS SIDE OF THE CHESAPEAKE.

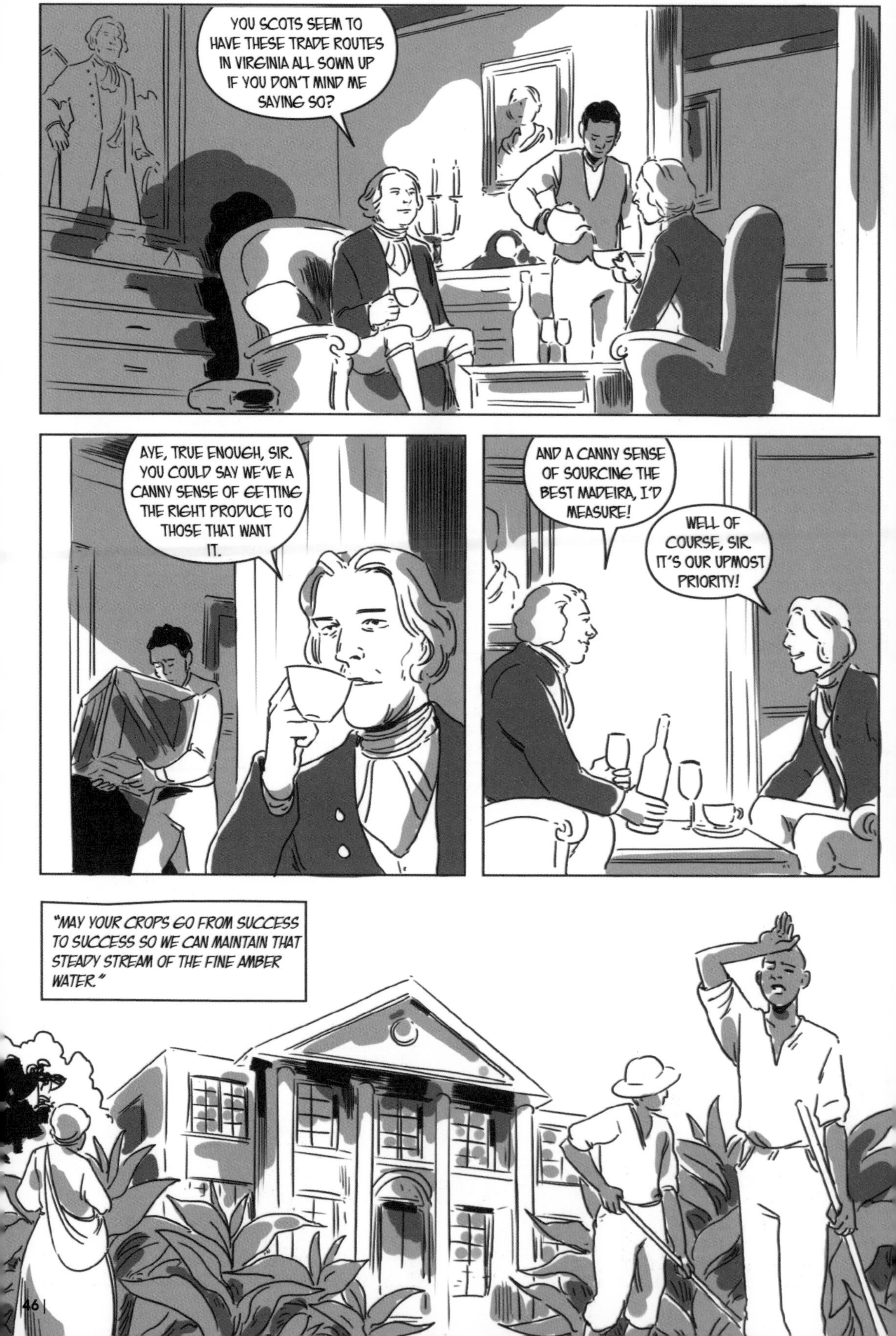
YOU SCOTS SEEM TO HAVE THESE TRADE ROUTES IN VIRGINIA ALL SOWN UP IF YOU DON'T MIND ME SAYING SO?
AYE, TRUE ENOUGH, SIR. YOU COULD SAY WE'VE A CANNY SENSE OF GETTING THE RIGHT PRODUCE TO THOSE THAT WANT IT.
AND A CANNY SENSE OF SOURCING THE BEST MADEIRA, I'D MEASURE!
WELL OF COURSE, SIR. IT'S OUR UPMOST PRIORITY!
"MAY YOUR CROPS GO FROM SUCCESS TO SUCCESS SO WE CAN MAINTAIN THAT STEADY STREAM OF THE FINE AMBER WATER."

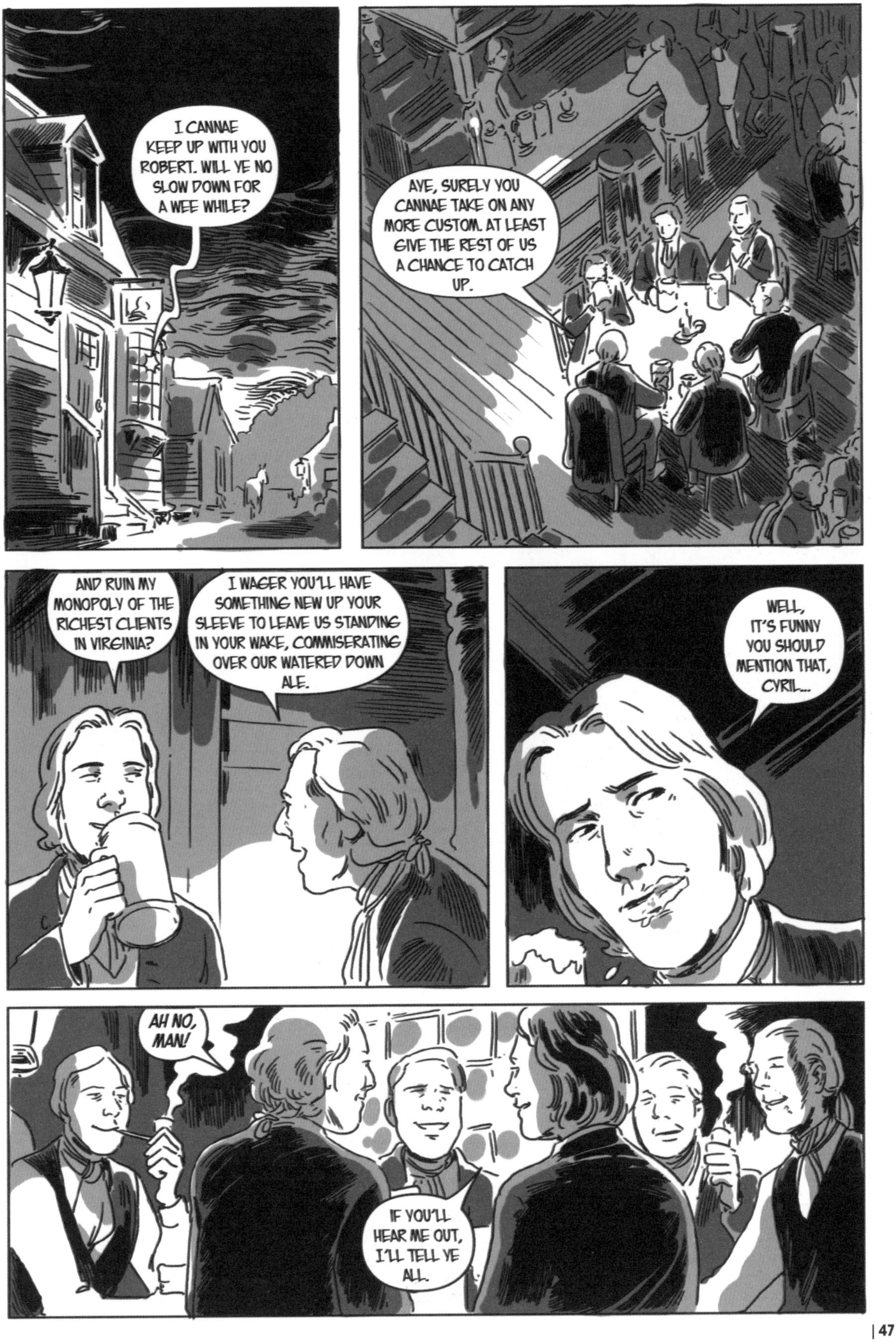

I CANNAE KEEP UP WITH YOU ROBERT. WILL YE NO SLOW DOWN FOR A WEE WHILE?
AYE, SURELY YOU CANNAE TAKE ON ANY MORE CUSTOM. AT LEAST GIVE THE REST OF US A CHANCE TO CATCH UP.
AND RUIN MY MONOPOLY OF THE RICHEST CLIENTS IN VIRGINIA?
I WAGER YOU'LL HAVE SOMETHING NEW UP YOUR SLEEVE TO LEAVE US STANDING IN YOUR WAKE, COMMISERATING OVER OUR WATERED DOWN ALE.
WELL, IT'S FUNNY YOU SHOULD MENTION THAT, CYRIL...
AH NO, MAN!
IF YOU'LL HEAR ME OUT, I'LL TELL YE ALL.

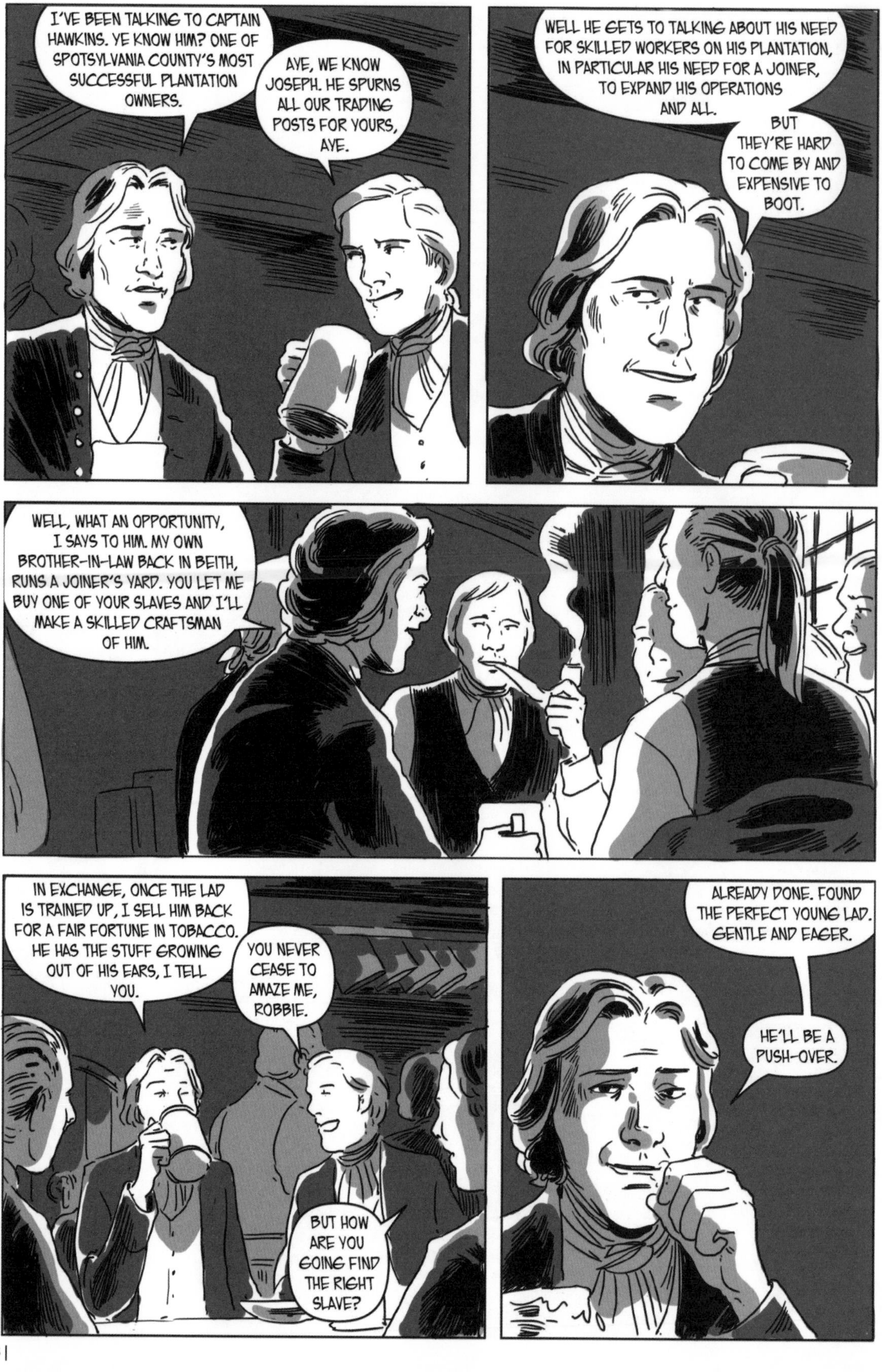
I'VE BEEN TALKING TO CAPTAIN HAWKINS. YE KNOW HIM? ONE OF SPOTSYLVANIA COUNTY'S MOST SUCCESSFUL PLANTATION OWNERS.
AYE, WE KNOW JOSEPH. HE SPURNS ALL OUR TRADING POSTS FOR YOURS, AYE.
WELL HE GETS TO TALKING ABOUT HIS NEED FOR SKILLED WORKERS ON HIS PLANTATION, IN PARTICULAR HIS NEED FOR A JOINER, TO EXPAND HIS OPERATIONS AND ALL.
BUT THEY'RE HARD TO COME BY AND EXPENSIVE TO BOOT.
WELL, WHAT AN OPPORTUNITY, I SAYS TO HIM. MY OWN BROTHER-IN-LAW BACK IN BEITH, RUNS A JOINER'S YARD. YOU LET ME BUY ONE OF YOUR SLAVES AND I'LL MAKE A SKILLED CRAFTSMAN OF HIM.
IN EXCHANGE, ONCE THE LAD IS TRAINED UP, I SELL HIM BACK FOR A FAIR FORTUNE IN TOBACCO. HE HAS THE STUFF GROWING OUT OF HIS EARS, I TELL YOU.
YOU NEVER CEASE TO AMAZE ME, ROBBIE.
BUT HOW ARE YOU GOING FIND THE RIGHT SLAVE?
ALREADY DONE. FOUND THE PERFECT YOUNG LAD. GENTLE AND EAGER.
HE'LL BE A PUSH-OVER.

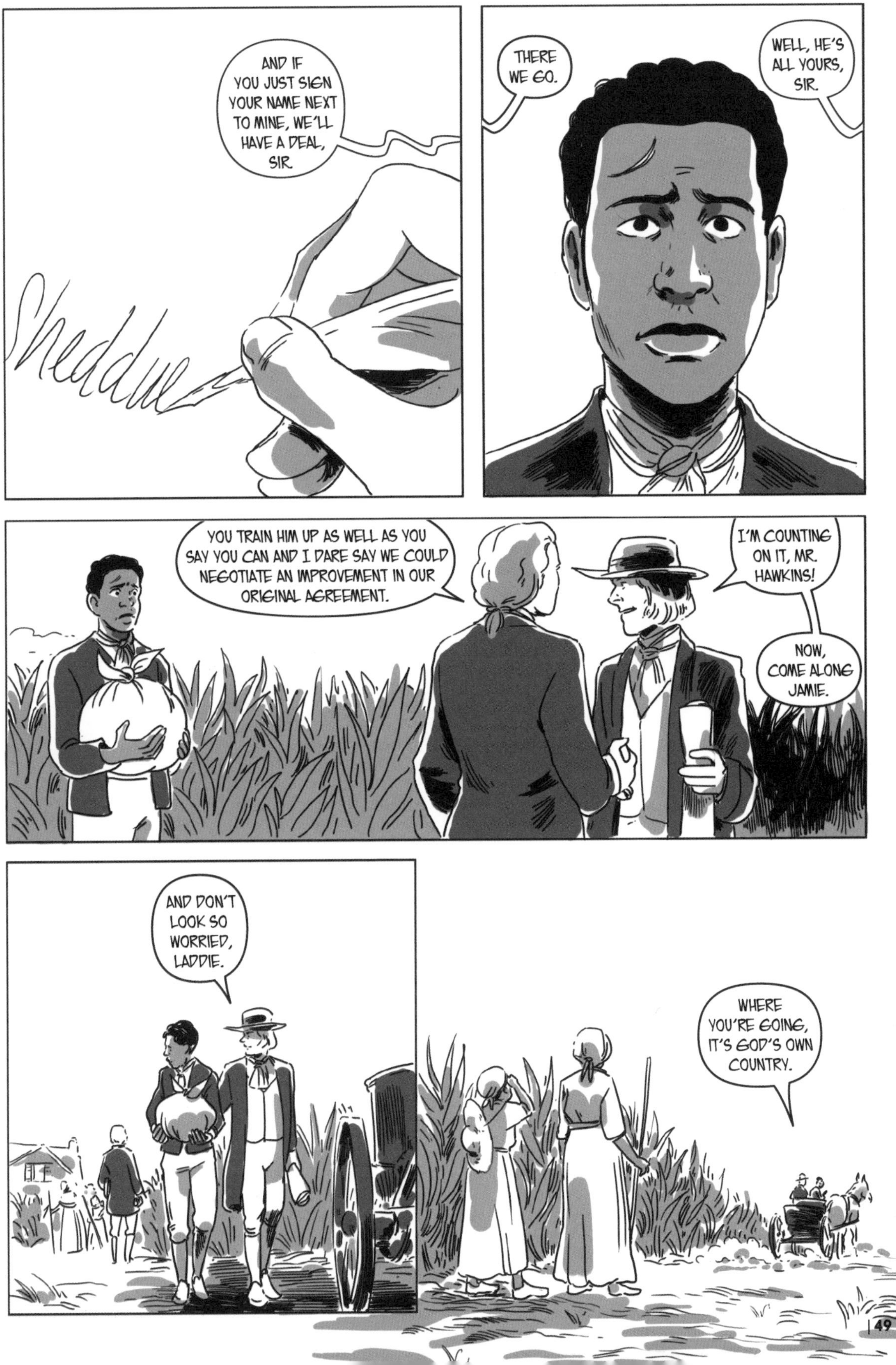
AND IF YOU JUST SIGN YOUR NAME NEXT TO MINE, WE'LL HAVE A DEAL, SIR.
THERE WE GO.
WELL, HE'S ALL YOURS, SIR.
YOU TRAIN HIM UP AS WELL AS YOU SAY YOU CAN AND I DARE SAY WE COULD NEGOTIATE AN IMPROVEMENT IN OUR ORIGINAL AGREEMENT.
I'M COUNTING ON IT, MR. HAWKINS!
NOW, COME ALONG JAMIE.
AND DON'T LOOK SO WORRIED, LADDIE.
WHERE YOU'RE GOING, IT'S GOD'S OWN COUNTRY.

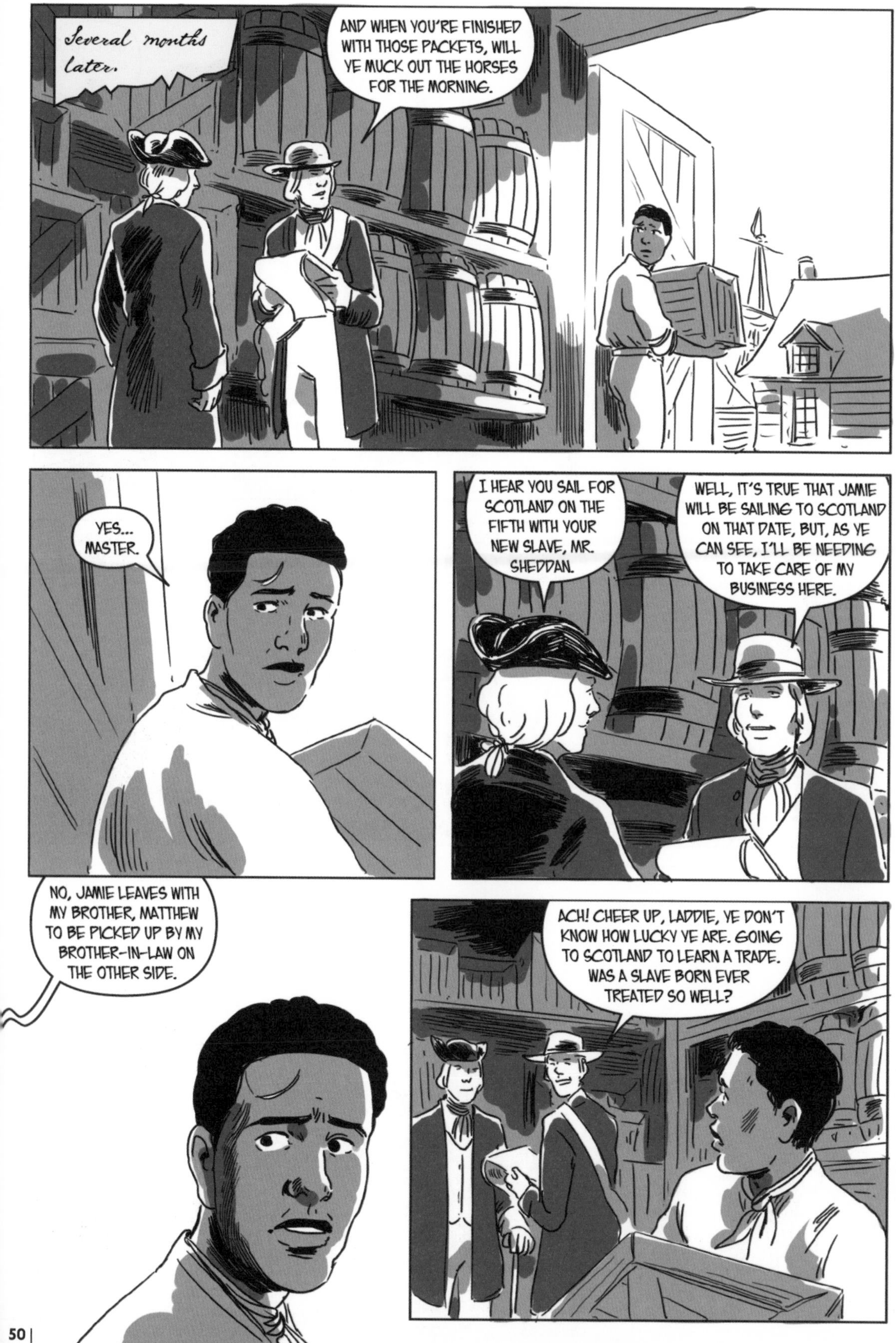
Several months later.
AND WHEN YOU'RE FINISHED WITH THOSE PACKETS, WILL YE MUCK OUT THE HORSES FOR THE MORNING.
YES... MASTER.
I HEAR YOU SAIL FOR SCOTLAND ON THE FIFTH WITH YOUR NEW SLAVE, MR. SHEDDAN.
WELL, IT'S TRUE THAT JAMIE WILL BE SAILING TO SCOTLAND ON THAT DATE, BUT, AS YE CAN SEE, I'LL BE NEEDING TO TAKE CARE OF MY BUSINESS HERE.
NO, JAMIE LEAVES WITH MY BROTHER, MATTHEW TO BE PICKED UP BY MY BROTHER-IN-LAW ON THE OTHER SIDE.
ACH! CHEER UP, LADDIE, YE DON'T KNOW HOW LUCKY YE ARE. GOING TO SCOTLAND TO LEARN A TRADE. WAS A SLAVE BORN EVER TREATED SO WELL?

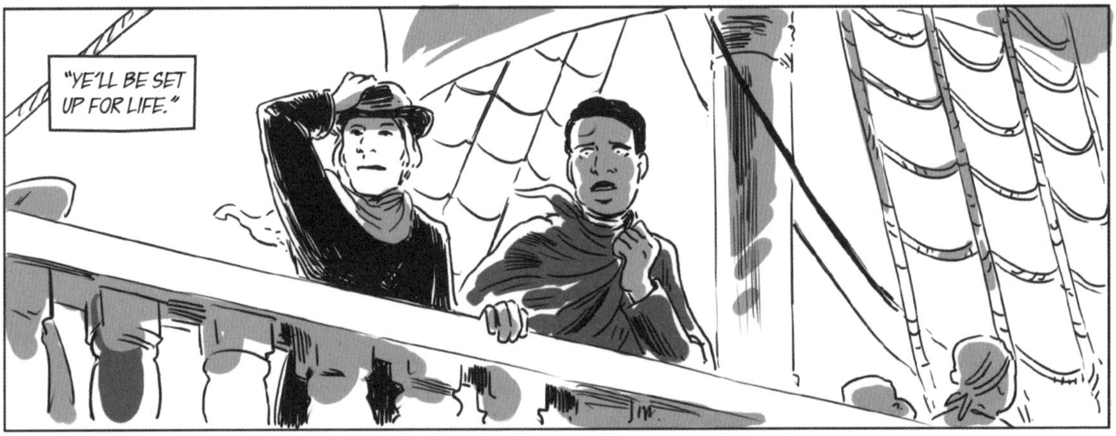
"YE'LL BE SET UP FOR LIFE."

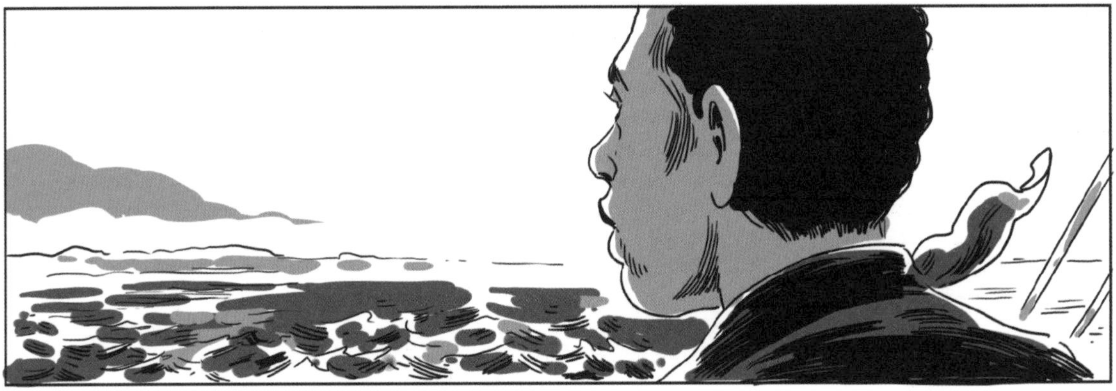

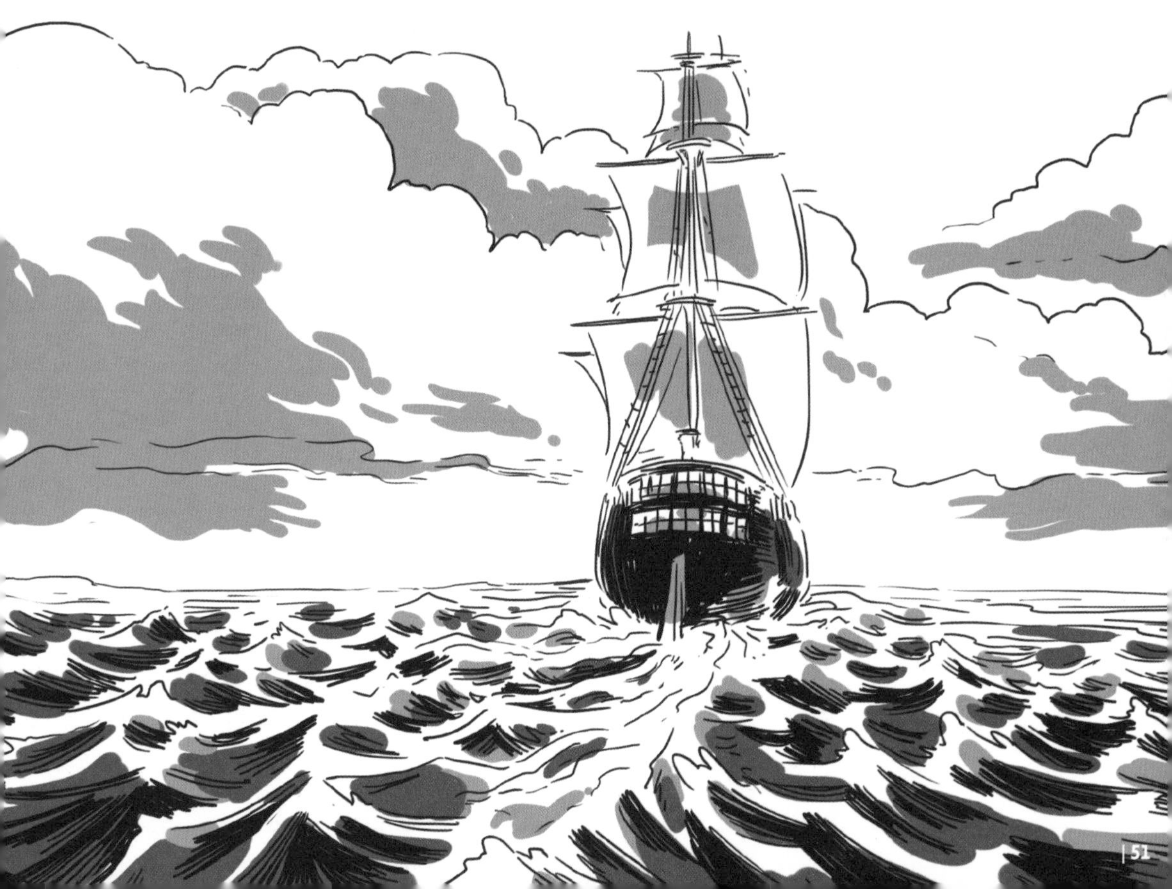

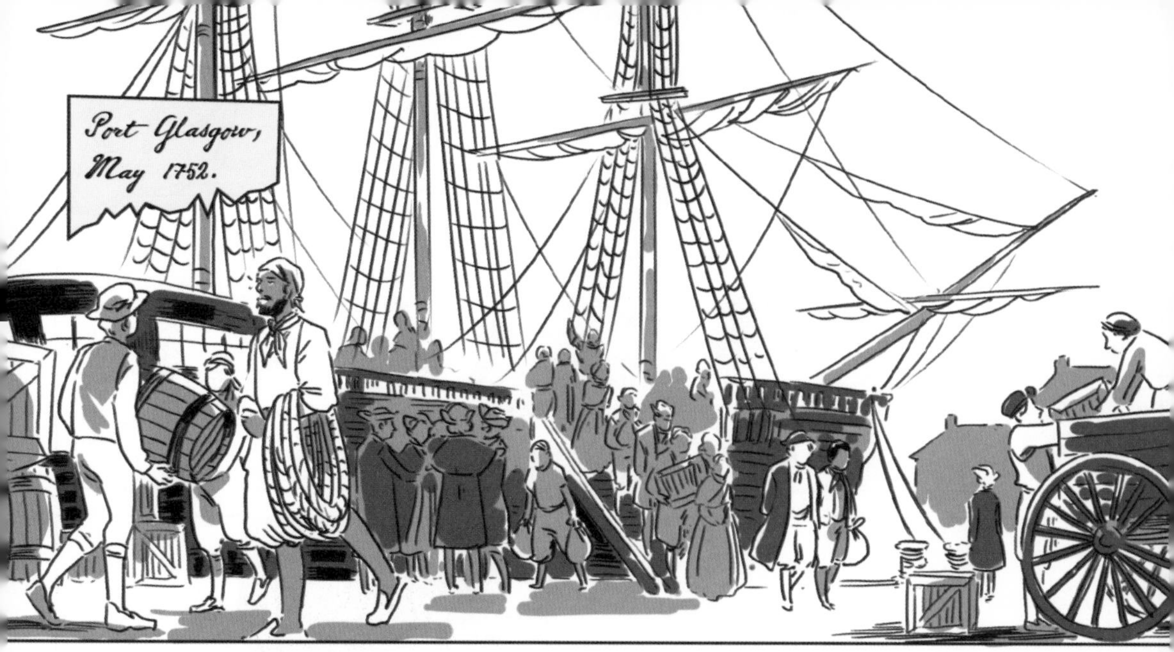
Port Glasgow, May 1752.

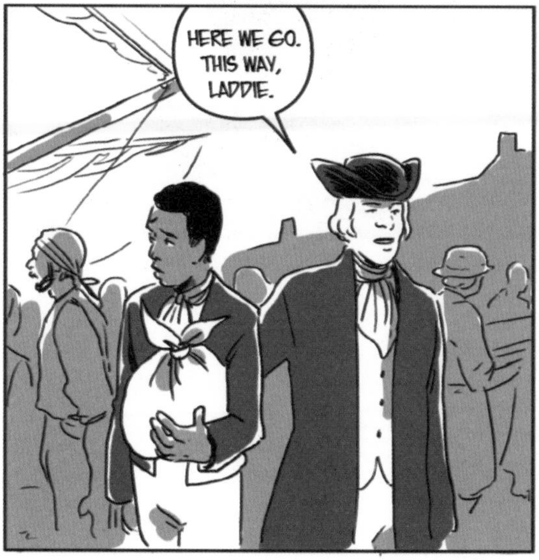
HERE WE GO. THIS WAY, LADDIE.

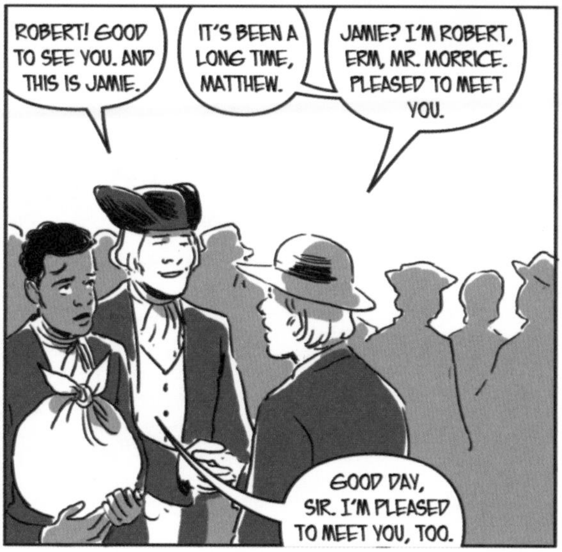
ROBERT! GOOD TO SEE YOU. AND THIS IS JAMIE.
IT'S BEEN A LONG TIME, MATTHEW.
JAMIE? I'M ROBERT, ERM, MR. MORRICE. PLEASED TO MEET YOU.
GOOD DAY, SIR. I'M PLEASED TO MEET YOU, TOO.

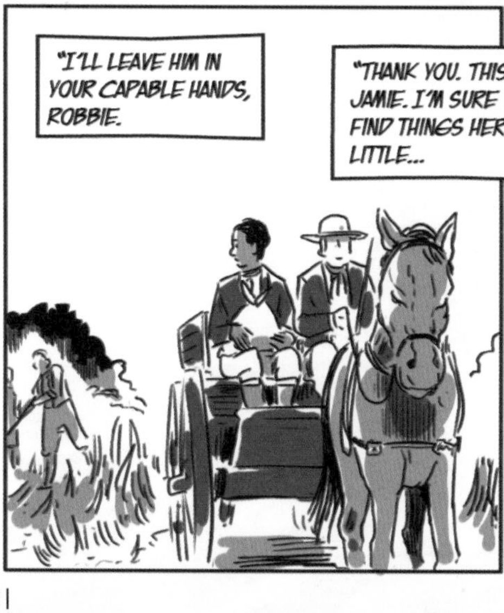
"I'LL LEAVE HIM IN YOUR CAPABLE HANDS, ROBBIE.
"THANK YOU. THIS WAY JAMIE. I'M SURE YOU'LL FIND THINGS HERE A LITTLE...

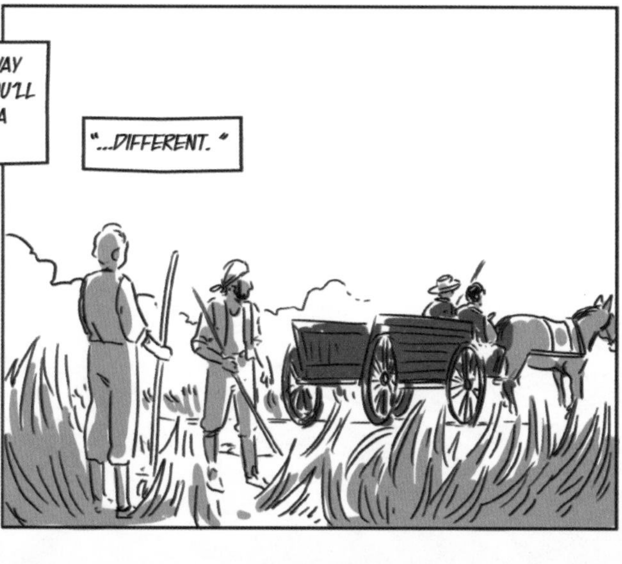
"...DIFFERENT."

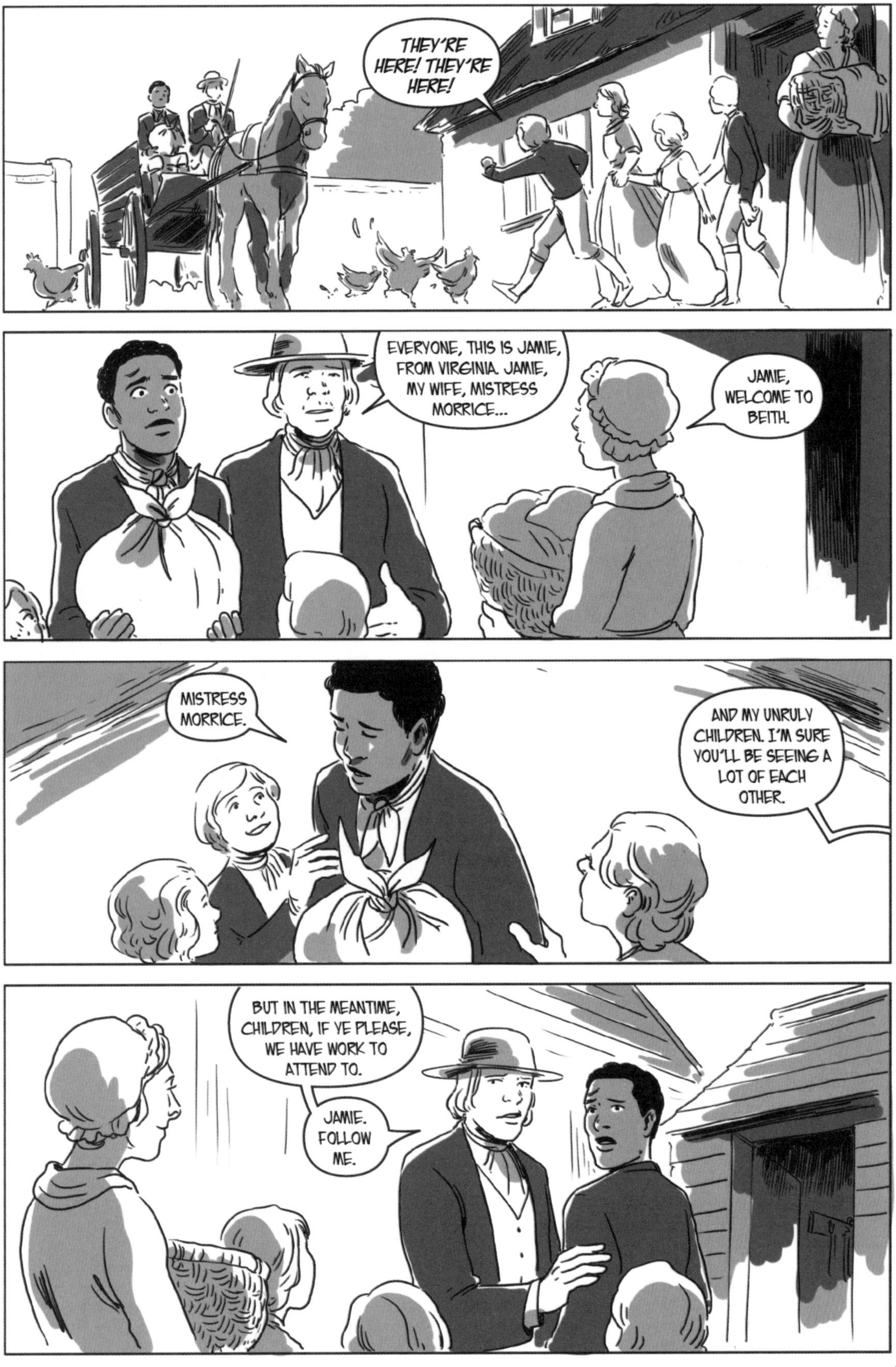
THEY'RE HERE! THEY'RE HERE!
EVERYONE, THIS IS JAMIE, FROM VIRGINIA. JAMIE, MY WIFE, MISTRESS MORRICE...
JAMIE, WELCOME TO BEITH.
MISTRESS MORRICE.
AND MY UNRULY CHILDREN. I'M SURE YOU'LL BE SEEING A LOT OF EACH OTHER.
BUT IN THE MEANTIME, CHILDREN, IF YE PLEASE, WE HAVE WORK TO ATTEND TO.
JAMIE. FOLLOW ME.

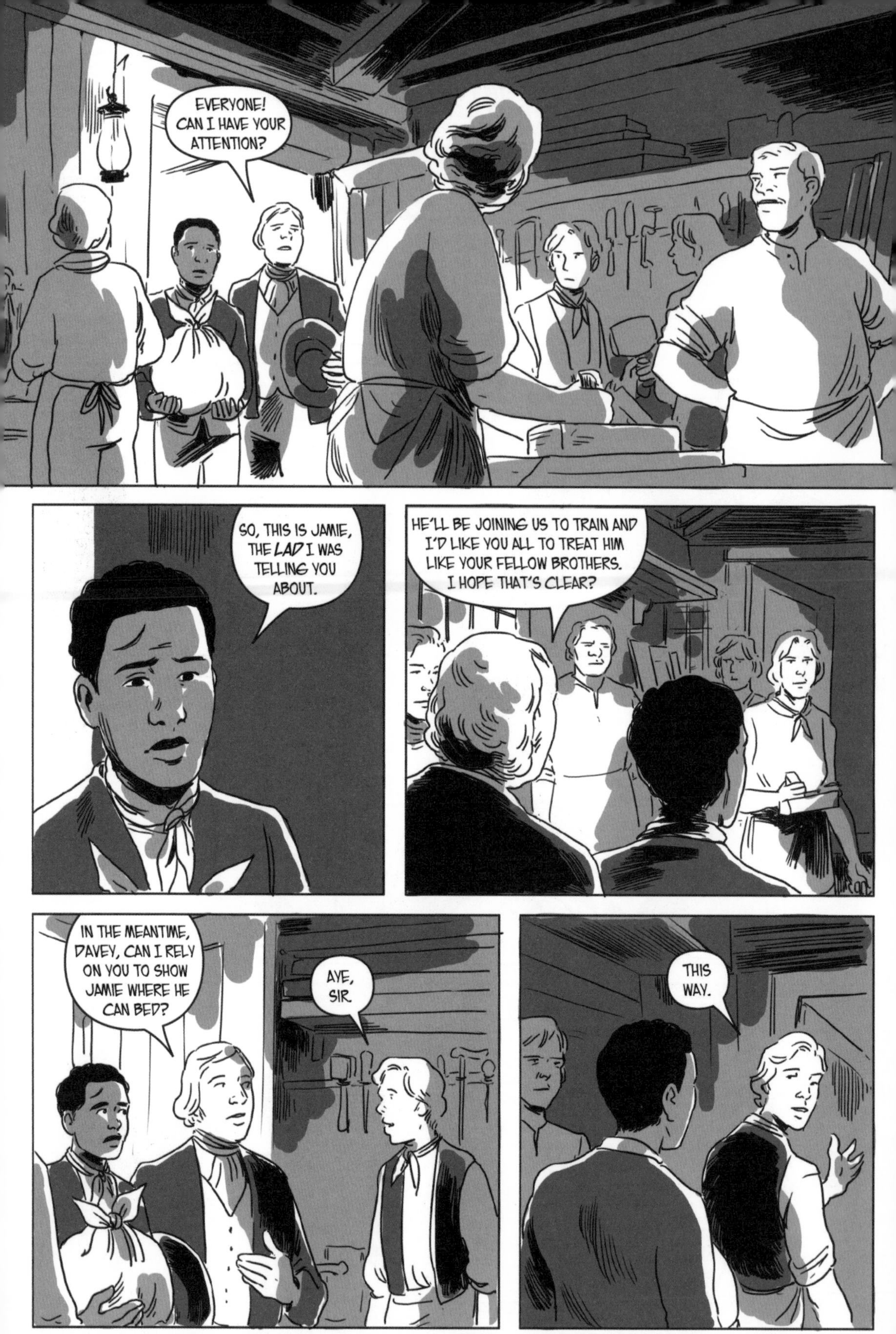
EVERYONE! CAN I HAVE YOUR ATTENTION?
SO, THIS IS JAMIE, THE LAD I WAS TELLING YOU ABOUT.
HE'LL BE JOINING US TO TRAIN AND I'D LIKE YOU ALL TO TREAT HIM LIKE YOUR FELLOW BROTHERS. I HOPE THAT'S CLEAR?
IN THE MEANTIME, DAVEY, CAN I RELY ON YOU TO SHOW JAMIE WHERE HE CAN BED?
AYE, SIR.
THIS WAY.

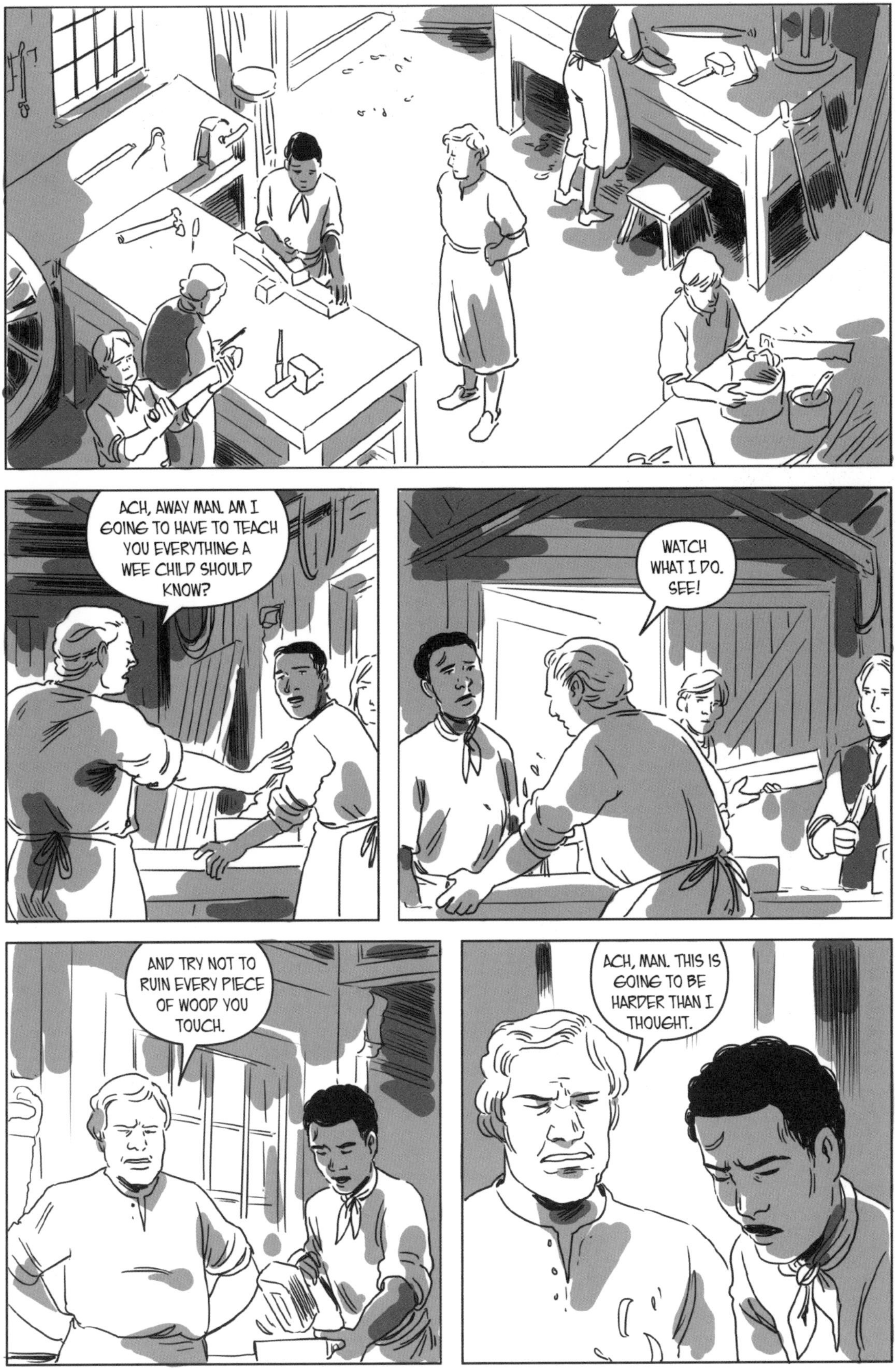
ACH, AWAY MAN. AM I GOING TO HAVE TO TEACH YOU EVERYTHING A WEE CHILD SHOULD KNOW?
WATCH WHAT I DO. SEE!
AND TRY NOT TO RUIN EVERY PIECE OF WOOD YOU TOUCH.
ACH, MAN. THIS IS GOING TO BE HARDER THAN I THOUGHT.

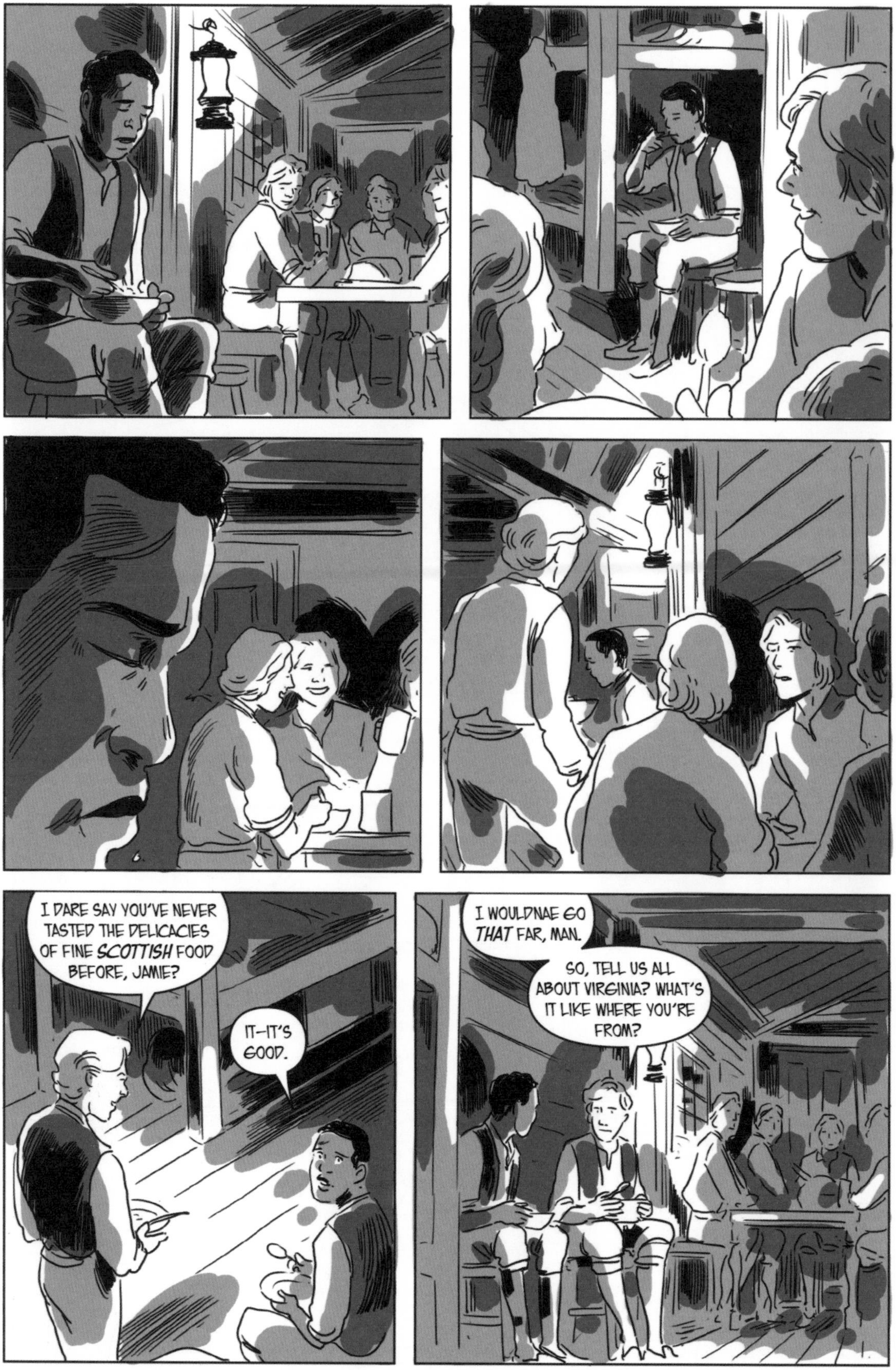

I DARE SAY YOU'VE NEVER TASTED THE DELICACIES OF FINE *SCOTTISH* FOOD BEFORE, JAMIE?
IT–IT'S GOOD.
I WOULDNAE GO *THAT* FAR, MAN.
SO, TELL US ALL ABOUT VIRGINIA? WHAT'S IT LIKE WHERE YOU'RE FROM?

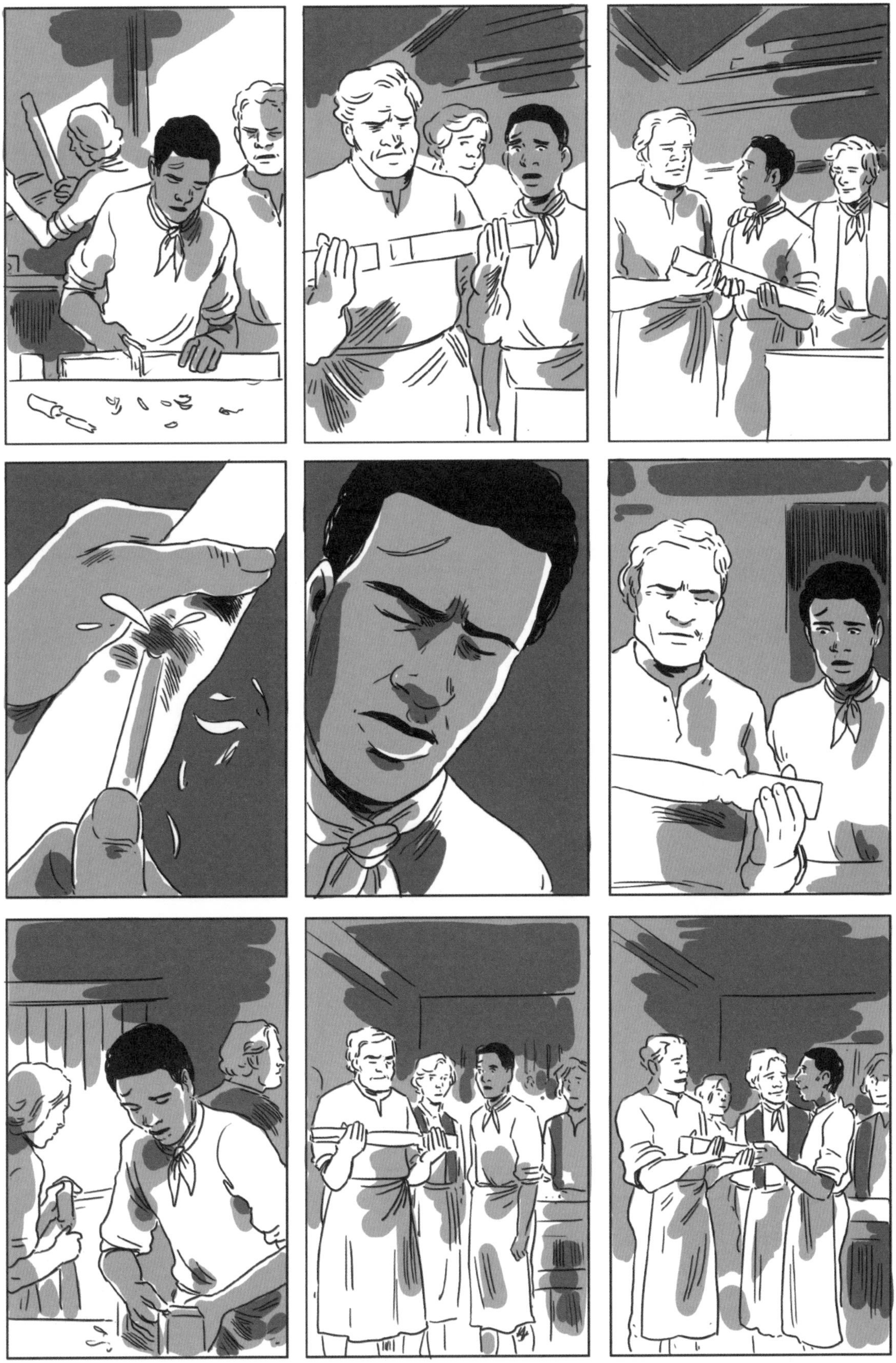

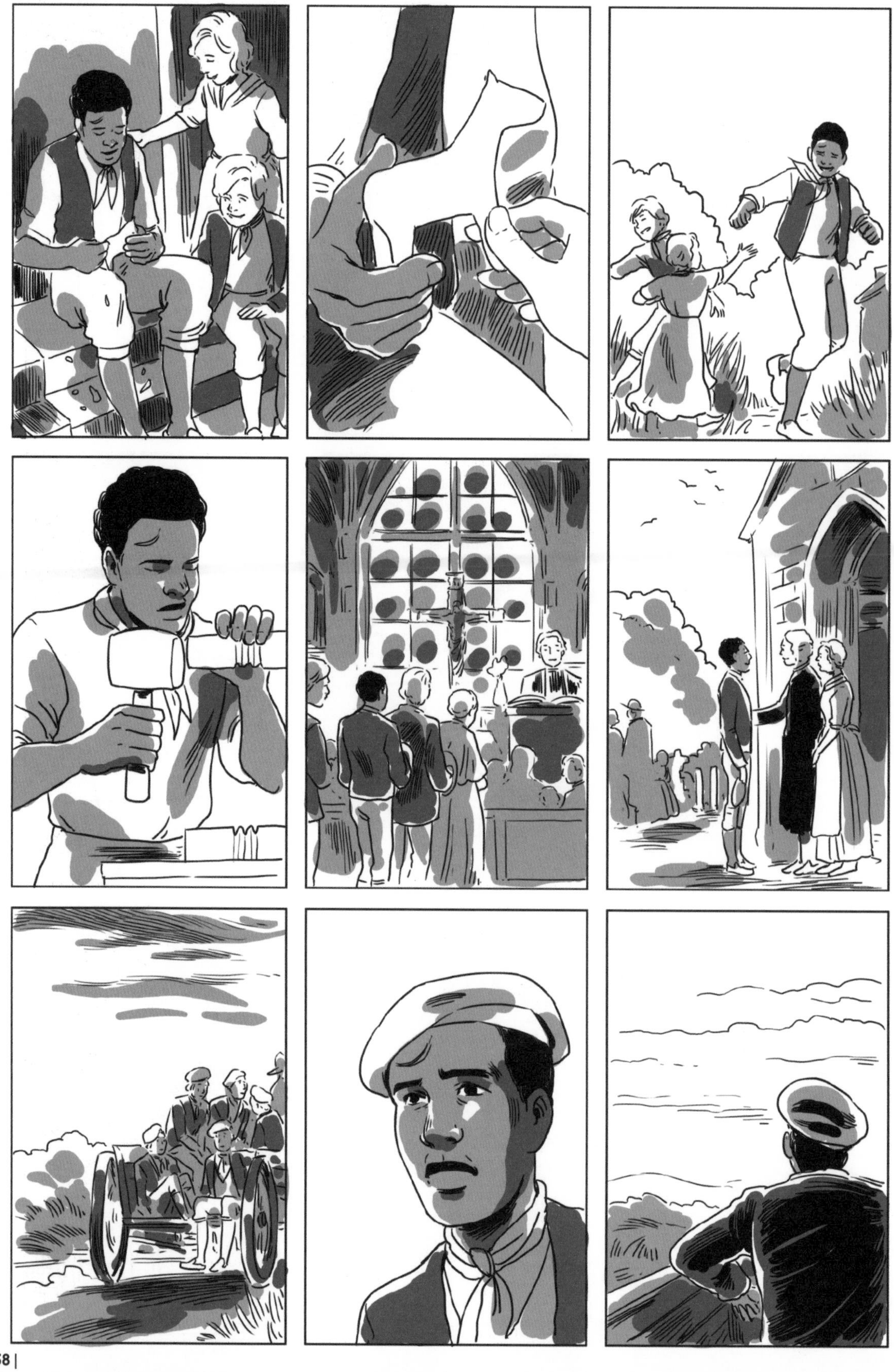

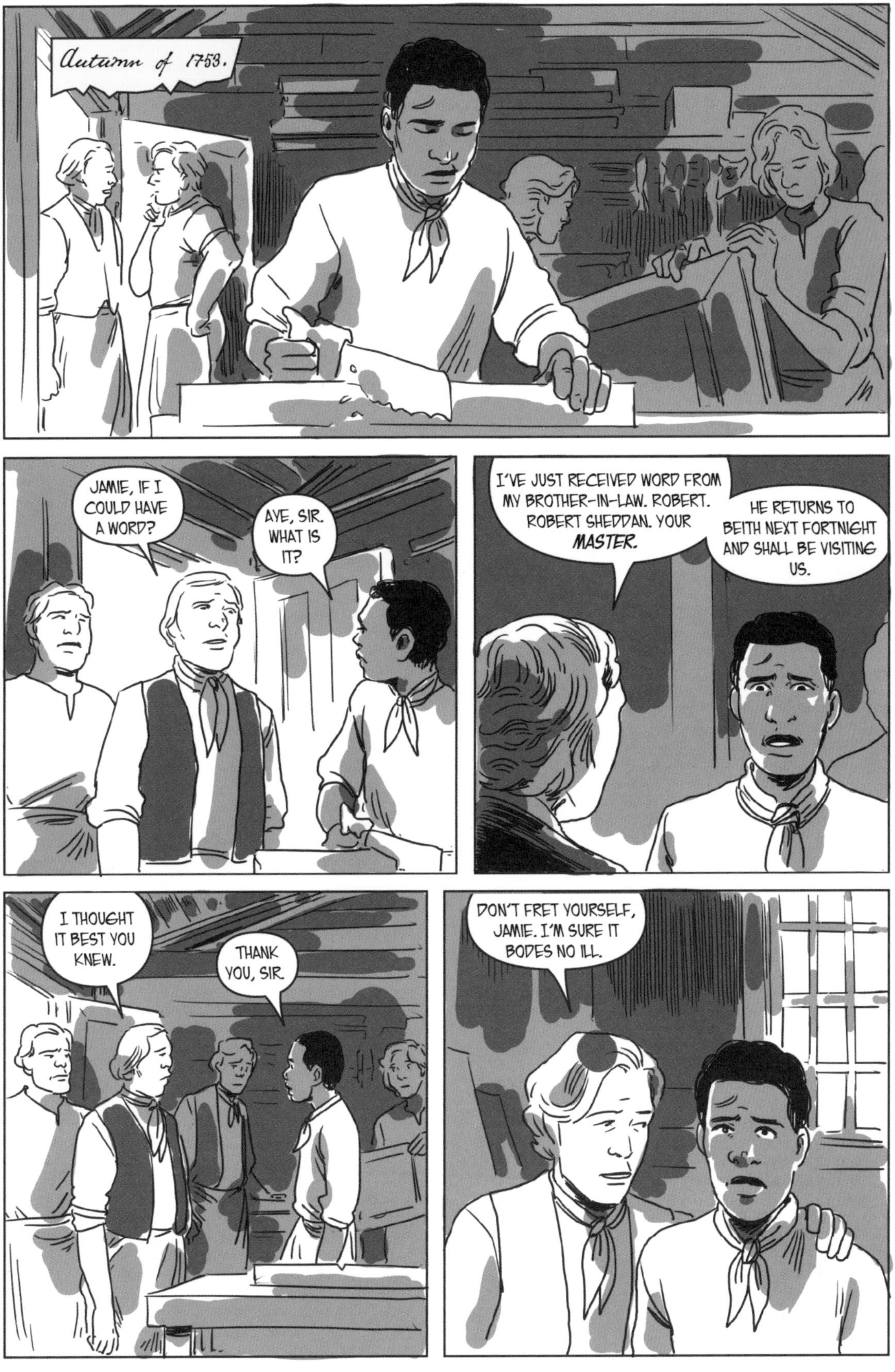
Autumn of 1753.
JAMIE, IF I COULD HAVE A WORD?
AYE, SIR. WHAT IS IT?
I'VE JUST RECEIVED WORD FROM MY BROTHER-IN-LAW. ROBERT. ROBERT SHEDDAN. YOUR *MASTER.*
HE RETURNS TO BEITH NEXT FORTNIGHT AND SHALL BE VISITING US.
I THOUGHT IT BEST YOU KNEW.
THANK YOU, SIR.
DON'T FRET YOURSELF, JAMIE. I'M SURE IT BODES NO ILL.

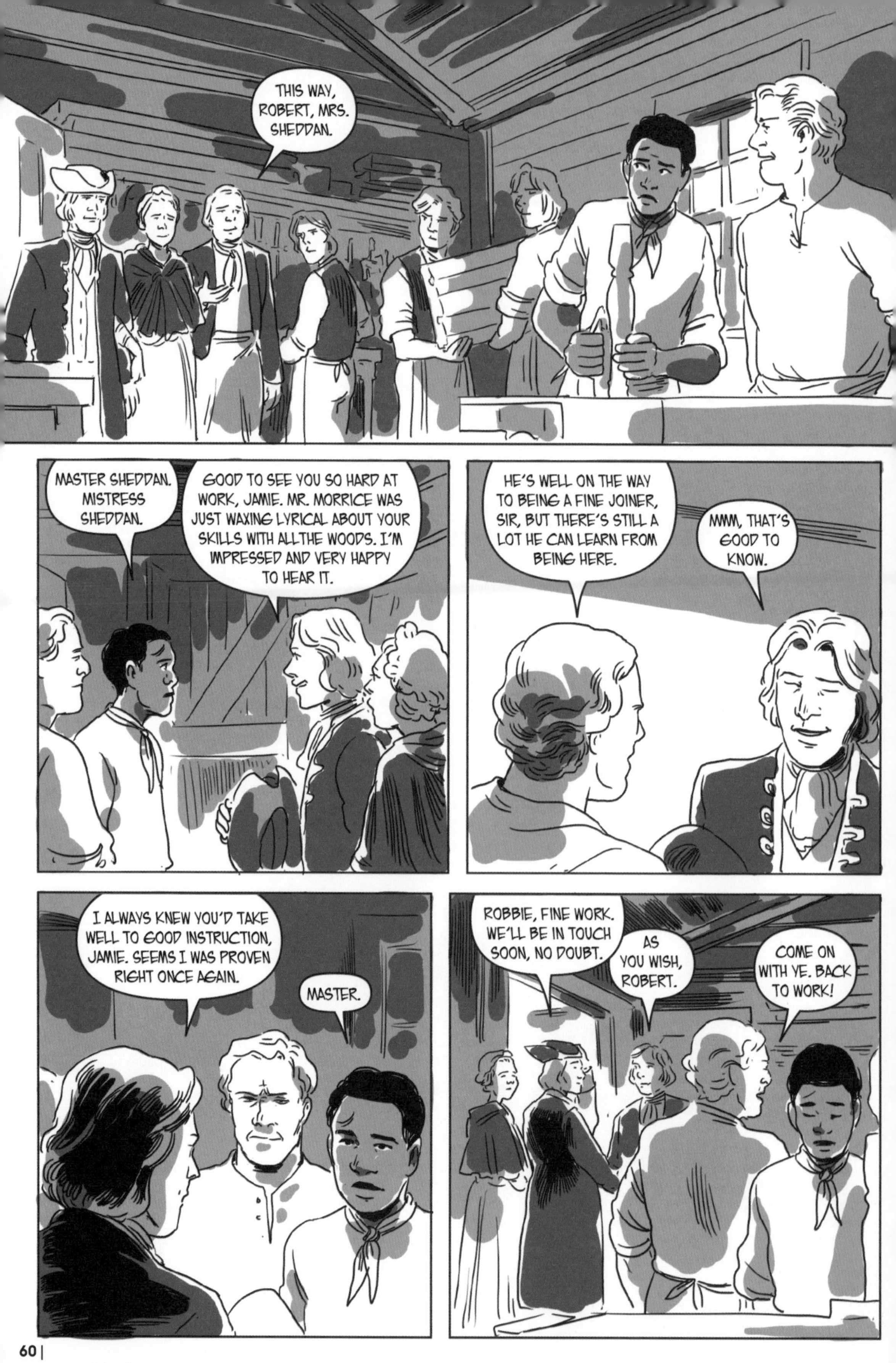
THIS WAY, ROBERT, MRS. SHEDDAN.
MASTER SHEDDAN. MISTRESS SHEDDAN.
GOOD TO SEE YOU SO HARD AT WORK, JAMIE. MR. MORRICE WAS JUST WAXING LYRICAL ABOUT YOUR SKILLS WITH ALLTHE WOODS. I'M IMPRESSED AND VERY HAPPY TO HEAR IT.
HE'S WELL ON THE WAY TO BEING A FINE JOINER, SIR, BUT THERE'S STILL A LOT HE CAN LEARN FROM BEING HERE.
MMM, THAT'S GOOD TO KNOW.
I ALWAYS KNEW YOU'D TAKE WELL TO GOOD INSTRUCTION, JAMIE. SEEMS I WAS PROVEN RIGHT ONCE AGAIN.
MASTER.
ROBBIE, FINE WORK. WE'LL BE IN TOUCH SOON, NO DOUBT.
AS YOU WISH, ROBERT.
COME ON WITH YE. BACK TO WORK!

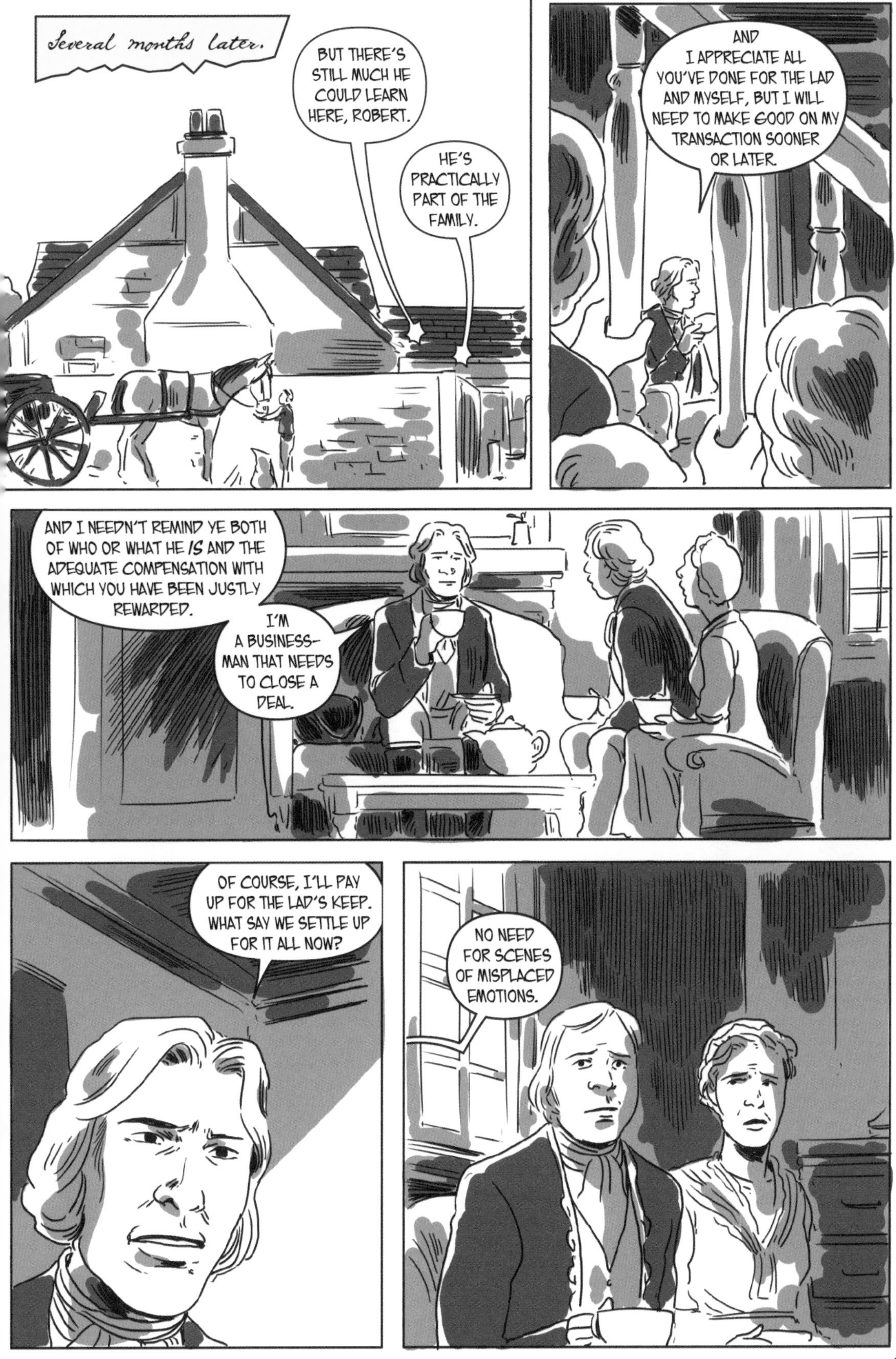
Several months later.
BUT THERE'S STILL MUCH HE COULD LEARN HERE, ROBERT.
HE'S PRACTICALLY PART OF THE FAMILY.
AND I APPRECIATE ALL YOU'VE DONE FOR THE LAD AND MYSELF, BUT I WILL NEED TO MAKE GOOD ON MY TRANSACTION SOONER OR LATER.
AND I NEEDN'T REMIND YE BOTH OF WHO OR WHAT HE IS AND THE ADEQUATE COMPENSATION WITH WHICH YOU HAVE BEEN JUSTLY REWARDED.
I'M A BUSINESS-MAN THAT NEEDS TO CLOSE A DEAL.
OF COURSE, I'LL PAY UP FOR THE LAD'S KEEP. WHAT SAY WE SETTLE UP FOR IT ALL NOW?
NO NEED FOR SCENES OF MISPLACED EMOTIONS.

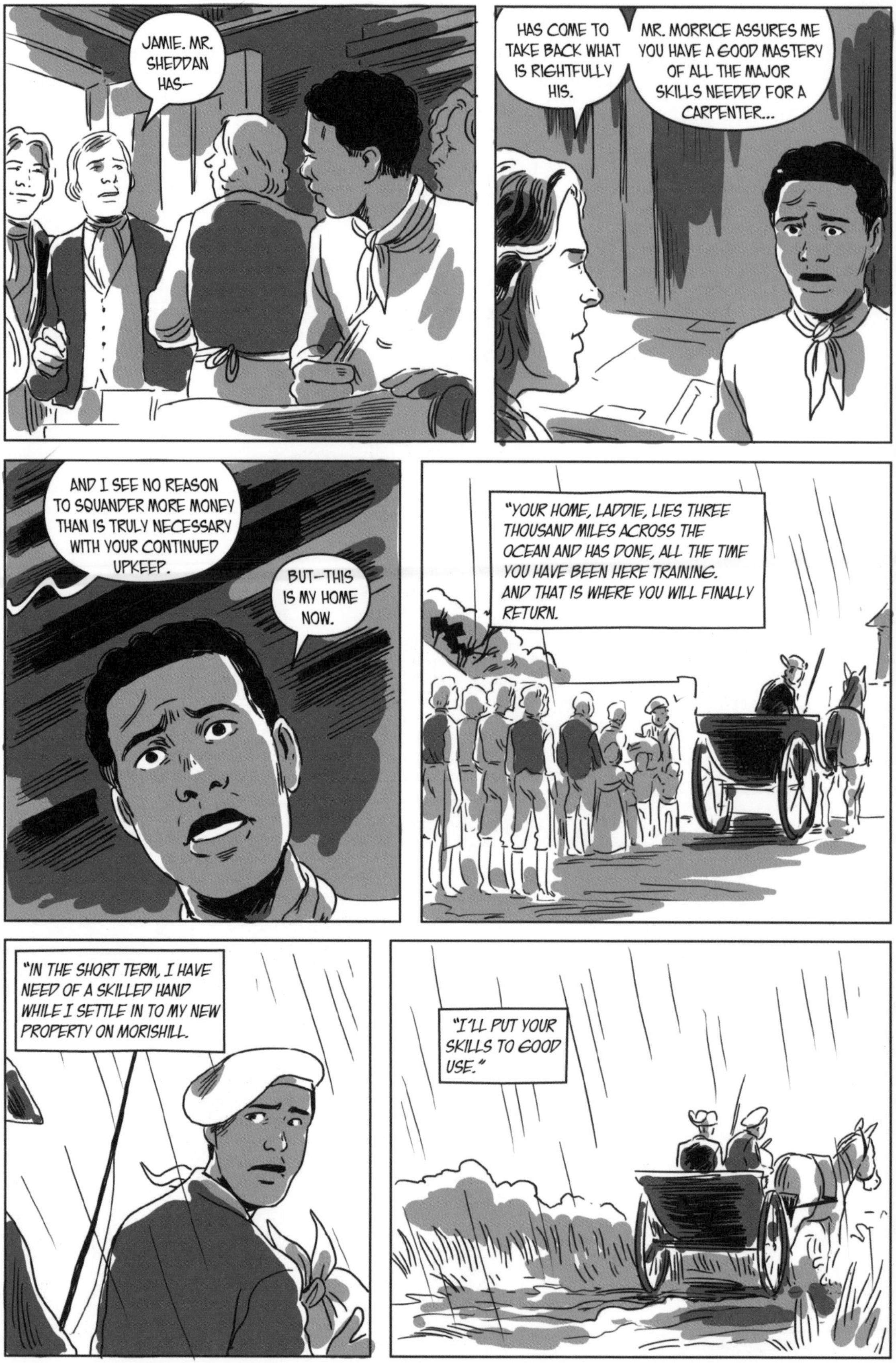
JAMIE. MR. SHEDDAN HAS–
HAS COME TO TAKE BACK WHAT IS RIGHTFULLY HIS.
MR. MORRICE ASSURES ME YOU HAVE A GOOD MASTERY OF ALL THE MAJOR SKILLS NEEDED FOR A CARPENTER...
AND I SEE NO REASON TO SQUANDER MORE MONEY THAN IS TRULY NECESSARY WITH YOUR CONTINUED UPKEEP.
BUT–THIS IS MY HOME NOW.
"YOUR HOME, LADDIE, LIES THREE THOUSAND MILES ACROSS THE OCEAN AND HAS DONE, ALL THE TIME YOU HAVE BEEN HERE TRAINING. AND THAT IS WHERE YOU WILL FINALLY RETURN.
"IN THE SHORT TERM, I HAVE NEED OF A SKILLED HAND WHILE I SETTLE IN TO MY NEW PROPERTY ON MORISHILL.
"I'LL PUT YOUR SKILLS TO GOOD USE."

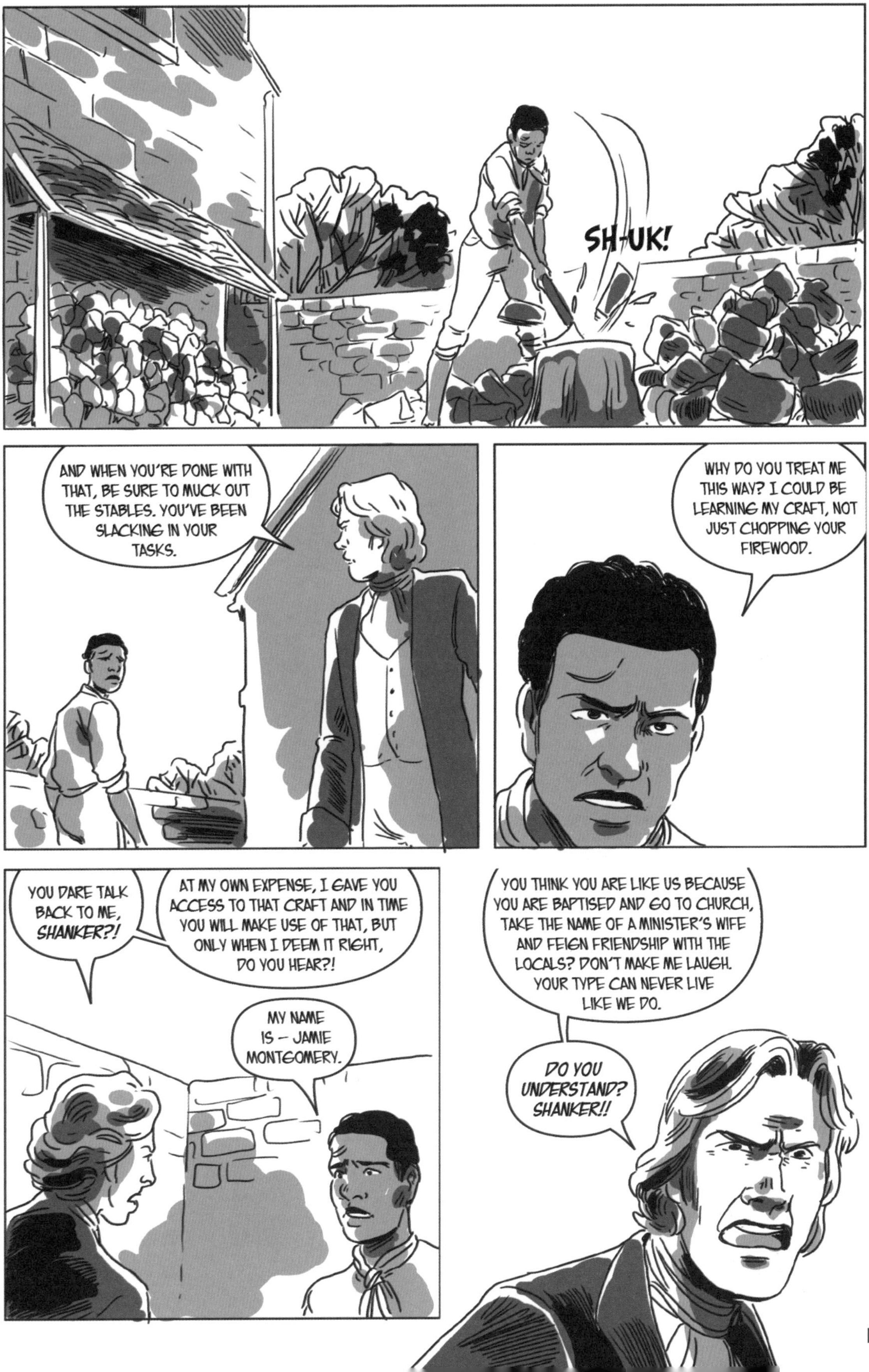
SH-UK!
AND WHEN YOU'RE DONE WITH THAT, BE SURE TO MUCK OUT THE STABLES. YOU'VE BEEN SLACKING IN YOUR TASKS.
WHY DO YOU TREAT ME THIS WAY? I COULD BE LEARNING MY CRAFT, NOT JUST CHOPPING YOUR FIREWOOD.
YOU DARE TALK BACK TO ME, SHANKER?!
AT MY OWN EXPENSE, I GAVE YOU ACCESS TO THAT CRAFT AND IN TIME YOU WILL MAKE USE OF THAT, BUT ONLY WHEN I DEEM IT RIGHT, DO YOU HEAR?!
MY NAME IS – JAMIE MONTGOMERY.
YOU THINK YOU ARE LIKE US BECAUSE YOU ARE BAPTISED AND GO TO CHURCH, TAKE THE NAME OF A MINISTER'S WIFE AND FEIGN FRIENDSHIP WITH THE LOCALS? DON'T MAKE ME LAUGH. YOUR TYPE CAN NEVER LIVE LIKE WE DO.
DO YOU UNDERSTAND? SHANKER!!

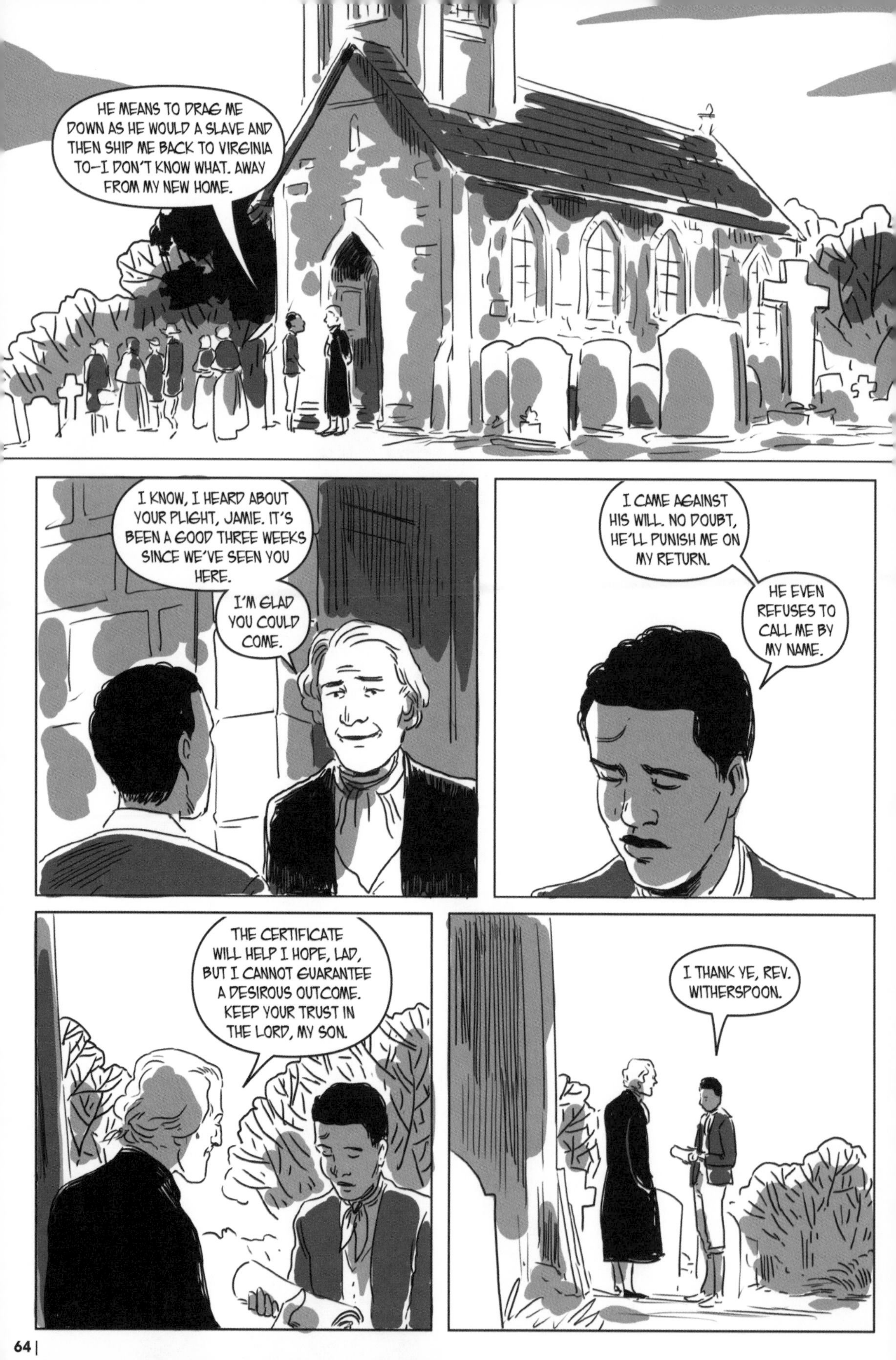
HE MEANS TO DRAG ME DOWN AS HE WOULD A SLAVE AND THEN SHIP ME BACK TO VIRGINIA TO—I DON'T KNOW WHAT. AWAY FROM MY NEW HOME.
I KNOW, I HEARD ABOUT YOUR PLIGHT, JAMIE. IT'S BEEN A GOOD THREE WEEKS SINCE WE'VE SEEN YOU HERE.
I'M GLAD YOU COULD COME.
I CAME AGAINST HIS WILL. NO DOUBT, HE'LL PUNISH ME ON MY RETURN.
HE EVEN REFUSES TO CALL ME BY MY NAME.
THE CERTIFICATE WILL HELP I HOPE, LAD, BUT I CANNOT GUARANTEE A DESIROUS OUTCOME. KEEP YOUR TRUST IN THE LORD, MY SON.
I THANK YE, REV. WITHERSPOON.

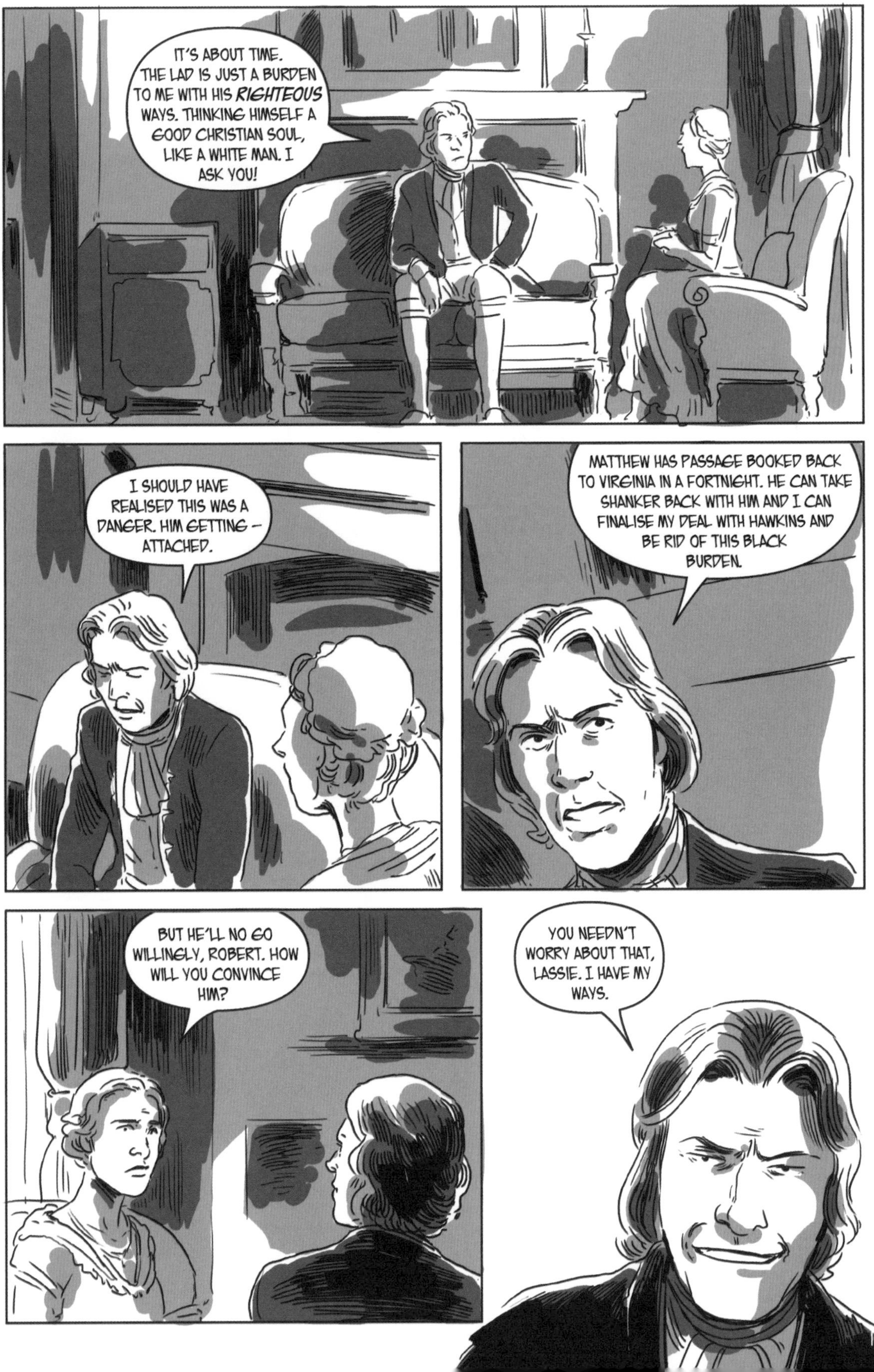
IT'S ABOUT TIME. THE LAD IS JUST A BURDEN TO ME WITH HIS *RIGHTEOUS* WAYS. THINKING HIMSELF A GOOD CHRISTIAN SOUL, LIKE A WHITE MAN. I ASK YOU!
I SHOULD HAVE REALISED THIS WAS A DANGER. HIM GETTING – ATTACHED.
MATTHEW HAS PASSAGE BOOKED BACK TO VIRGINIA IN A FORTNIGHT. HE CAN TAKE SHANKER BACK WITH HIM AND I CAN FINALISE MY DEAL WITH HAWKINS AND BE RID OF THIS BLACK BURDEN.
BUT HE'LL NO GO WILLINGLY, ROBERT. HOW WILL YOU CONVINCE HIM?
YOU NEEDN'T WORRY ABOUT THAT, LASSIE. I HAVE MY WAYS.

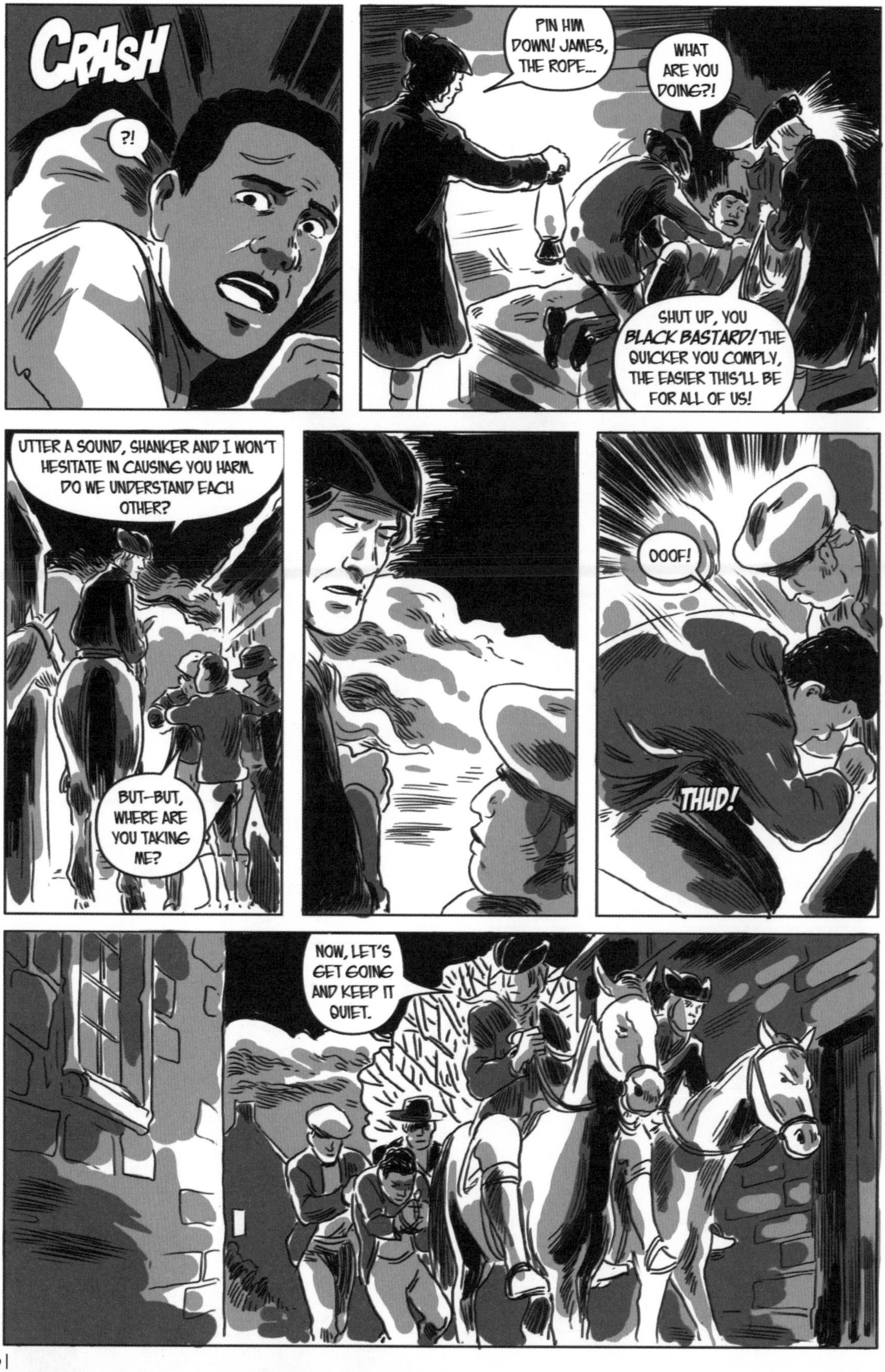
CRASH
?!
PIN HIM DOWN! JAMES, THE ROPE...
WHAT ARE YOU DOING?!
SHUT UP, YOU BLACK BASTARD! THE QUICKER YOU COMPLY, THE EASIER THIS'LL BE FOR ALL OF US!
UTTER A SOUND, SHANKER AND I WON'T HESITATE IN CAUSING YOU HARM. DO WE UNDERSTAND EACH OTHER?
BUT--BUT, WHERE ARE YOU TAKING ME?
OOOF!
THUD!
NOW, LET'S GET GOING AND KEEP IT QUIET.

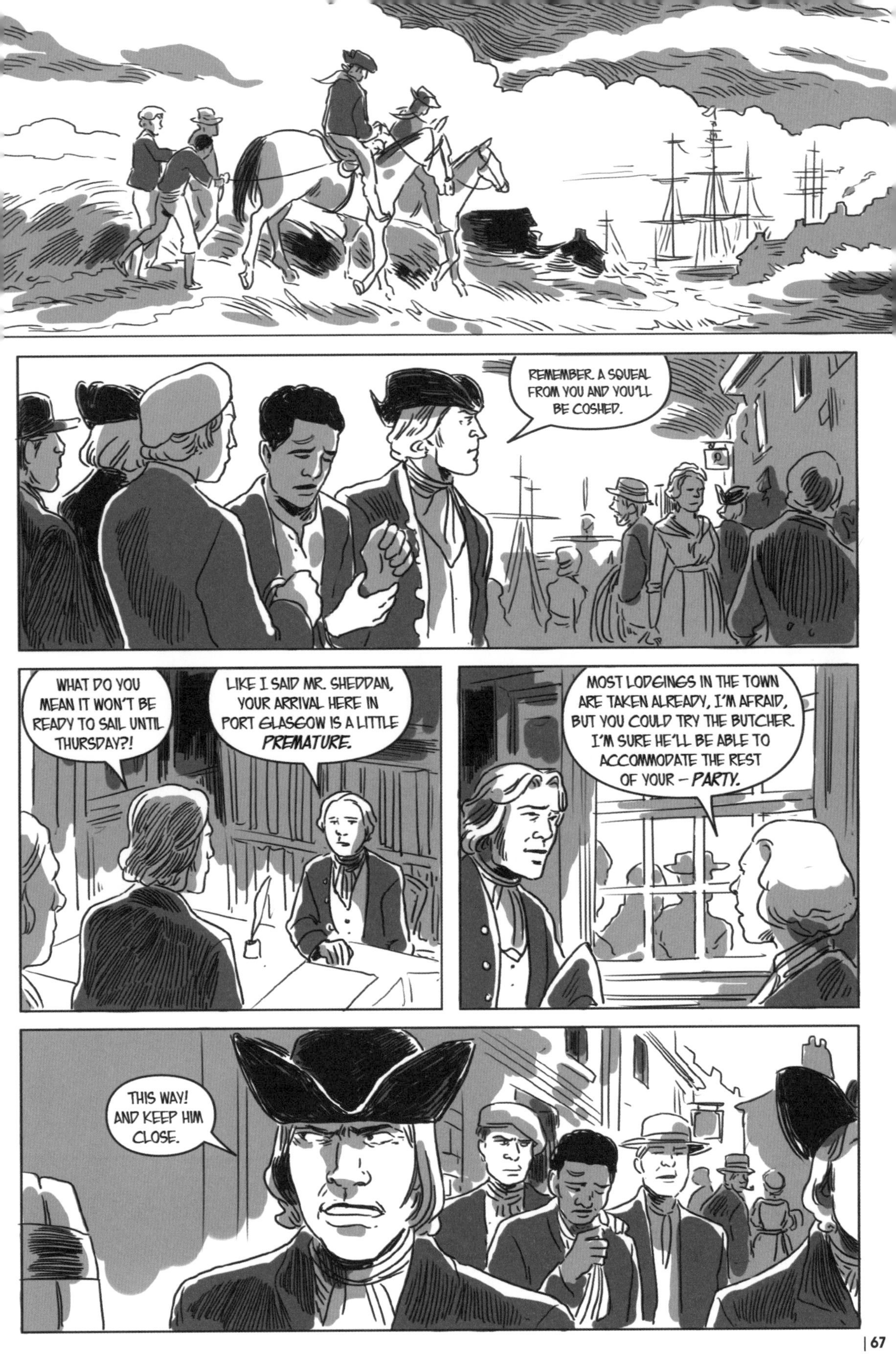
REMEMBER. A SQUEAL FROM YOU AND YOU'LL BE COSHED.
WHAT DO YOU MEAN IT WON'T BE READY TO SAIL UNTIL THURSDAY?!
LIKE I SAID MR. SHEDDAN, YOUR ARRIVAL HERE IN PORT GLASGOW IS A LITTLE *PREMATURE.*
MOST LODGINGS IN THE TOWN ARE TAKEN ALREADY, I'M AFRAID, BUT YOU COULD TRY THE BUTCHER. I'M SURE HE'LL BE ABLE TO ACCOMMODATE THE REST OF YOUR – *PARTY.*
THIS WAY! AND KEEP HIM CLOSE.

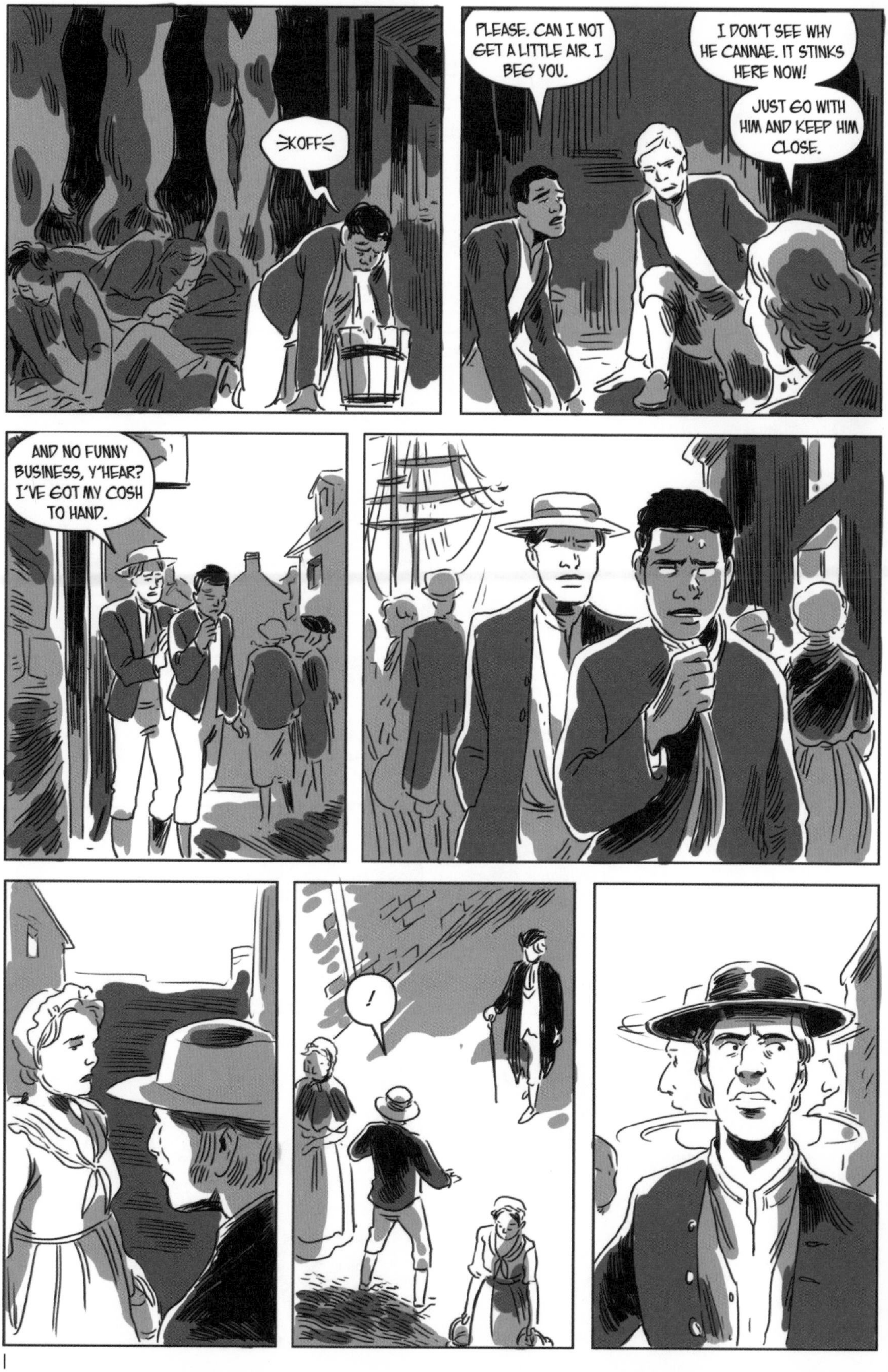
KOFF
PLEASE. CAN I NOT GET A LITTLE AIR. I BEG YOU.
I DON'T SEE WHY HE CANNAE. IT STINKS HERE NOW!
JUST GO WITH HIM AND KEEP HIM CLOSE.
AND NO FUNNY BUSINESS, Y'HEAR? I'VE GOT MY COSH TO HAND.
!

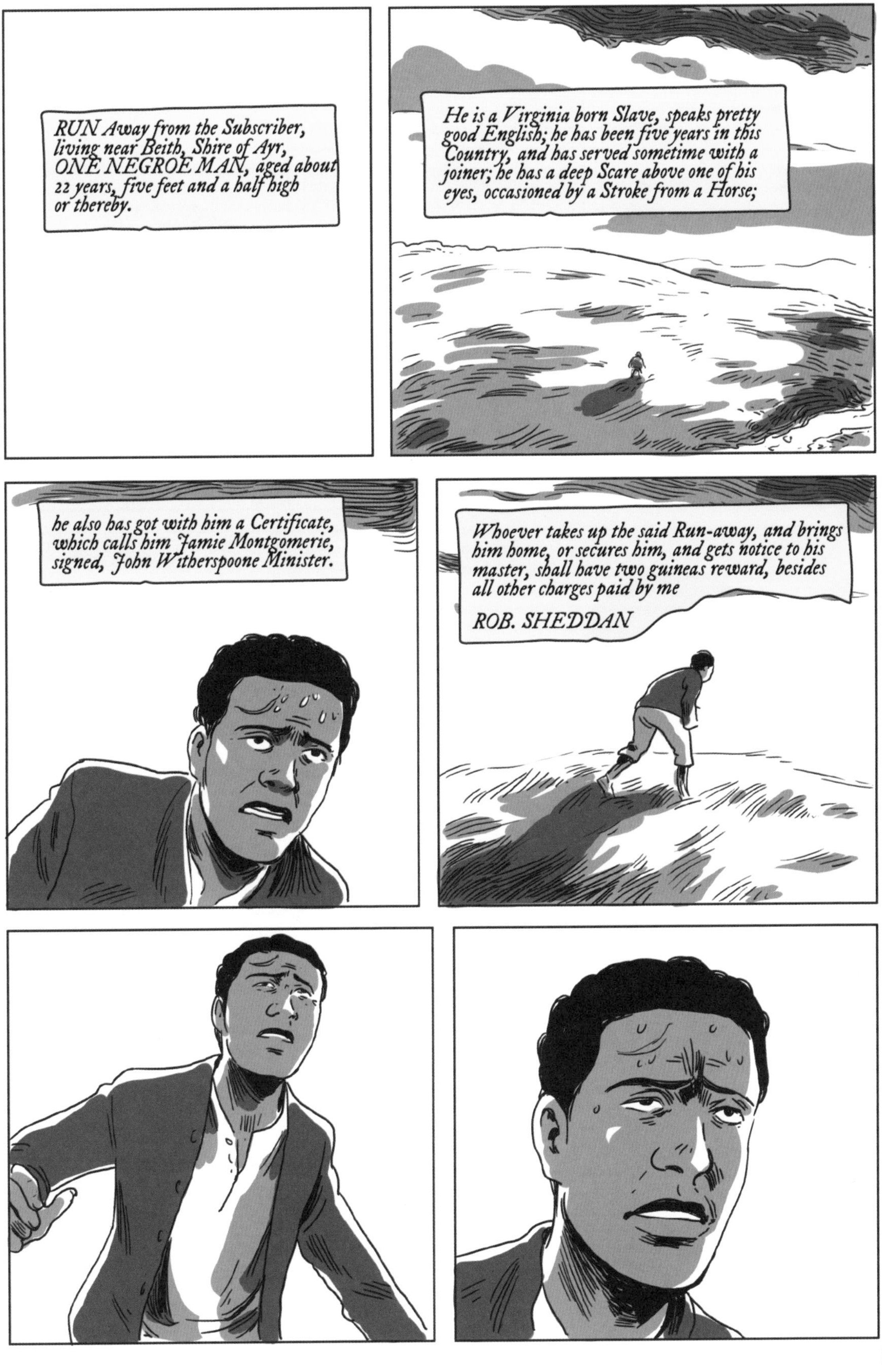
RUN Away from the Subscriber,
living near Beith, Shire of Ayr,
ONE NEGROE MAN, aged about
22 years, five feet and a half high
or thereby.
He is a Virginia born Slave, speaks pretty
good English; he has been five years in this
Country, and has served sometime with a
joiner; he has a deep Scare above one of his
eyes, occasioned by a Stroke from a Horse;
he also has got with him a Certificate,
which calls him Jamie Montgomerie,
signed, John Witherspoone Minister.
Whoever takes up the said Run-away, and brings
him home, or secures him, and gets notice to his
master, shall have two guineas reward, besides
all other charges paid by me
ROB. SHEDDAN

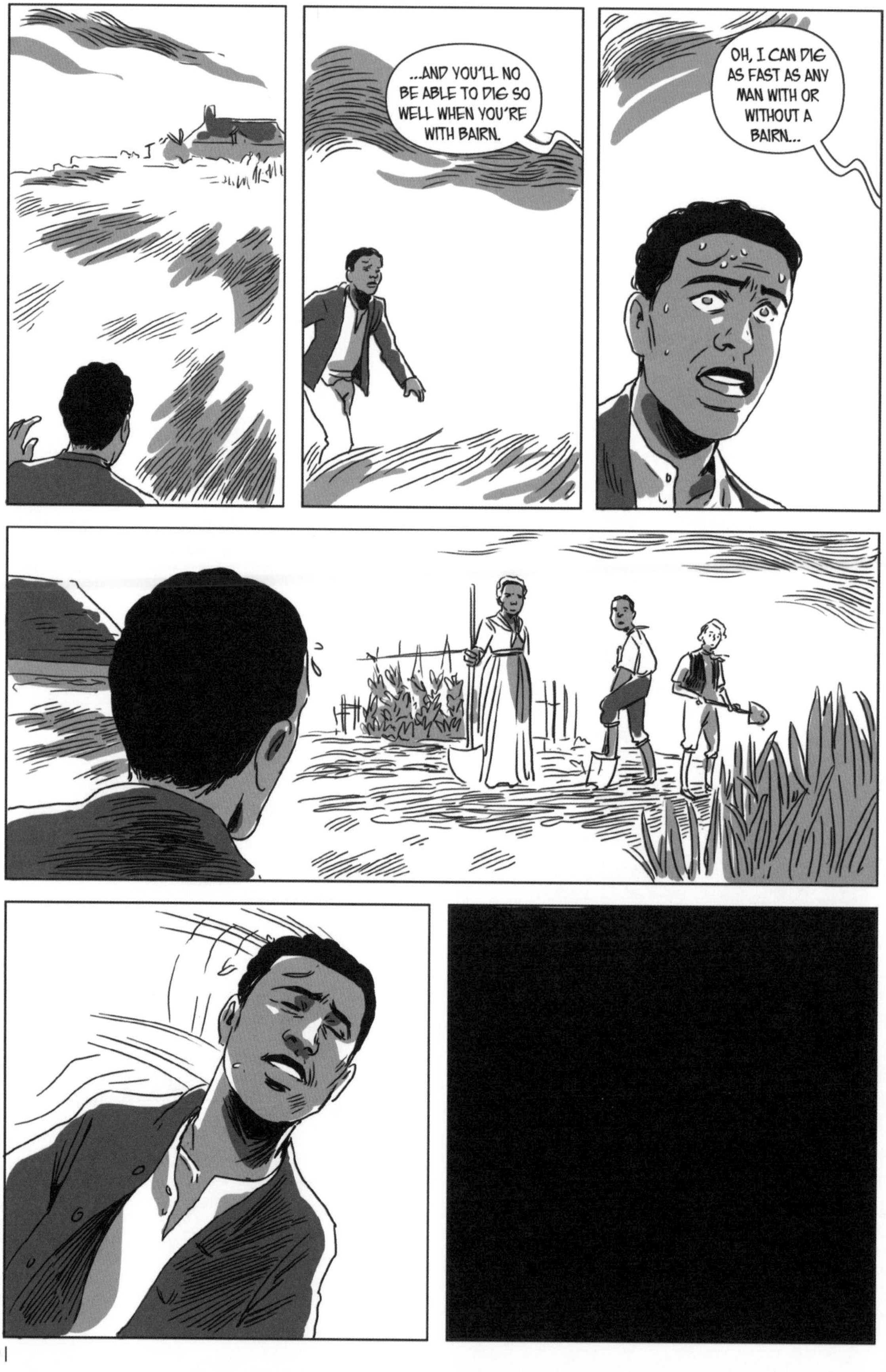
...AND YOU'LL NO BE ABLE TO DIG SO WELL WHEN YOU'RE WITH BAIRN.
OH, I CAN DIG AS FAST AS ANY MAN WITH OR WITHOUT A BAIRN...

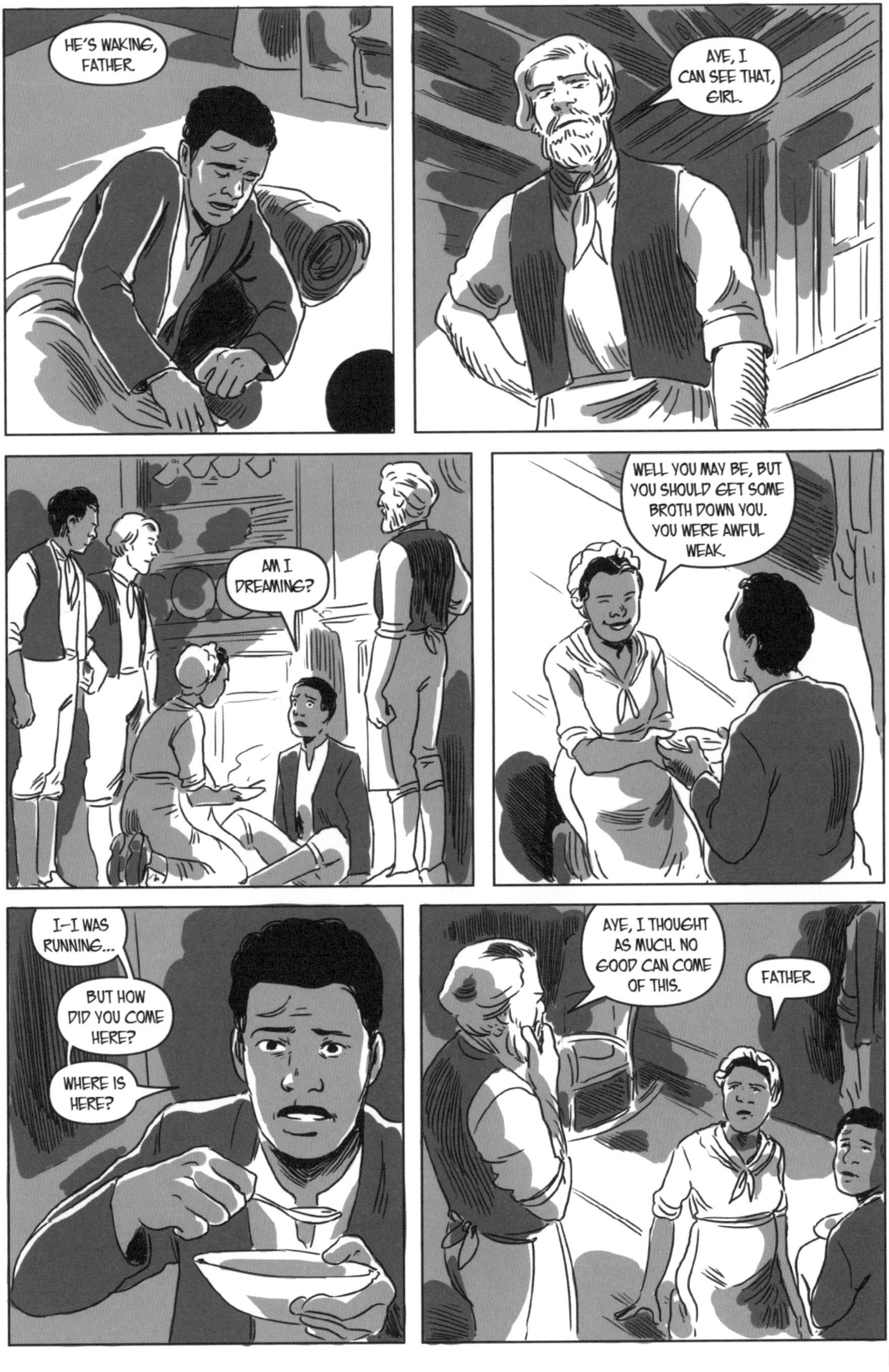
HE'S WAKING, FATHER.
AYE, I CAN SEE THAT, GIRL.
AM I DREAMING?
WELL YOU MAY BE, BUT YOU SHOULD GET SOME BROTH DOWN YOU. YOU WERE AWFUL WEAK.
I—I WAS RUNNING...
BUT HOW DID YOU COME HERE?
WHERE IS HERE?
AYE, I THOUGHT AS MUCH. NO GOOD CAN COME OF THIS.
FATHER.

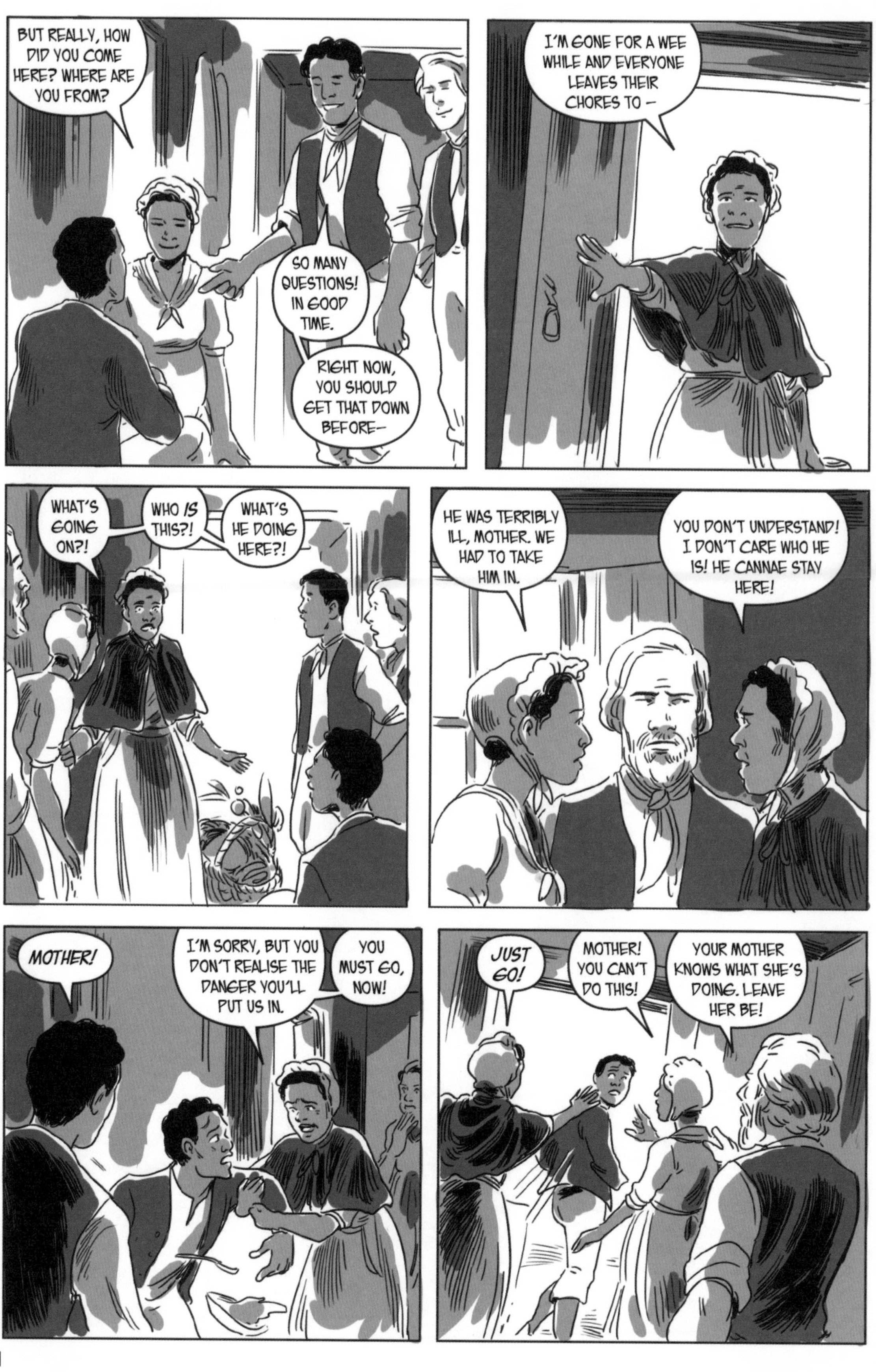
BUT REALLY, HOW DID YOU COME HERE? WHERE ARE YOU FROM?
SO MANY QUESTIONS! IN GOOD TIME.
RIGHT NOW, YOU SHOULD GET THAT DOWN BEFORE–
I'M GONE FOR A WEE WHILE AND EVERYONE LEAVES THEIR CHORES TO –
WHAT'S GOING ON?!
WHO *IS* THIS?!
WHAT'S HE DOING HERE?!
HE WAS TERRIBLY ILL, MOTHER. WE HAD TO TAKE HIM IN.
YOU DON'T UNDERSTAND! I DON'T CARE WHO HE IS! HE CANNAE STAY HERE!
*MOTHER!*
I'M SORRY, BUT YOU DON'T REALISE THE DANGER YOU'LL PUT US IN.
YOU MUST GO, NOW!
*JUST GO!*
MOTHER! YOU CAN'T DO THIS!
YOUR MOTHER KNOWS WHAT SHE'S DOING. LEAVE HER BE!

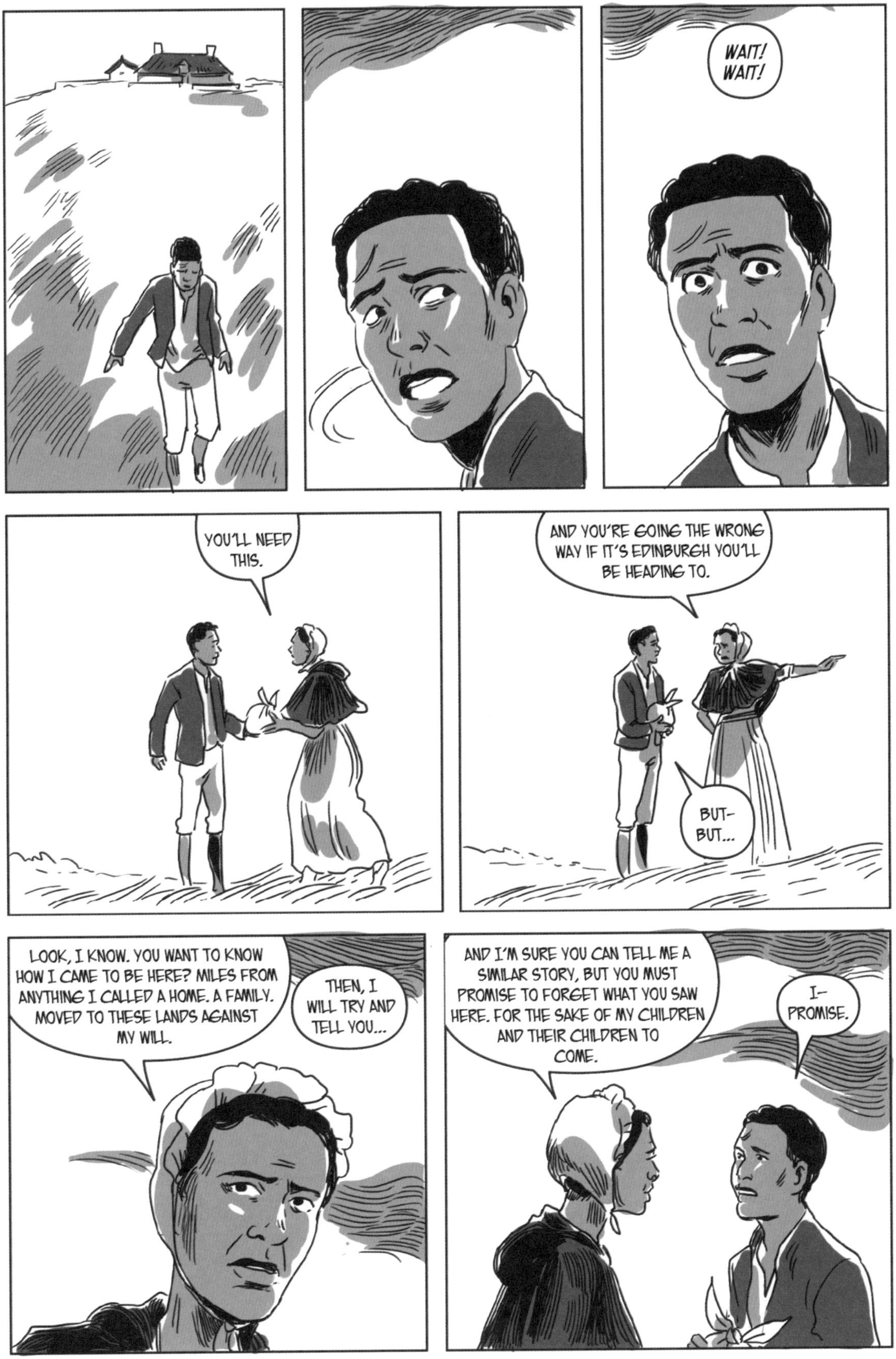
WAIT! WAIT!
YOU'LL NEED THIS.
AND YOU'RE GOING THE WRONG WAY IF IT'S EDINBURGH YOU'LL BE HEADING TO.
BUT- BUT...
LOOK, I KNOW. YOU WANT TO KNOW HOW I CAME TO BE HERE? MILES FROM ANYTHING I CALLED A HOME. A FAMILY. MOVED TO THESE LANDS AGAINST MY WILL.
THEN, I WILL TRY AND TELL YOU...
AND I'M SURE YOU CAN TELL ME A SIMILAR STORY, BUT YOU MUST PROMISE TO FORGET WHAT YOU SAW HERE. FOR THE SAKE OF MY CHILDREN AND THEIR CHILDREN TO COME.
I- PROMISE.

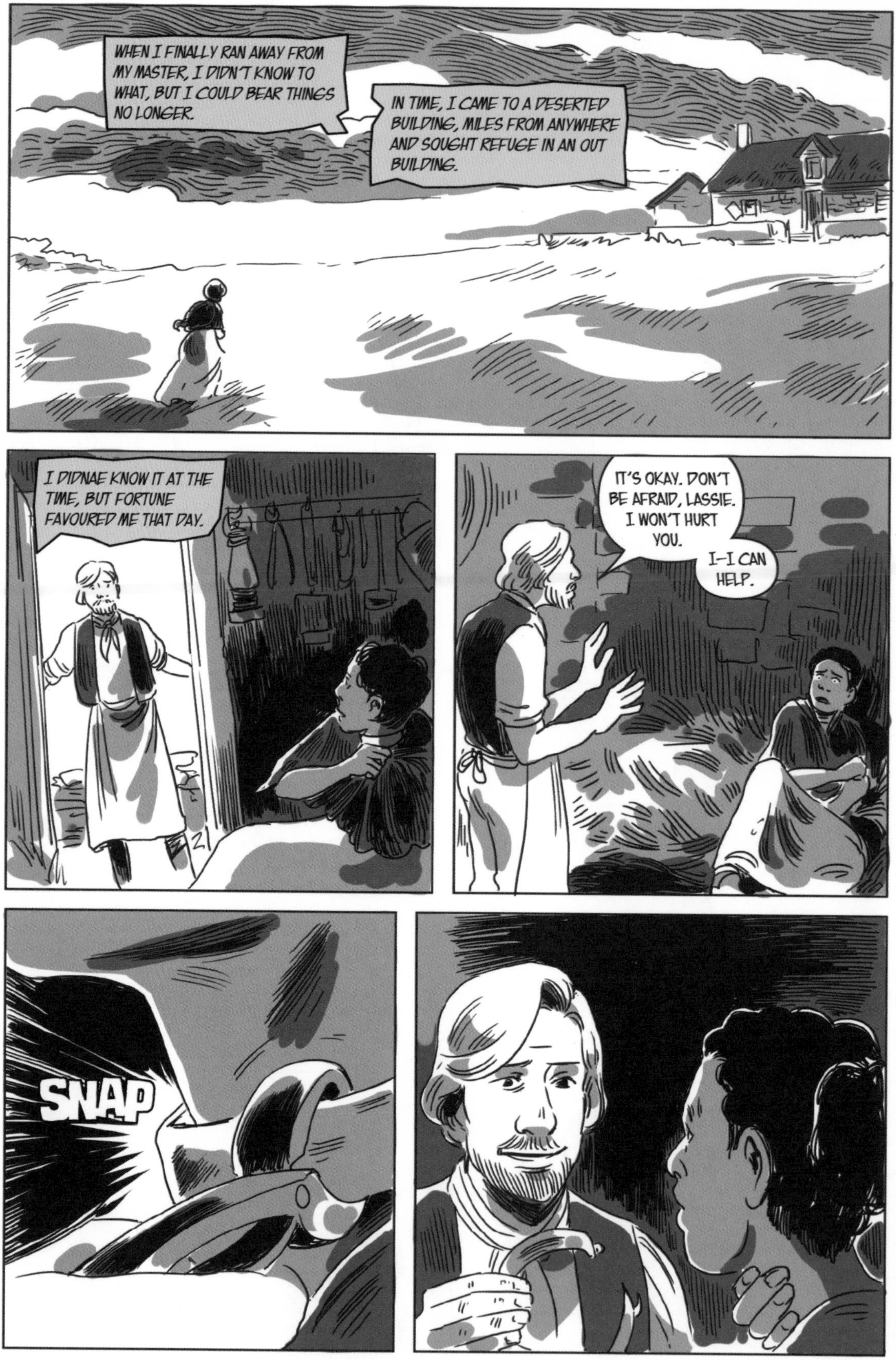
WHEN I FINALLY RAN AWAY FROM MY MASTER, I DIDN'T KNOW TO WHAT, BUT I COULD BEAR THINGS NO LONGER.
IN TIME, I CAME TO A DESERTED BUILDING, MILES FROM ANYWHERE AND SOUGHT REFUGE IN AN OUT BUILDING.
I DIDNAE KNOW IT AT THE TIME, BUT FORTUNE FAVOURED ME THAT DAY.
IT'S OKAY. DON'T BE AFRAID, LASSIE. I WON'T HURT YOU.
I—I CAN HELP.
SNAP

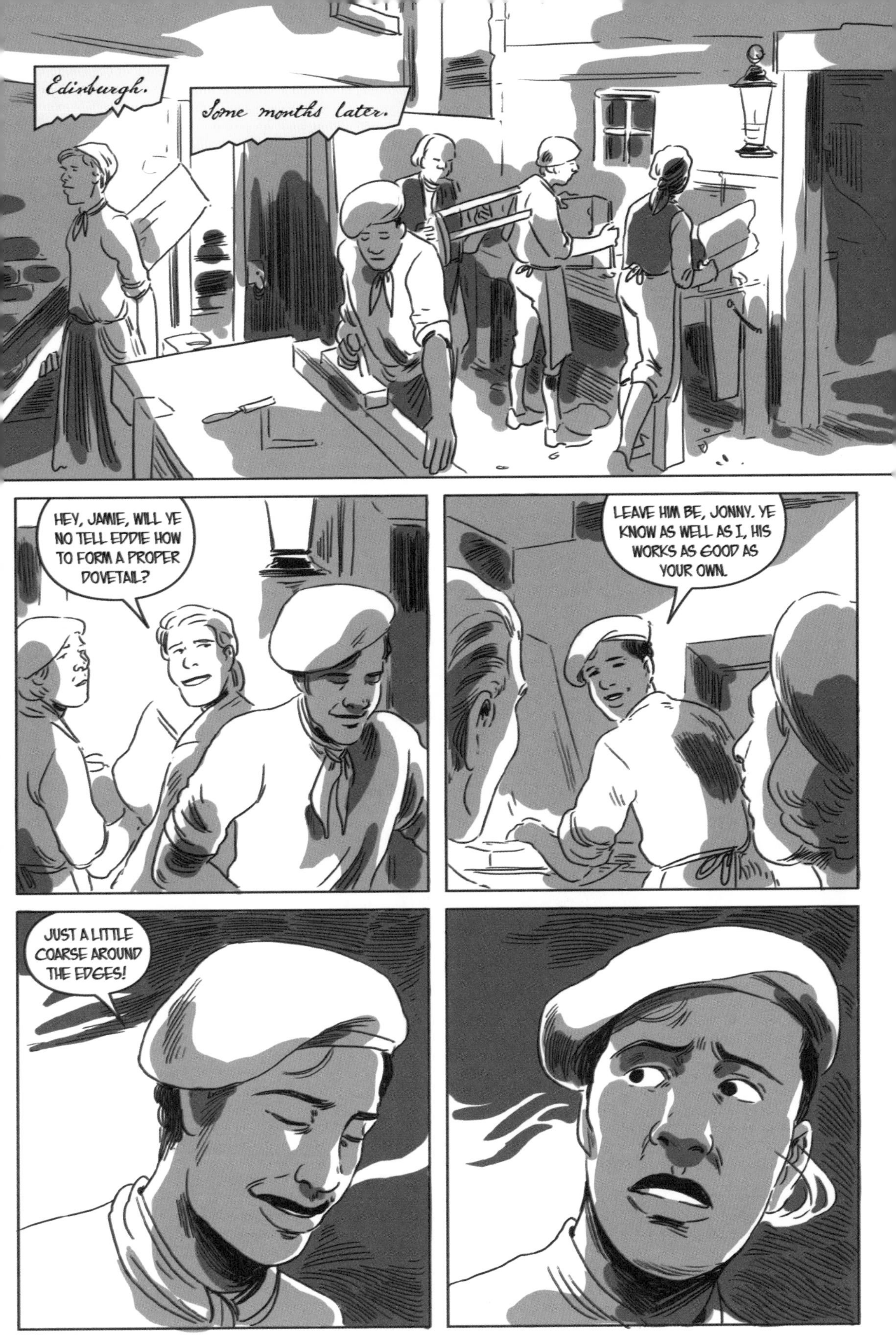
Edinburgh.
Some months later.
HEY, JAMIE, WILL YE NO TELL EDDIE HOW TO FORM A PROPER DOVETAIL?
LEAVE HIM BE, JONNY. YE KNOW AS WELL AS I, HIS WORKS AS GOOD AS YOUR OWN.
JUST A LITTLE COARSE AROUND THE EDGES!

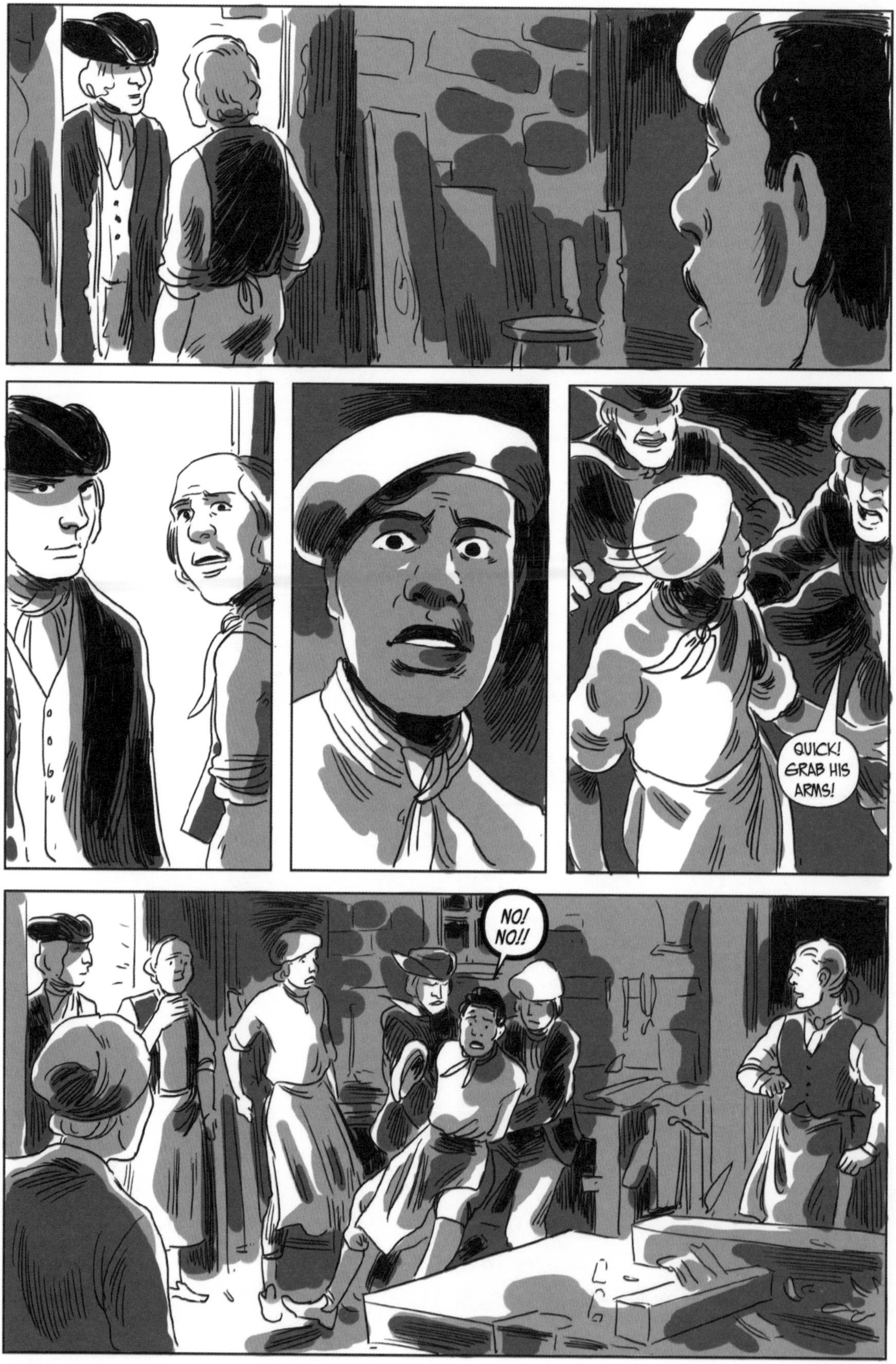
QUICK! GRAB HIS ARMS!
NO! NO!!

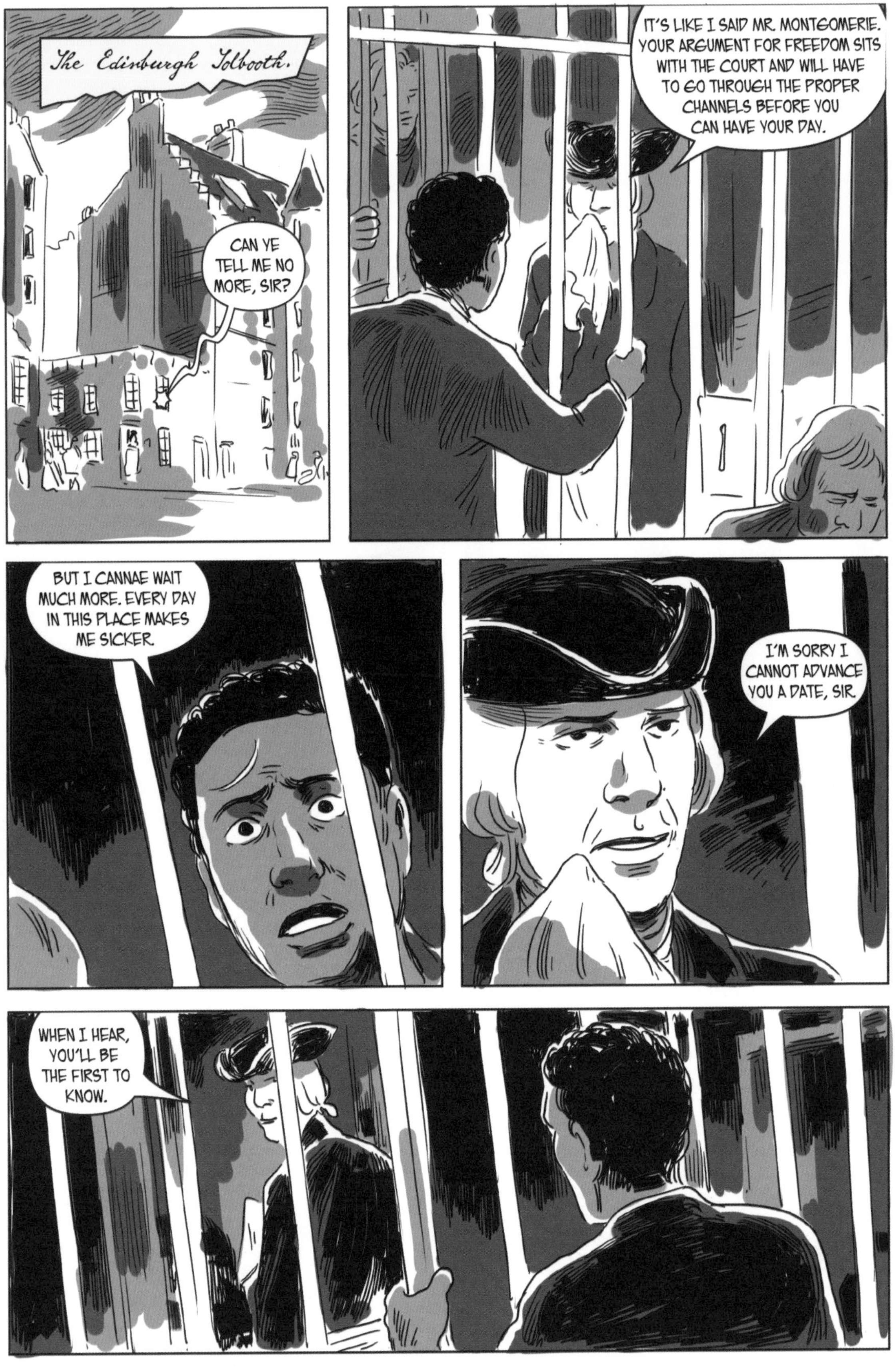
The Edinburgh Tolbooth.
CAN YE TELL ME NO MORE, SIR?
IT'S LIKE I SAID MR. MONTGOMERIE. YOUR ARGUMENT FOR FREEDOM SITS WITH THE COURT AND WILL HAVE TO GO THROUGH THE PROPER CHANNELS BEFORE YOU CAN HAVE YOUR DAY.
BUT I CANNAE WAIT MUCH MORE. EVERY DAY IN THIS PLACE MAKES ME SICKER.
I'M SORRY I CANNOT ADVANCE YOU A DATE, SIR.
WHEN I HEAR, YOU'LL BE THE FIRST TO KNOW.

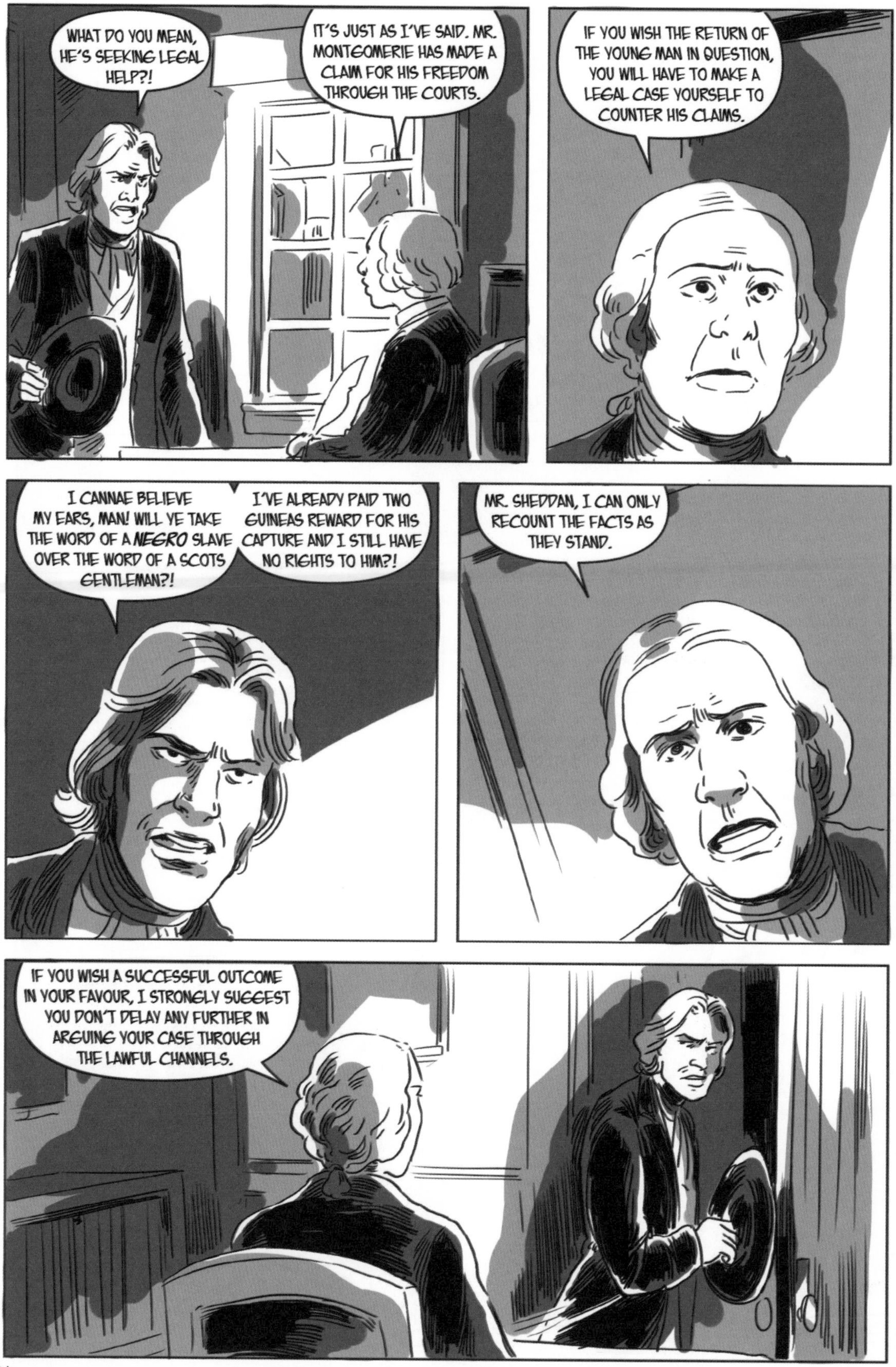
WHAT DO YOU MEAN, HE'S SEEKING LEGAL HELP?!
IT'S JUST AS I'VE SAID. MR. MONTGOMERIE HAS MADE A CLAIM FOR HIS FREEDOM THROUGH THE COURTS.
IF YOU WISH THE RETURN OF THE YOUNG MAN IN QUESTION, YOU WILL HAVE TO MAKE A LEGAL CASE YOURSELF TO COUNTER HIS CLAIMS.
I CANNAE BELIEVE MY EARS, MAN! WILL YE TAKE THE WORD OF A *NEGRO* SLAVE OVER THE WORD OF A SCOTS GENTLEMAN?!
I'VE ALREADY PAID TWO GUINEAS REWARD FOR HIS CAPTURE AND I STILL HAVE NO RIGHTS TO HIM?!
MR. SHEDDAN, I CAN ONLY RECOUNT THE FACTS AS THEY STAND.
IF YOU WISH A SUCCESSFUL OUTCOME IN YOUR FAVOUR, I STRONGLY SUGGEST YOU DON'T DELAY ANY FURTHER IN ARGUING YOUR CASE THROUGH THE LAWFUL CHANNELS.

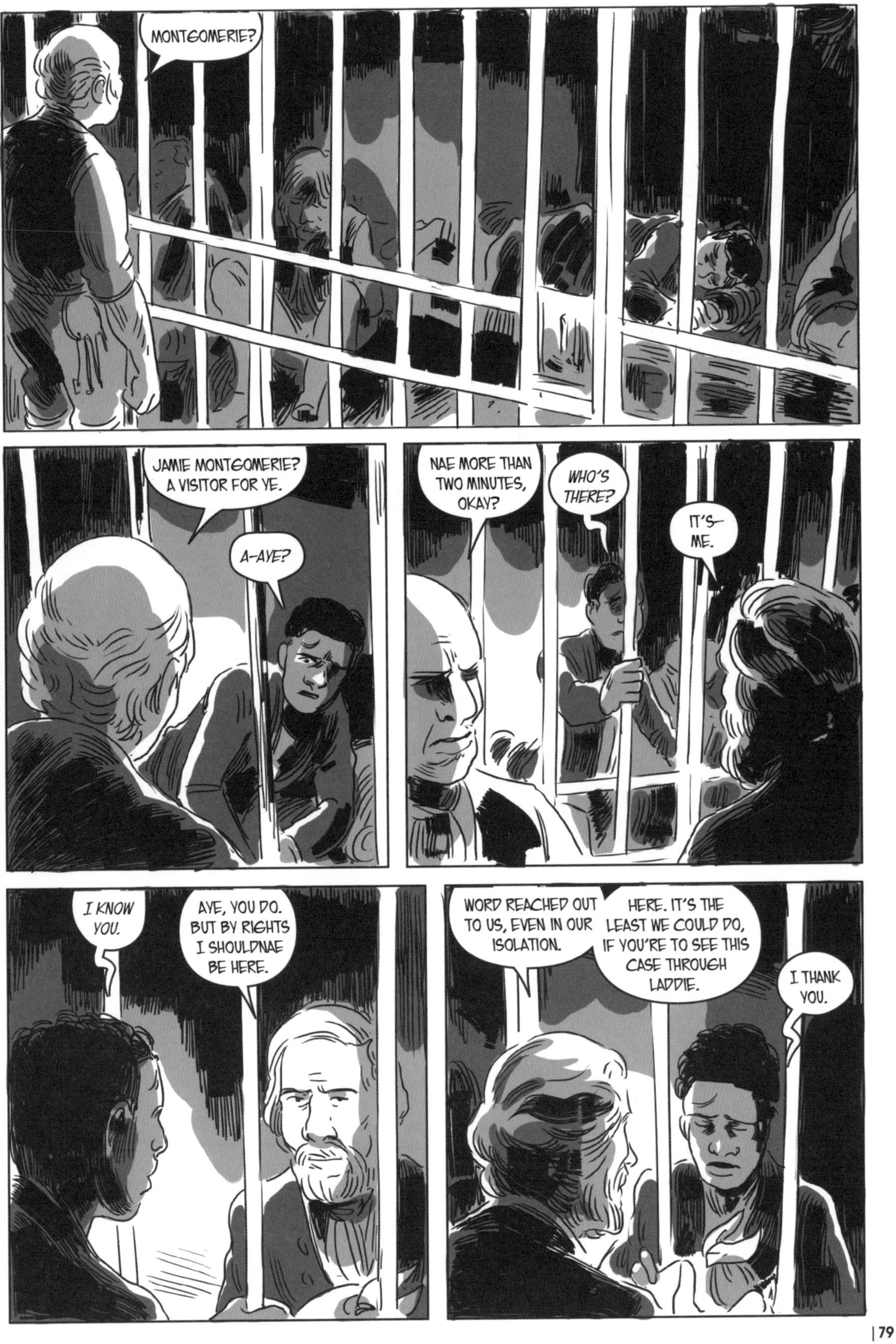
MONTGOMERIE?
JAMIE MONTGOMERIE? A VISITOR FOR YE.
A-AYE?
NAE MORE THAN TWO MINUTES, OKAY?
WHO'S THERE?
IT'S— ME.
I KNOW YOU.
AYE, YOU DO. BUT BY RIGHTS I SHOULDNAE BE HERE.
WORD REACHED OUT TO US, EVEN IN OUR ISOLATION.
HERE. IT'S THE LEAST WE COULD DO, IF YOU'RE TO SEE THIS CASE THROUGH LADDIE.
I THANK YOU.

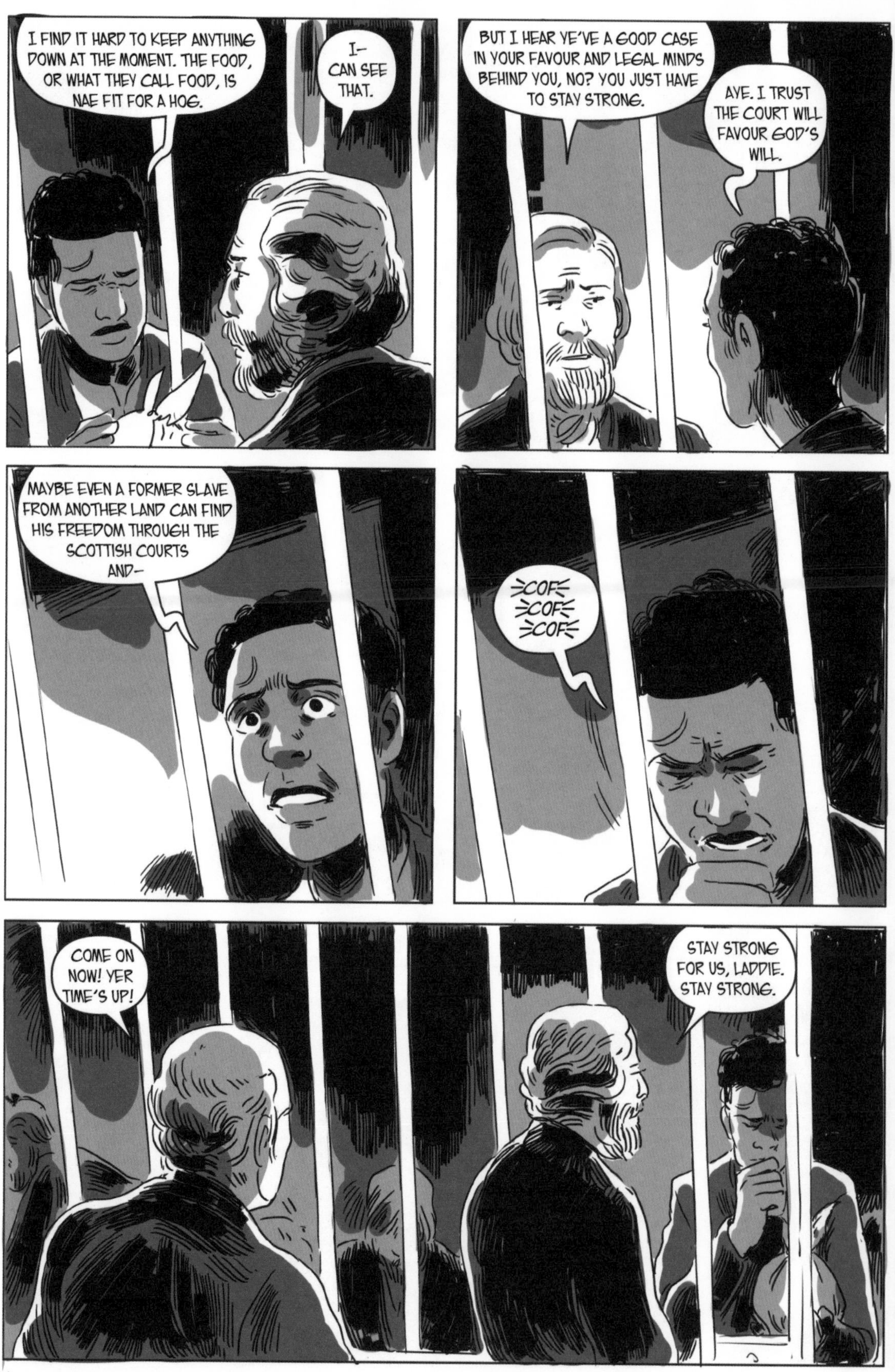

I FIND IT HARD TO KEEP ANYTHING DOWN AT THE MOMENT. THE FOOD, OR WHAT THEY CALL FOOD, IS NAE FIT FOR A HOG.
I– CAN SEE THAT.
BUT I HEAR YE'VE A GOOD CASE IN YOUR FAVOUR AND LEGAL MINDS BEHIND YOU, NO? YOU JUST HAVE TO STAY STRONG.
AYE. I TRUST THE COURT WILL FAVOUR GOD'S WILL.
MAYBE EVEN A FORMER SLAVE FROM ANOTHER LAND CAN FIND HIS FREEDOM THROUGH THE SCOTTISH COURTS AND–
COF COF COF
COME ON NOW! YER TIME'S UP!
STAY STRONG FOR US, LADDIE. STAY STRONG.

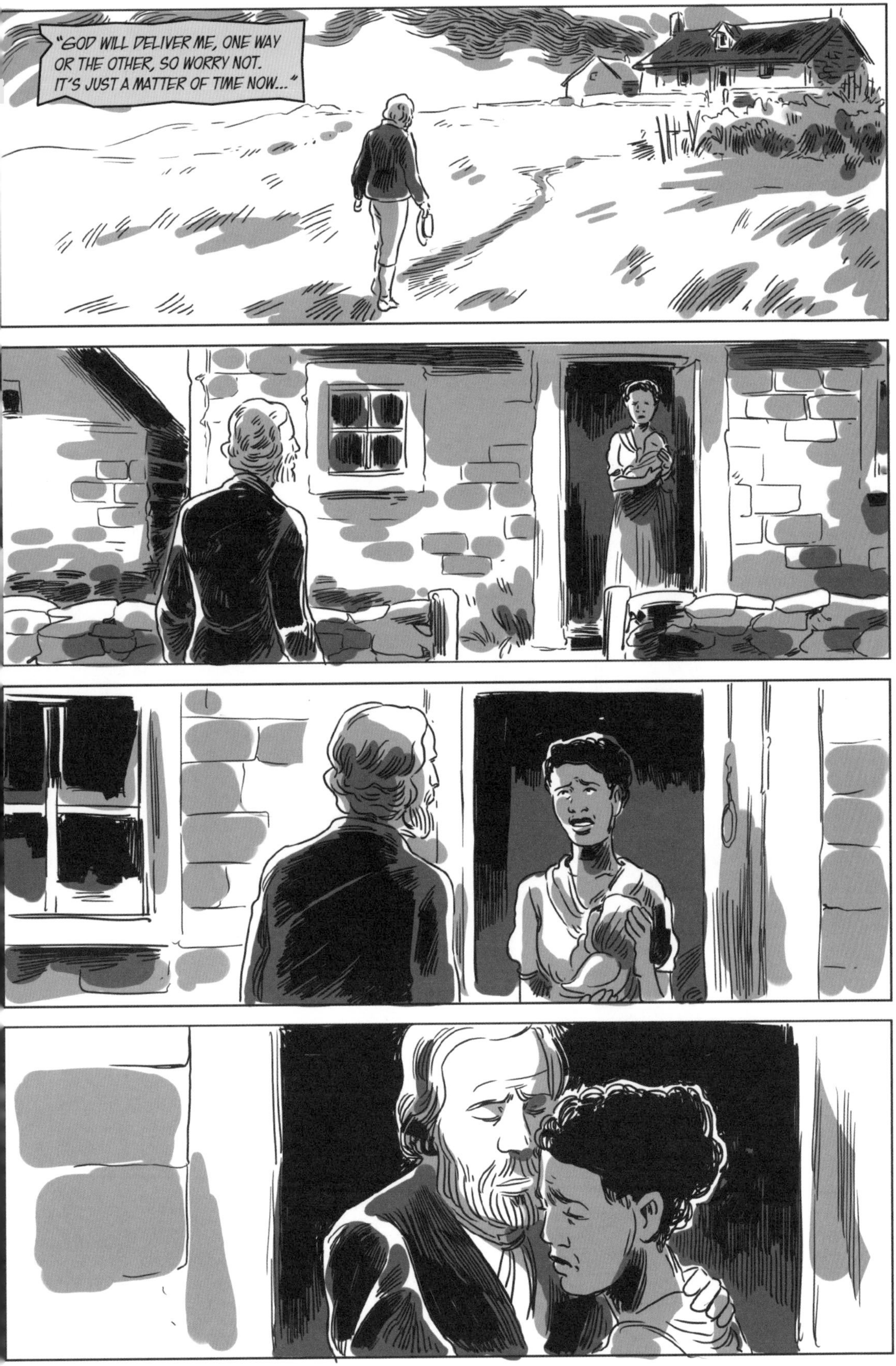
"GOD WILL DELIVER ME, ONE WAY OR THE OTHER, SO WORRY NOT. IT'S JUST A MATTER OF TIME NOW..."

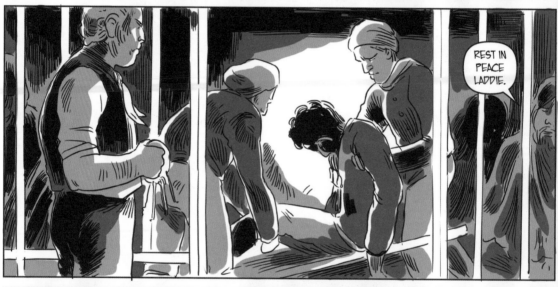

REST IN PEACE LADDIE.

WE'LL SEE YOU ALL SOON IN A BETTER PLACE THAN THIS.

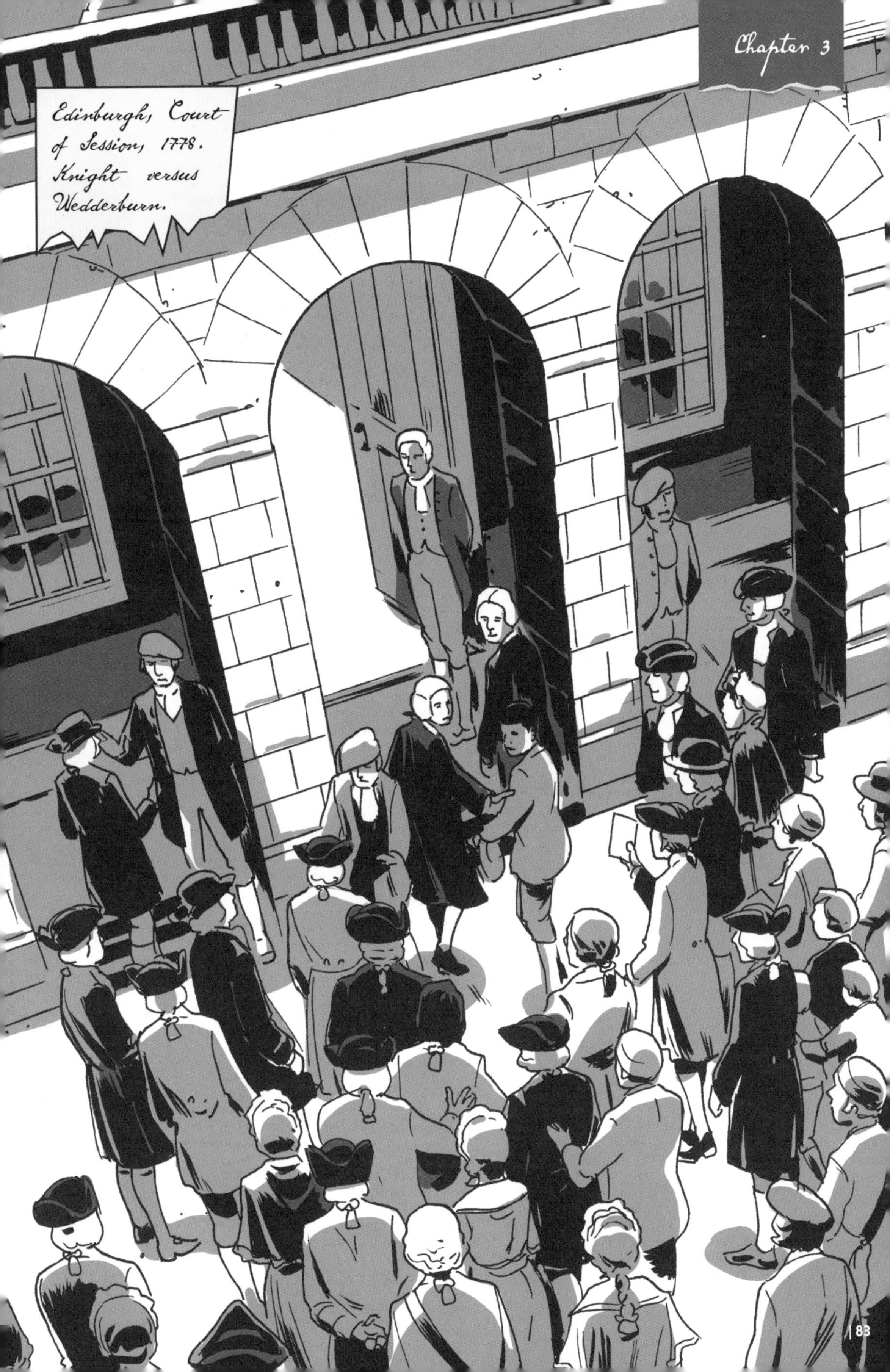
Chapter 3
Edinburgh, Court of Session, 1778. Knight versus Wedderburn.

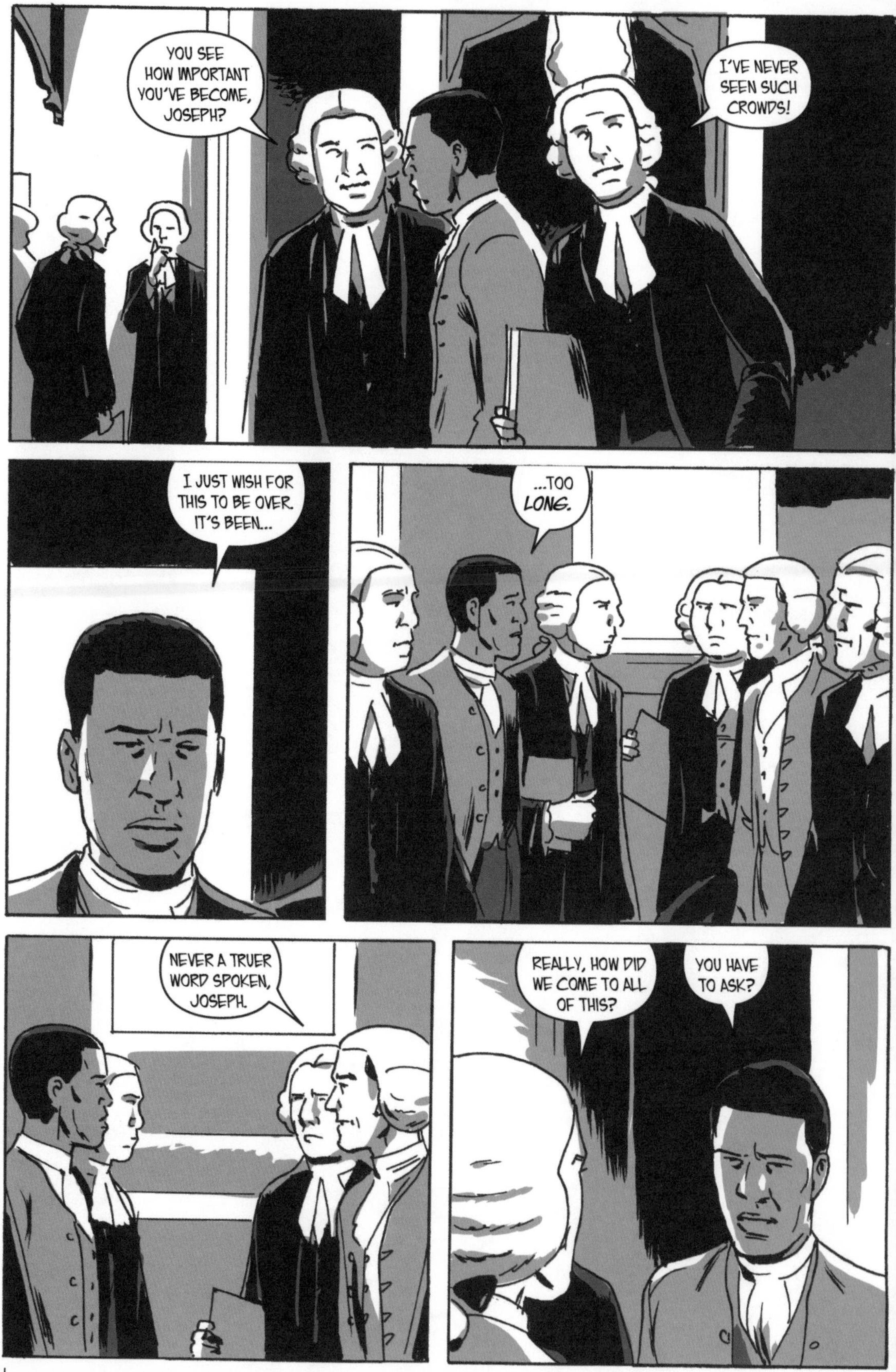
YOU SEE HOW IMPORTANT YOU'VE BECOME, JOSEPH?
I'VE NEVER SEEN SUCH CROWDS!
I JUST WISH FOR THIS TO BE OVER. IT'S BEEN...
...TOO LONG.
NEVER A TRUER WORD SPOKEN, JOSEPH.
REALLY, HOW DID WE COME TO ALL OF THIS?
YOU HAVE TO ASK?

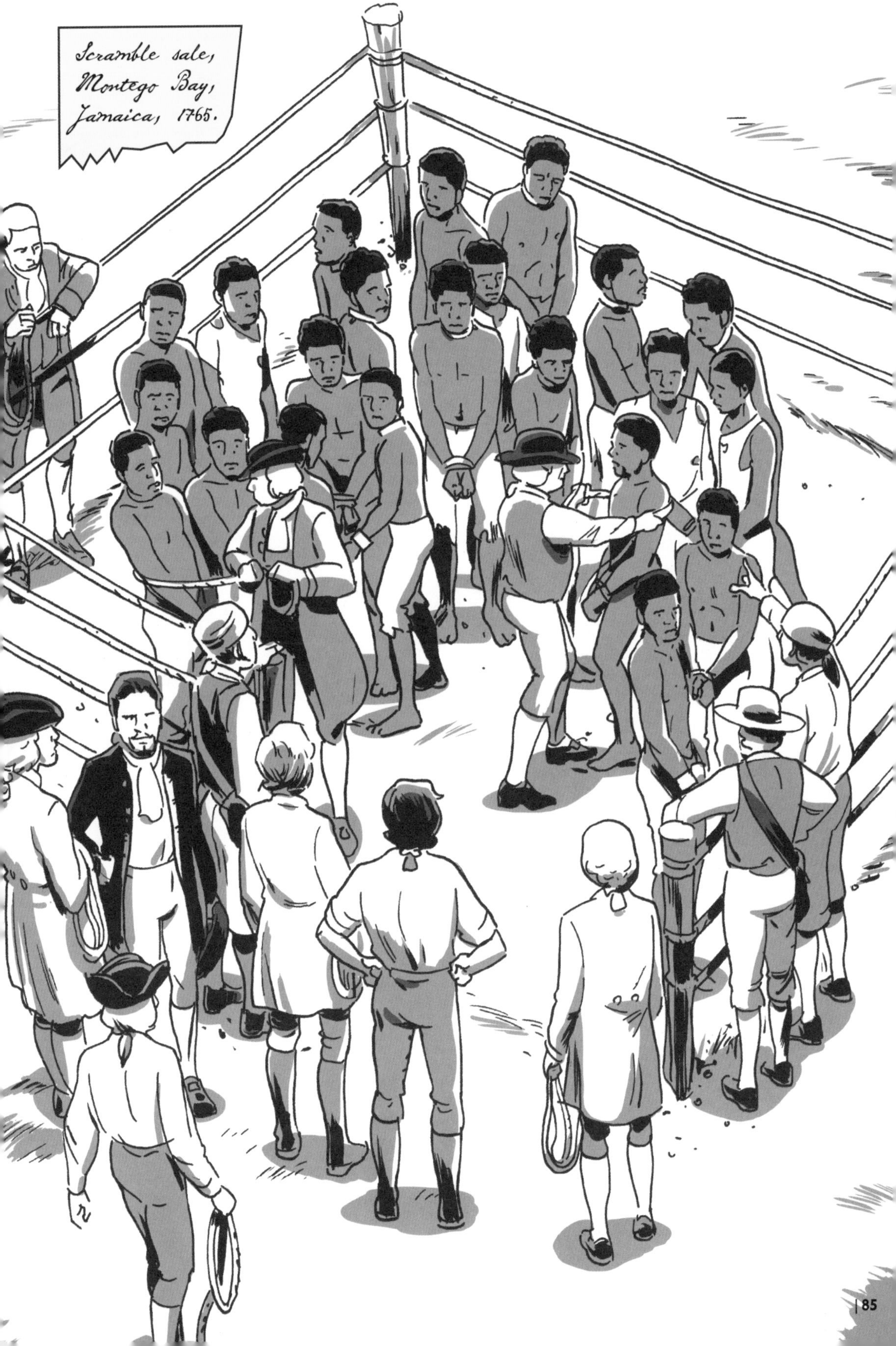
Scramble sale, Montego Bay, Jamaica, 1765.

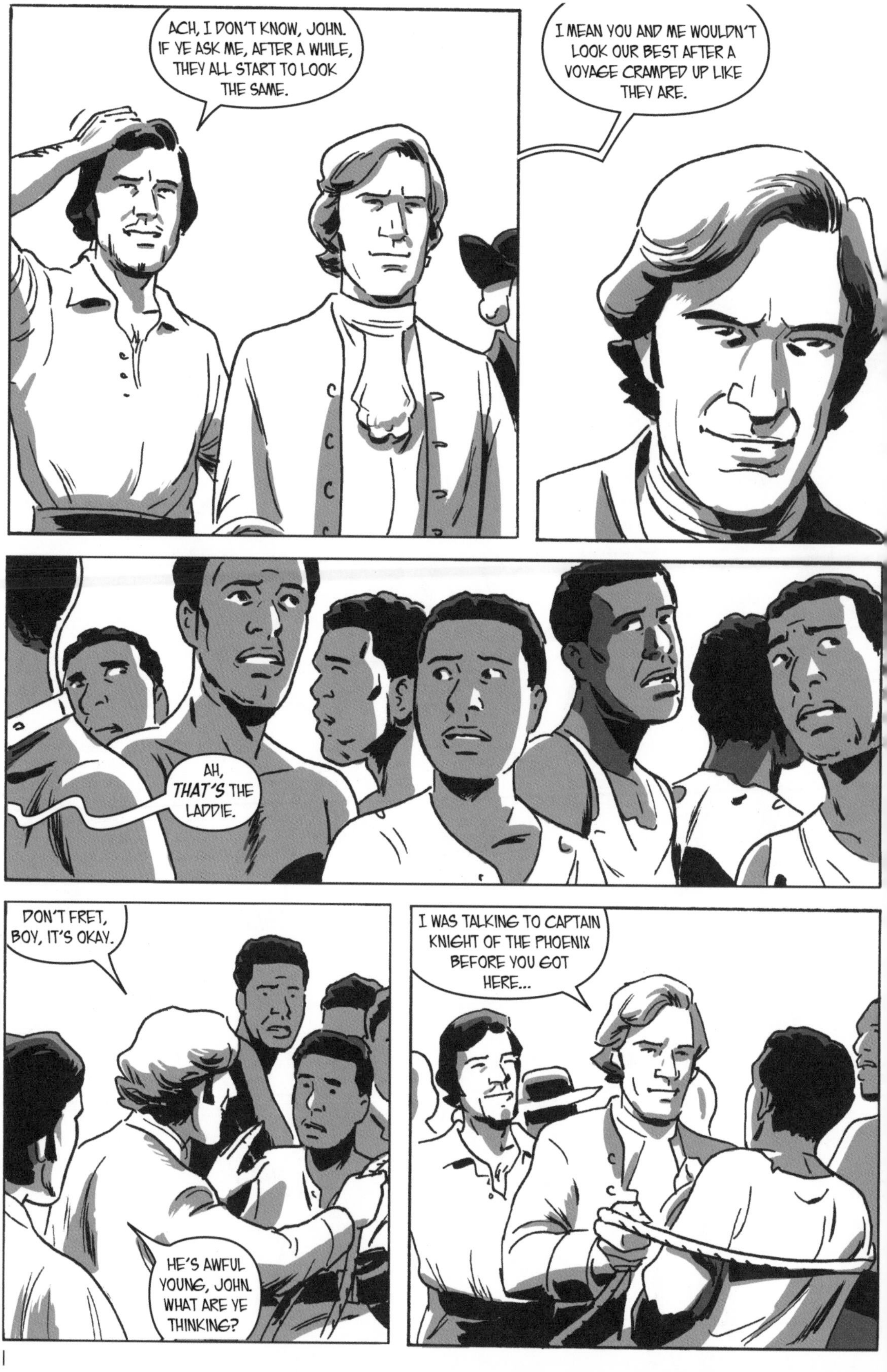
ACH, I DON'T KNOW, JOHN. IF YE ASK ME, AFTER A WHILE, THEY ALL START TO LOOK THE SAME.
I MEAN YOU AND ME WOULDN'T LOOK OUR BEST AFTER A VOYAGE CRAMPED UP LIKE THEY ARE.
AH, *THAT'S* THE LADDIE.
DON'T FRET, BOY, IT'S OKAY.
HE'S AWFUL YOUNG, JOHN. WHAT ARE YE THINKING?
I WAS TALKING TO CAPTAIN KNIGHT OF THE PHOENIX BEFORE YOU GOT HERE...

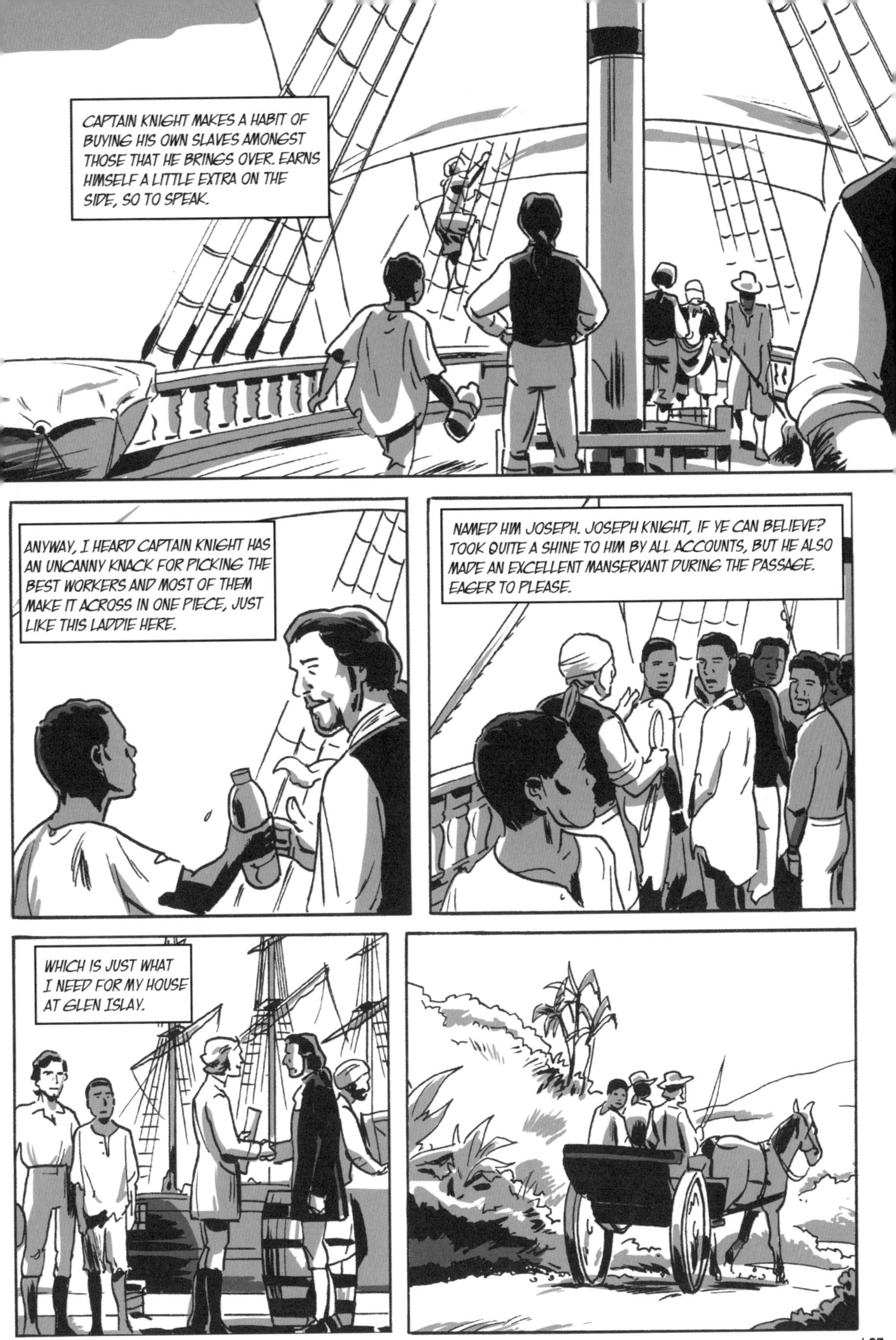
CAPTAIN KNIGHT MAKES A HABIT OF BUYING HIS OWN SLAVES AMONGST THOSE THAT HE BRINGS OVER. EARNS HIMSELF A LITTLE EXTRA ON THE SIDE, SO TO SPEAK.
ANYWAY, I HEARD CAPTAIN KNIGHT HAS AN UNCANNY KNACK FOR PICKING THE BEST WORKERS AND MOST OF THEM MAKE IT ACROSS IN ONE PIECE, JUST LIKE THIS LADDIE HERE.
NAMED HIM JOSEPH. JOSEPH KNIGHT, IF YE CAN BELIEVE? TOOK QUITE A SHINE TO HIM BY ALL ACCOUNTS, BUT HE ALSO MADE AN EXCELLENT MANSERVANT DURING THE PASSAGE. EAGER TO PLEASE.
WHICH IS JUST WHAT I NEED FOR MY HOUSE AT GLEN ISLAY.

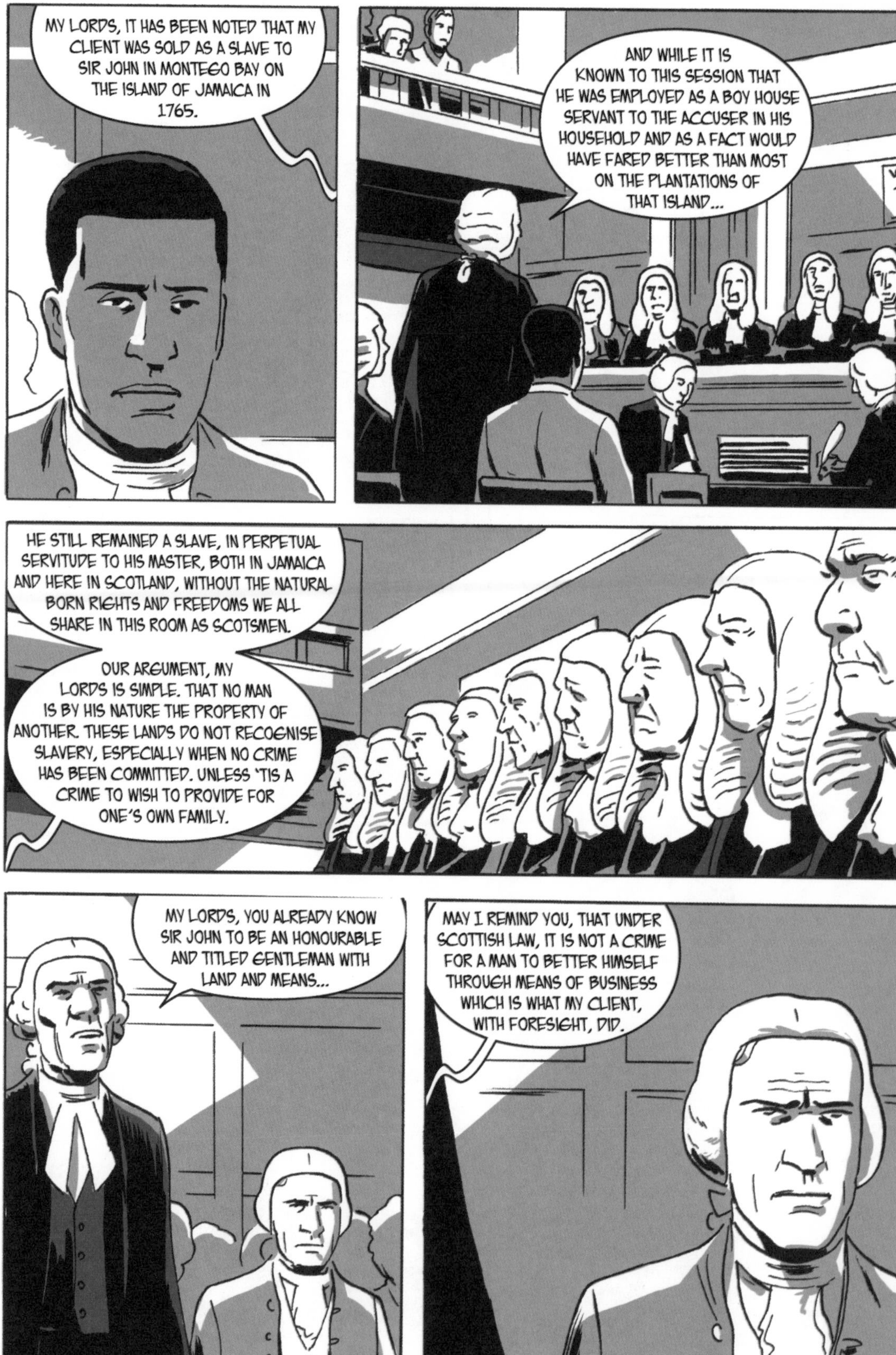
MY LORDS, IT HAS BEEN NOTED THAT MY CLIENT WAS SOLD AS A SLAVE TO SIR JOHN IN MONTEGO BAY ON THE ISLAND OF JAMAICA IN 1765.
AND WHILE IT IS KNOWN TO THIS SESSION THAT HE WAS EMPLOYED AS A BOY HOUSE SERVANT TO THE ACCUSER IN HIS HOUSEHOLD AND AS A FACT WOULD HAVE FARED BETTER THAN MOST ON THE PLANTATIONS OF THAT ISLAND...
HE STILL REMAINED A SLAVE, IN PERPETUAL SERVITUDE TO HIS MASTER, BOTH IN JAMAICA AND HERE IN SCOTLAND, WITHOUT THE NATURAL BORN RIGHTS AND FREEDOMS WE ALL SHARE IN THIS ROOM AS SCOTSMEN.
OUR ARGUMENT, MY LORDS IS SIMPLE. THAT NO MAN IS BY HIS NATURE THE PROPERTY OF ANOTHER. THESE LANDS DO NOT RECOGNISE SLAVERY, ESPECIALLY WHEN NO CRIME HAS BEEN COMMITTED. UNLESS 'TIS A CRIME TO WISH TO PROVIDE FOR ONE'S OWN FAMILY.
MY LORDS, YOU ALREADY KNOW SIR JOHN TO BE AN HONOURABLE AND TITLED GENTLEMAN WITH LAND AND MEANS...
MAY I REMIND YOU, THAT UNDER SCOTTISH LAW, IT IS NOT A CRIME FOR A MAN TO BETTER HIMSELF THROUGH MEANS OF BUSINESS WHICH IS WHAT MY CLIENT, WITH FORESIGHT, DID.

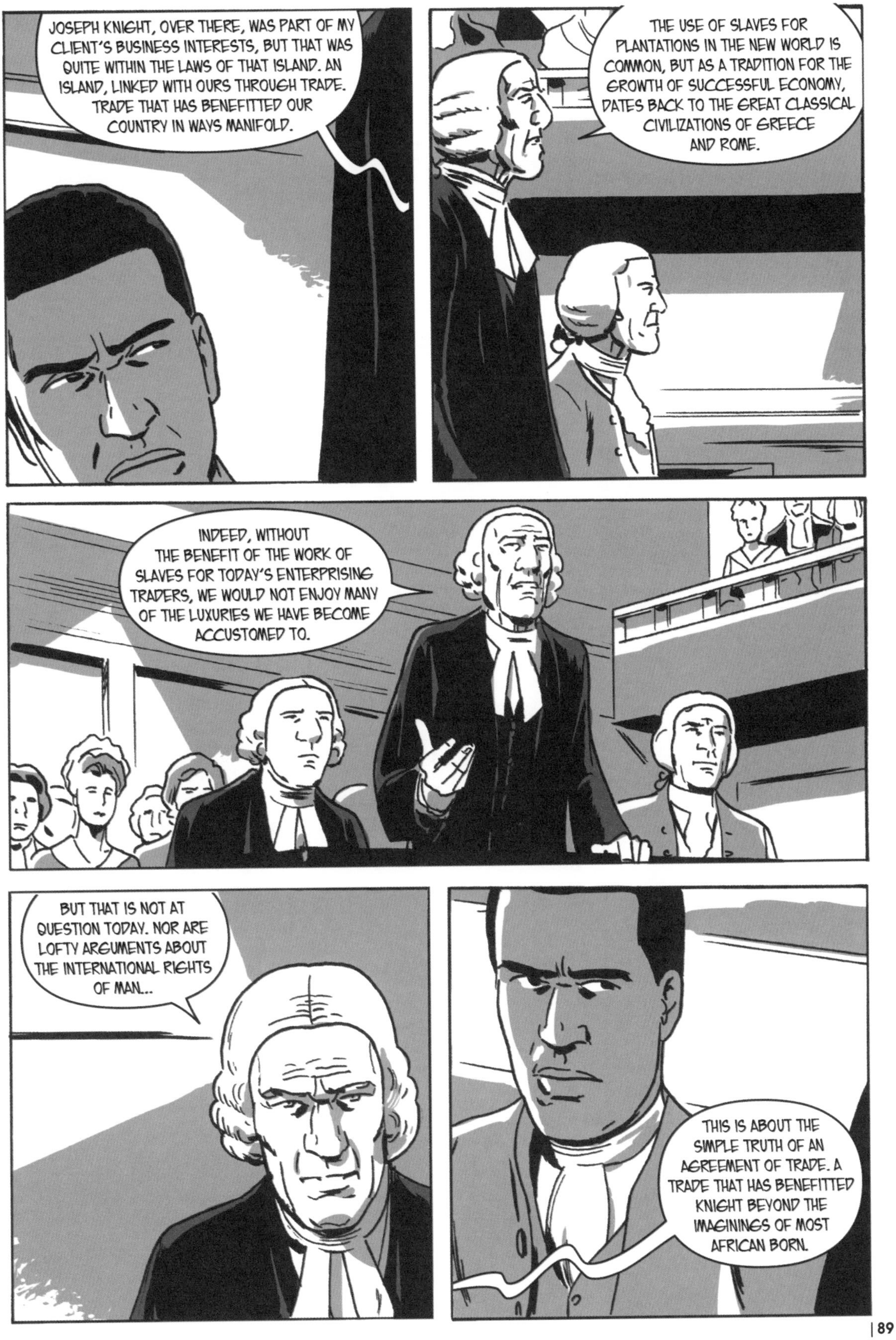
JOSEPH KNIGHT, OVER THERE, WAS PART OF MY CLIENT'S BUSINESS INTERESTS, BUT THAT WAS QUITE WITHIN THE LAWS OF THAT ISLAND. AN ISLAND, LINKED WITH OURS THROUGH TRADE. TRADE THAT HAS BENEFITTED OUR COUNTRY IN WAYS MANIFOLD.
THE USE OF SLAVES FOR PLANTATIONS IN THE NEW WORLD IS COMMON, BUT AS A TRADITION FOR THE GROWTH OF SUCCESSFUL ECONOMY, DATES BACK TO THE GREAT CLASSICAL CIVILIZATIONS OF GREECE AND ROME.
INDEED, WITHOUT THE BENEFIT OF THE WORK OF SLAVES FOR TODAY'S ENTERPRISING TRADERS, WE WOULD NOT ENJOY MANY OF THE LUXURIES WE HAVE BECOME ACCUSTOMED TO.
BUT THAT IS NOT AT QUESTION TODAY. NOR ARE LOFTY ARGUMENTS ABOUT THE INTERNATIONAL RIGHTS OF MAN...
THIS IS ABOUT THE SIMPLE TRUTH OF AN AGREEMENT OF TRADE. A TRADE THAT HAS BENEFITTED KNIGHT BEYOND THE IMAGININGS OF MOST AFRICAN BORN.

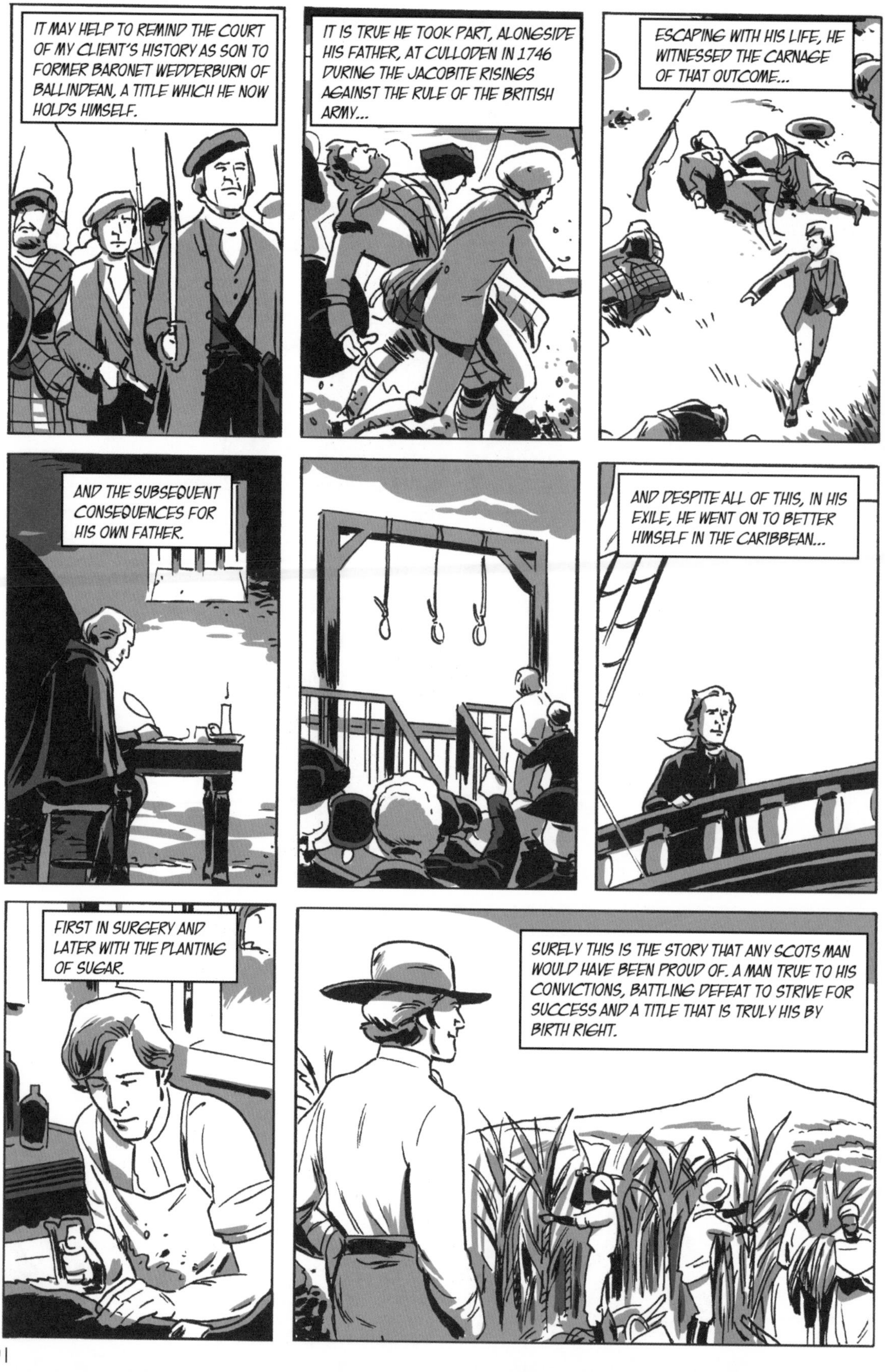
IT MAY HELP TO REMIND THE COURT OF MY CLIENT'S HISTORY AS SON TO FORMER BARONET WEDDERBURN OF BALLINDEAN, A TITLE WHICH HE NOW HOLDS HIMSELF.
IT IS TRUE HE TOOK PART, ALONGSIDE HIS FATHER, AT CULLODEN IN 1746 DURING THE JACOBITE RISINGS AGAINST THE RULE OF THE BRITISH ARMY...
ESCAPING WITH HIS LIFE, HE WITNESSED THE CARNAGE OF THAT OUTCOME...
AND THE SUBSEQUENT CONSEQUENCES FOR HIS OWN FATHER.
AND DESPITE ALL OF THIS, IN HIS EXILE, HE WENT ON TO BETTER HIMSELF IN THE CARIBBEAN...
FIRST IN SURGERY AND LATER WITH THE PLANTING OF SUGAR.
SURELY THIS IS THE STORY THAT ANY SCOTS MAN WOULD HAVE BEEN PROUD OF. A MAN TRUE TO HIS CONVICTIONS, BATTLING DEFEAT TO STRIVE FOR SUCCESS AND A TITLE THAT IS TRULY HIS BY BIRTH RIGHT.

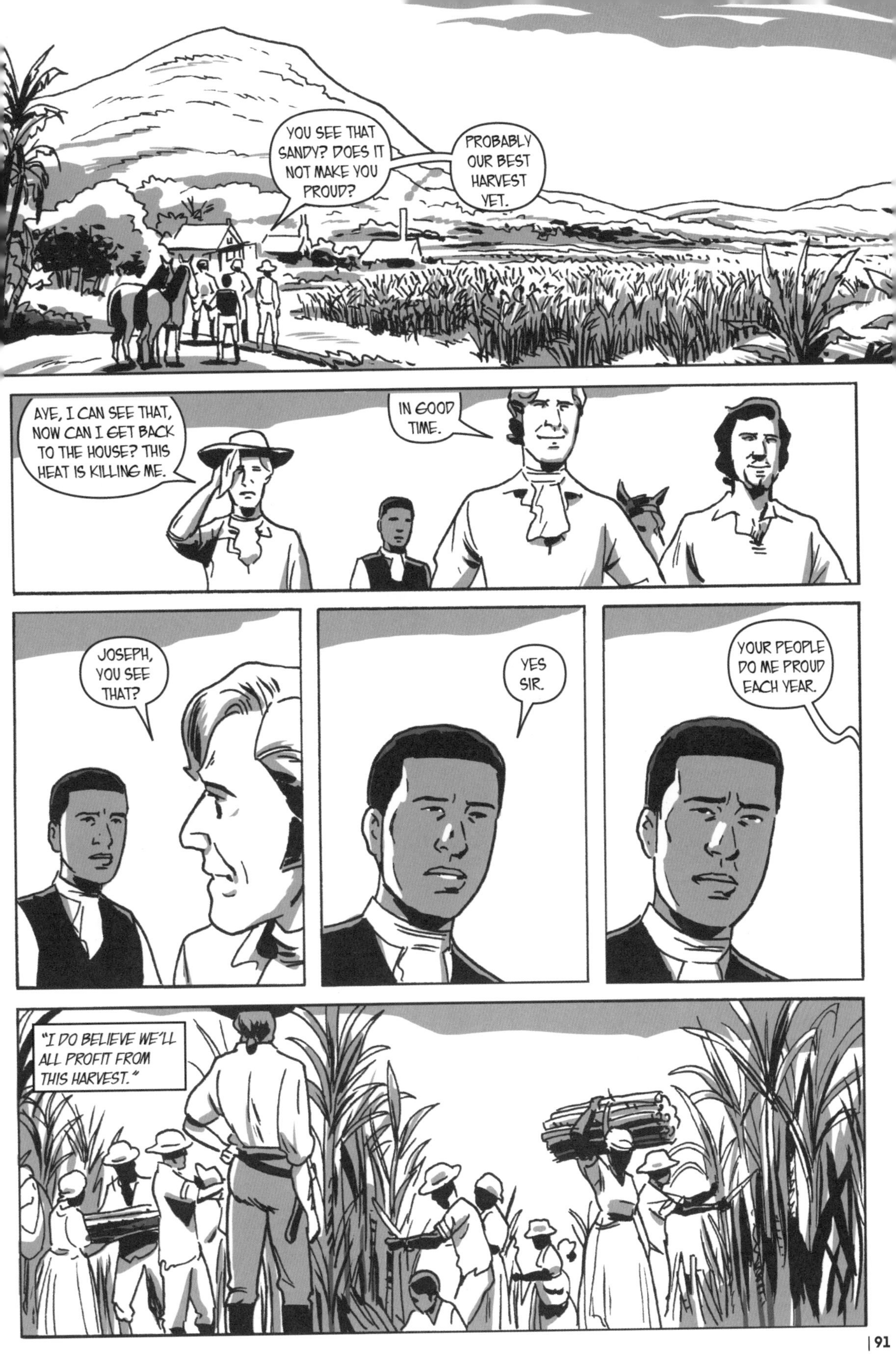
YOU SEE THAT SANDY? DOES IT NOT MAKE YOU PROUD?
PROBABLY OUR BEST HARVEST YET.
AYE, I CAN SEE THAT, NOW CAN I GET BACK TO THE HOUSE? THIS HEAT IS KILLING ME.
IN GOOD TIME.
JOSEPH, YOU SEE THAT?
YES SIR.
YOUR PEOPLE DO ME PROUD EACH YEAR.
"I DO BELIEVE WE'LL ALL PROFIT FROM THIS HARVEST."

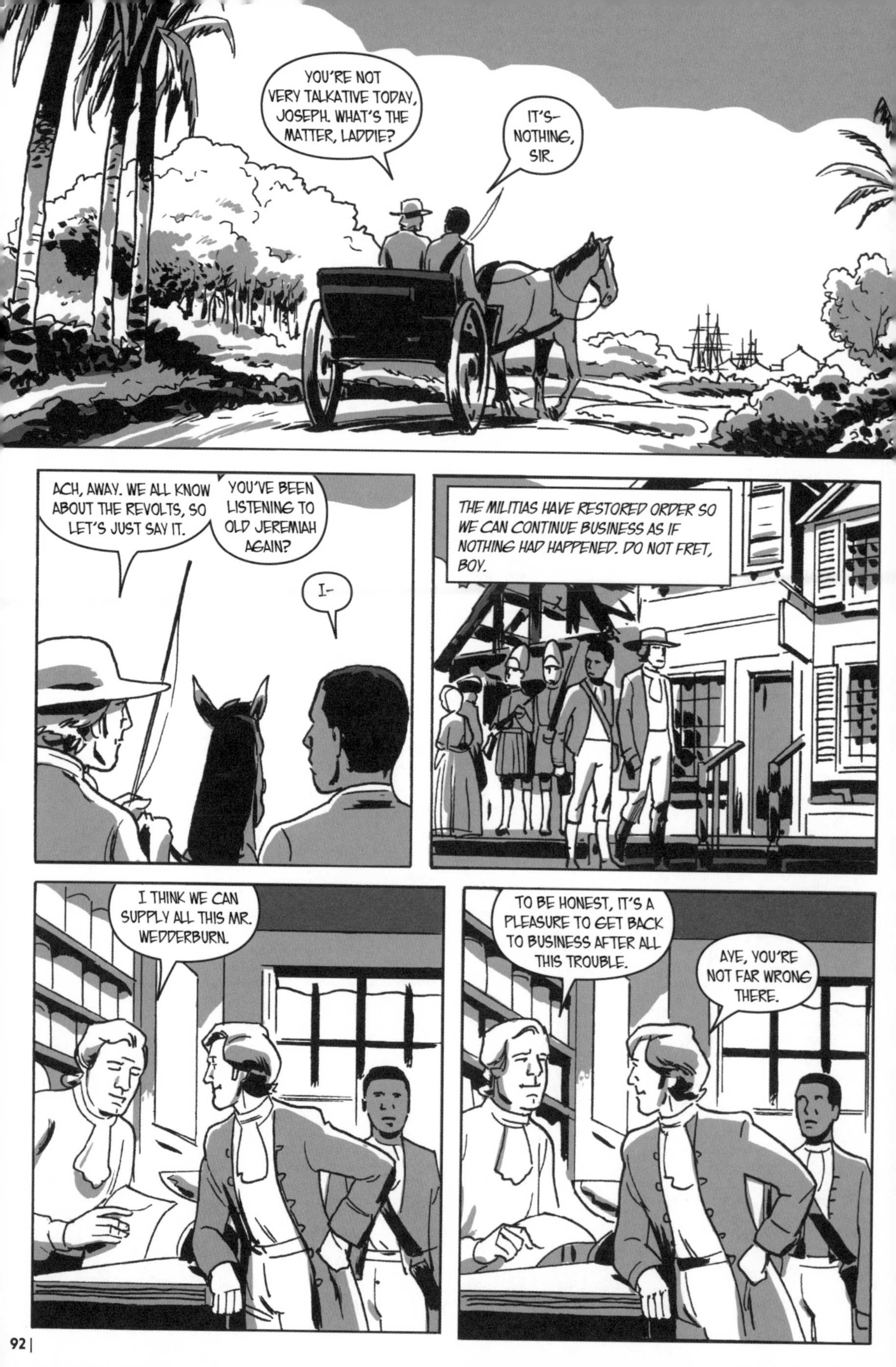
YOU'RE NOT VERY TALKATIVE TODAY, JOSEPH. WHAT'S THE MATTER, LADDIE?
IT'S- NOTHING, SIR.
ACH, AWAY. WE ALL KNOW ABOUT THE REVOLTS, SO LET'S JUST SAY IT.
YOU'VE BEEN LISTENING TO OLD JEREMIAH AGAIN?
I-
THE MILITIAS HAVE RESTORED ORDER SO WE CAN CONTINUE BUSINESS AS IF NOTHING HAD HAPPENED. DO NOT FRET, BOY.
I THINK WE CAN SUPPLY ALL THIS MR. WEDDERBURN.
TO BE HONEST, IT'S A PLEASURE TO GET BACK TO BUSINESS AFTER ALL THIS TROUBLE.
AYE, YOU'RE NOT FAR WRONG THERE.

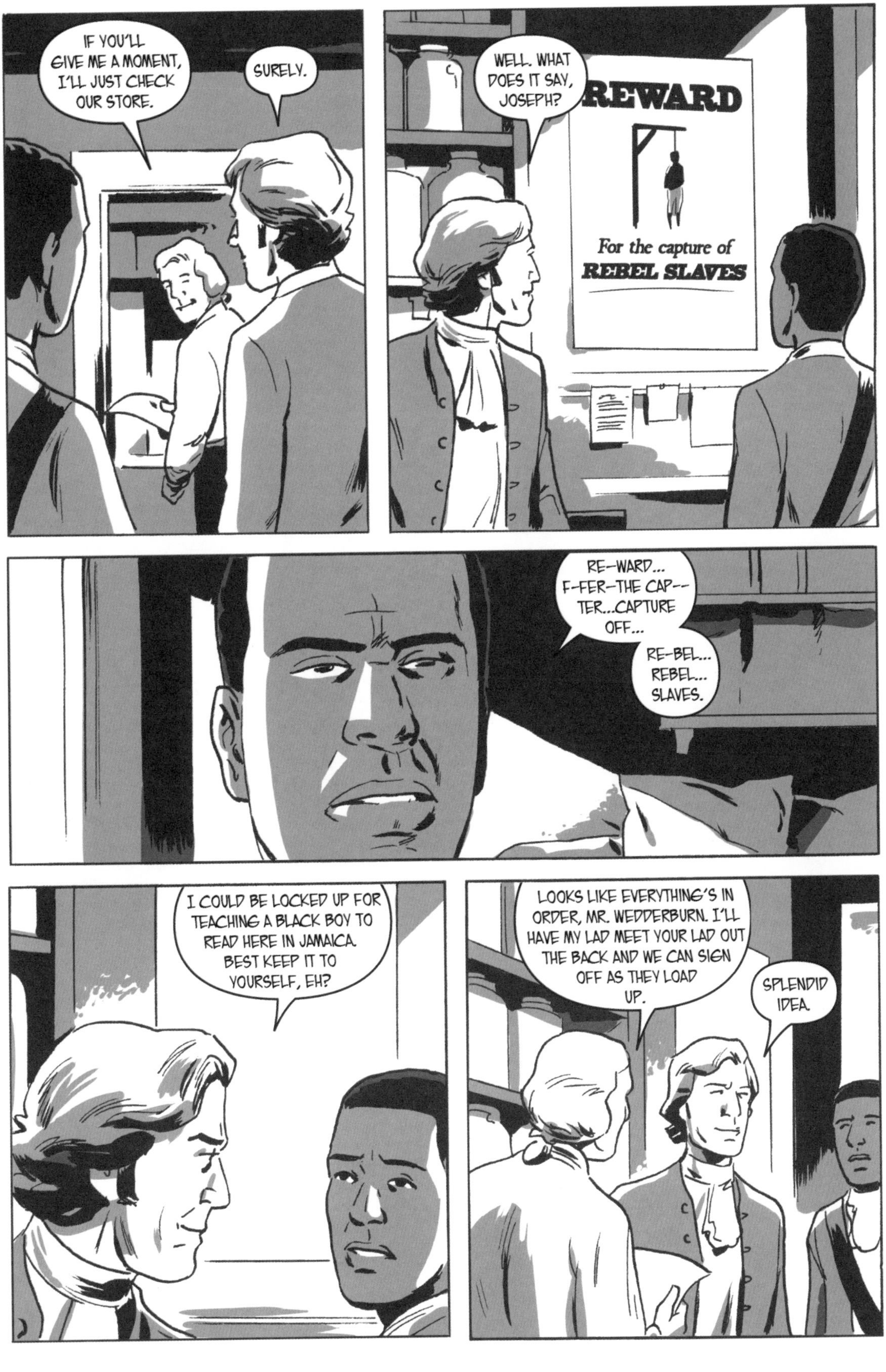

IF YOU'LL GIVE ME A MOMENT, I'LL JUST CHECK OUR STORE.
SURELY.
WELL. WHAT DOES IT SAY, JOSEPH?
REWARD
For the capture of
REBEL SLAVES
RE–WARD... F–FER–THE CAP–– TER...CAPTURE OFF...
RE–BEL... REBEL... SLAVES.
I COULD BE LOCKED UP FOR TEACHING A BLACK BOY TO READ HERE IN JAMAICA. BEST KEEP IT TO YOURSELF, EH?
LOOKS LIKE EVERYTHING'S IN ORDER, MR. WEDDERBURN. I'LL HAVE MY LAD MEET YOUR LAD OUT THE BACK AND WE CAN SIGN OFF AS THEY LOAD UP.
SPLENDID IDEA.

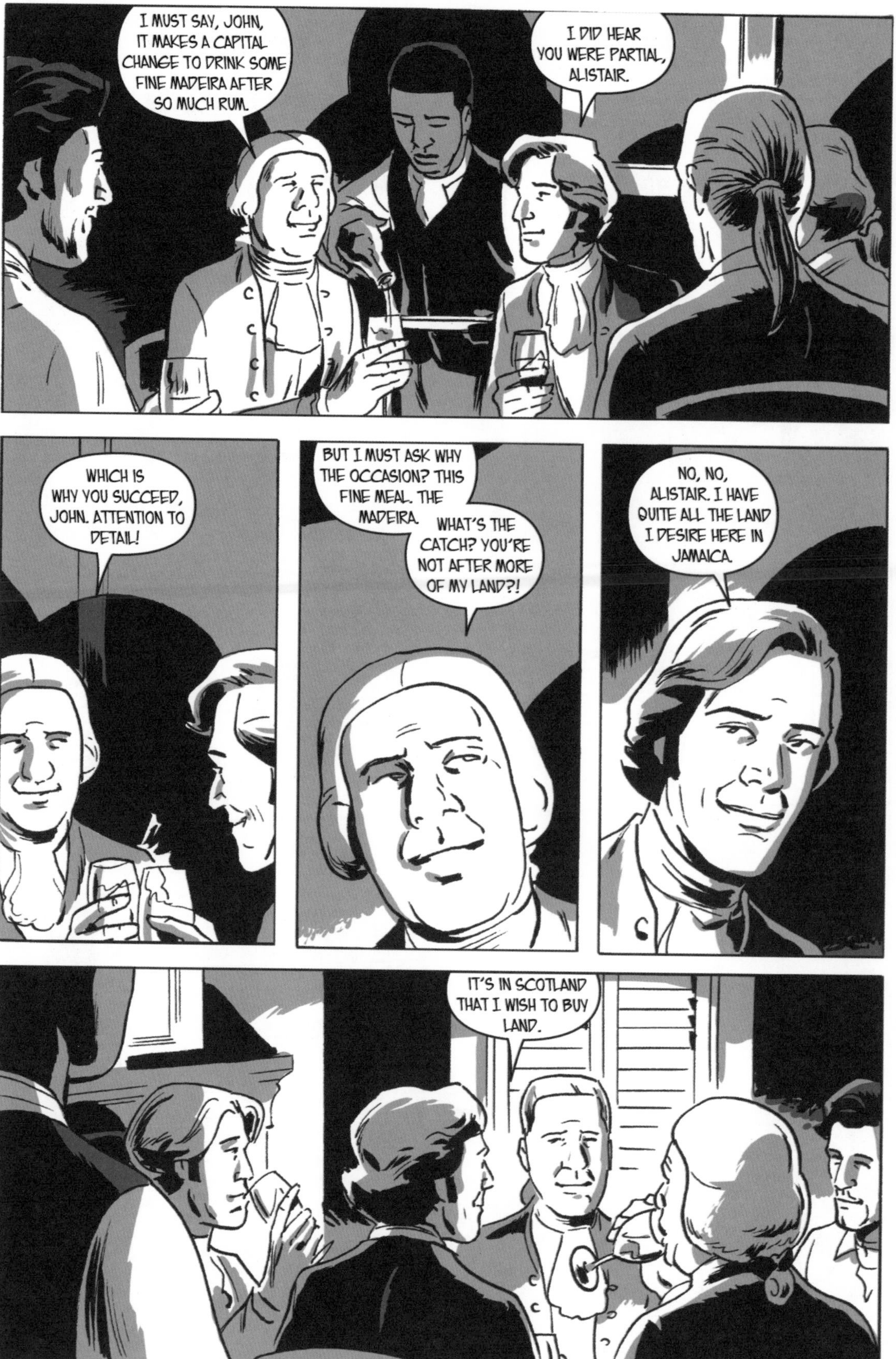
I MUST SAY, JOHN, IT MAKES A CAPITAL CHANGE TO DRINK SOME FINE MADEIRA AFTER SO MUCH RUM.
I DID HEAR YOU WERE PARTIAL, ALISTAIR.
WHICH IS WHY YOU SUCCEED, JOHN. ATTENTION TO DETAIL!
BUT I MUST ASK WHY THE OCCASION? THIS FINE MEAL. THE MADEIRA.
WHAT'S THE CATCH? YOU'RE NOT AFTER MORE OF MY LAND?!
NO, NO, ALISTAIR. I HAVE QUITE ALL THE LAND I DESIRE HERE IN JAMAICA.
IT'S IN SCOTLAND THAT I WISH TO BUY LAND.

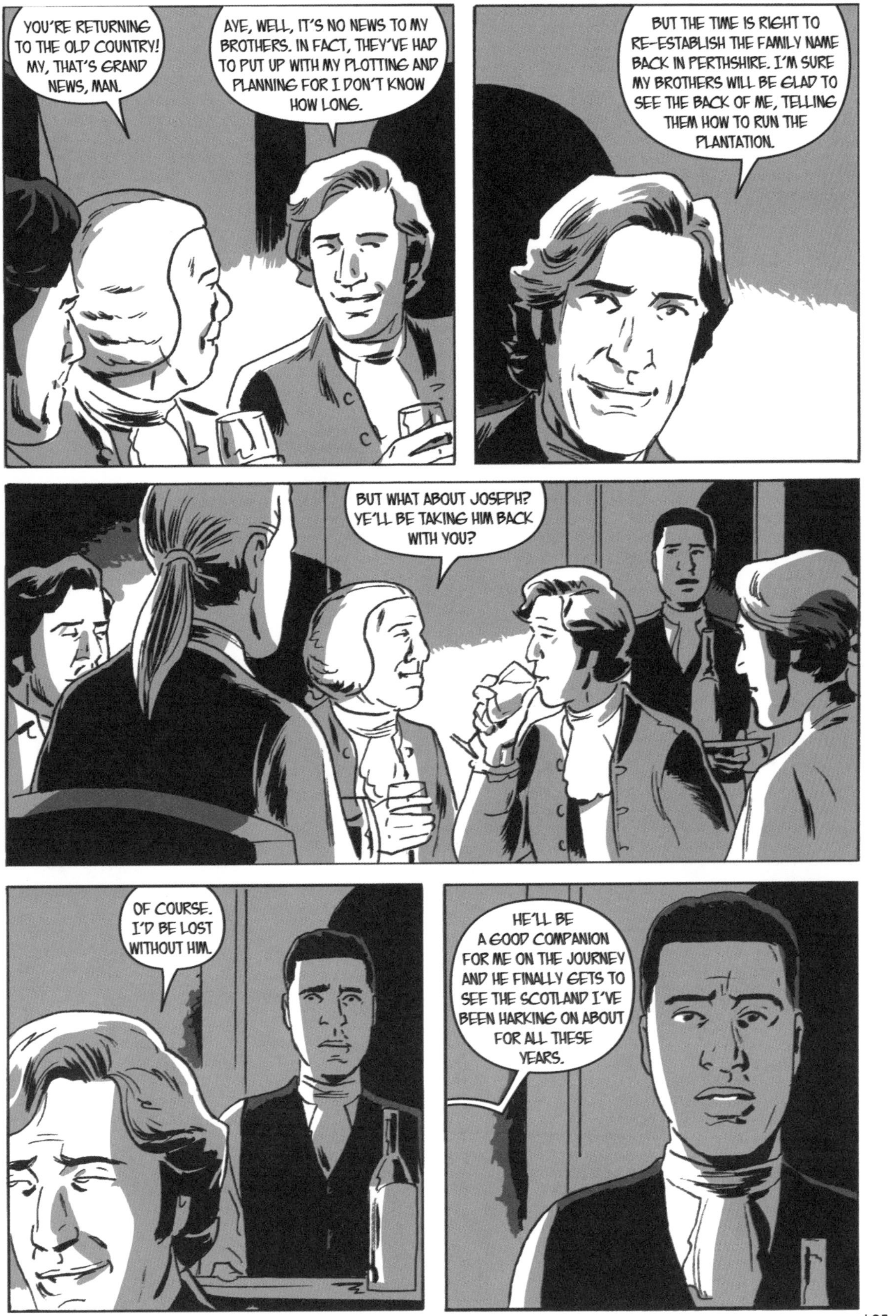
YOU'RE RETURNING TO THE OLD COUNTRY! MY, THAT'S GRAND NEWS, MAN.
AYE, WELL, IT'S NO NEWS TO MY BROTHERS. IN FACT, THEY'VE HAD TO PUT UP WITH MY PLOTTING AND PLANNING FOR I DON'T KNOW HOW LONG.
BUT THE TIME IS RIGHT TO RE-ESTABLISH THE FAMILY NAME BACK IN PERTHSHIRE. I'M SURE MY BROTHERS WILL BE GLAD TO SEE THE BACK OF ME, TELLING THEM HOW TO RUN THE PLANTATION.
BUT WHAT ABOUT JOSEPH? YE'LL BE TAKING HIM BACK WITH YOU?
OF COURSE. I'D BE LOST WITHOUT HIM.
HE'LL BE A GOOD COMPANION FOR ME ON THE JOURNEY AND HE FINALLY GETS TO SEE THE SCOTLAND I'VE BEEN HARKING ON ABOUT FOR ALL THESE YEARS.

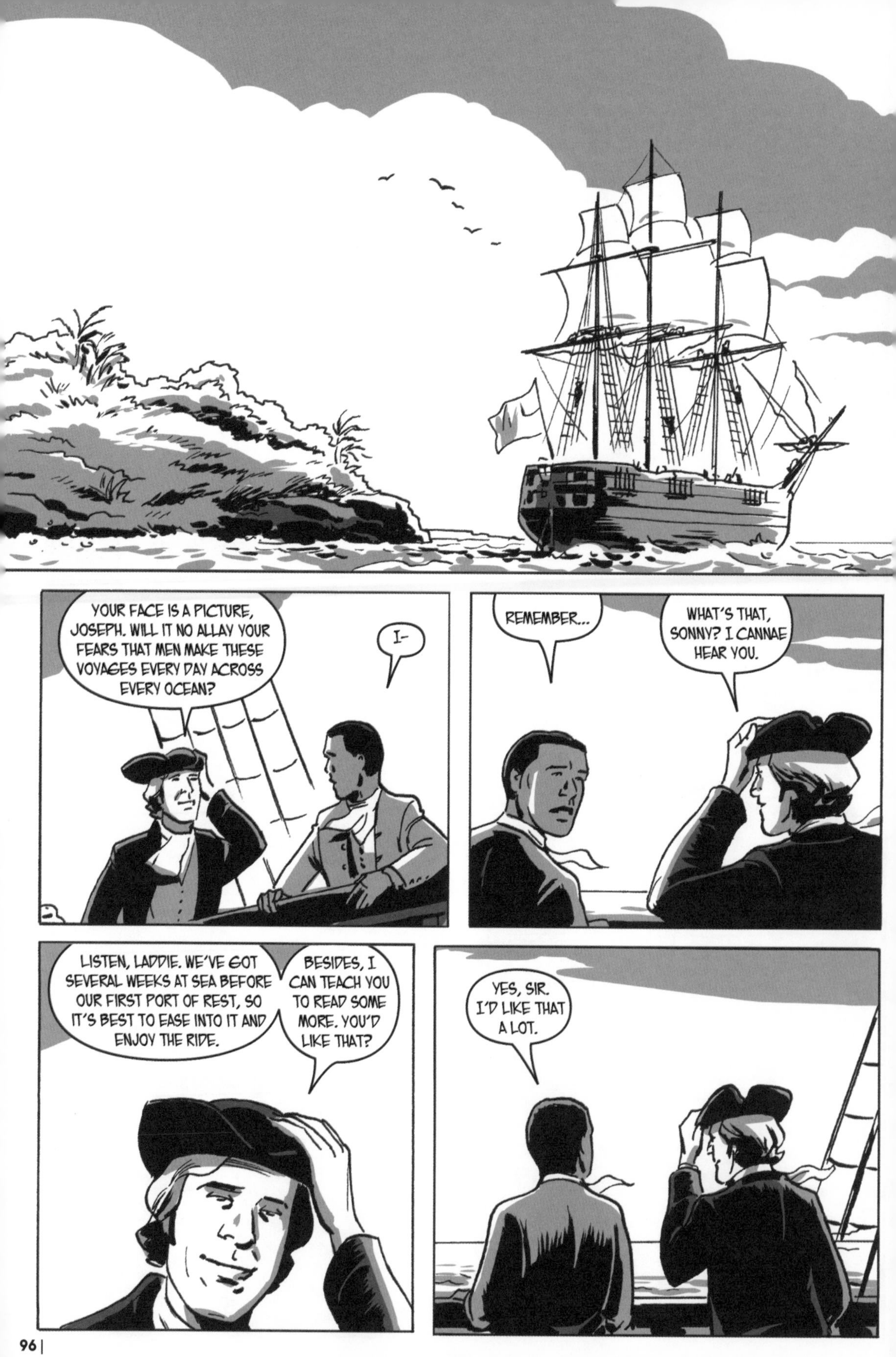
YOUR FACE IS A PICTURE, JOSEPH. WILL IT NO ALLAY YOUR FEARS THAT MEN MAKE THESE VOYAGES EVERY DAY ACROSS EVERY OCEAN?
I-
REMEMBER...
WHAT'S THAT, SONNY? I CANNAE HEAR YOU.
LISTEN, LADDIE. WE'VE GOT SEVERAL WEEKS AT SEA BEFORE OUR FIRST PORT OF REST, SO IT'S BEST TO EASE INTO IT AND ENJOY THE RIDE.
BESIDES, I CAN TEACH YOU TO READ SOME MORE. YOU'D LIKE THAT?
YES, SIR. I'D LIKE THAT A LOT.

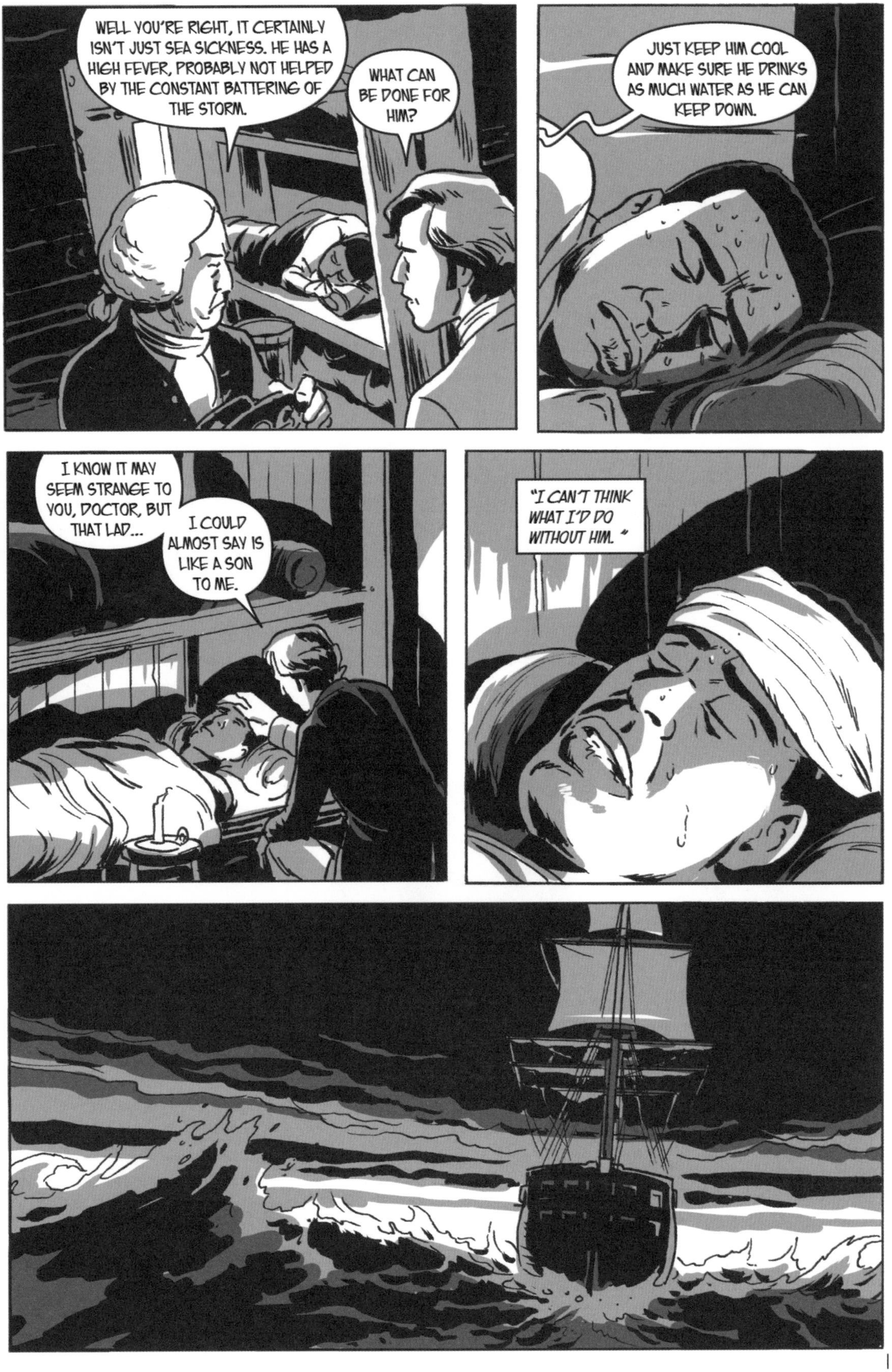
WELL YOU'RE RIGHT, IT CERTAINLY ISN'T JUST SEA SICKNESS. HE HAS A HIGH FEVER, PROBABLY NOT HELPED BY THE CONSTANT BATTERING OF THE STORM.
WHAT CAN BE DONE FOR HIM?
JUST KEEP HIM COOL AND MAKE SURE HE DRINKS AS MUCH WATER AS HE CAN KEEP DOWN.
I KNOW IT MAY SEEM STRANGE TO YOU, DOCTOR, BUT THAT LAD...
I COULD ALMOST SAY IS LIKE A SON TO ME.
"I CAN'T THINK WHAT I'D DO WITHOUT HIM."

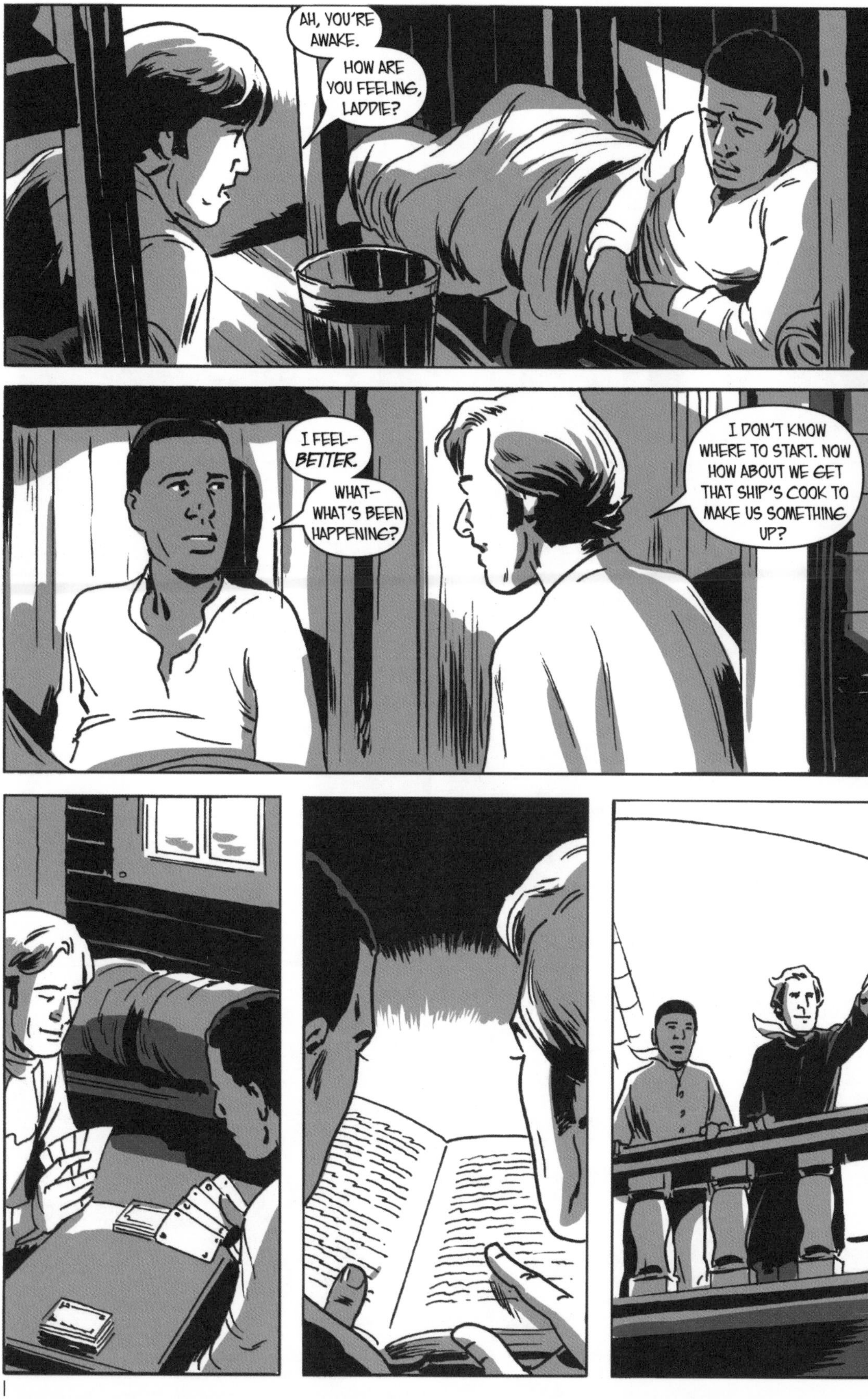
AH, YOU'RE AWAKE.
HOW ARE YOU FEELING, LADDIE?
I FEEL- **BETTER.**
WHAT- WHAT'S BEEN HAPPENING?
I DON'T KNOW WHERE TO START. NOW HOW ABOUT WE GET THAT SHIP'S COOK TO MAKE US SOMETHING UP?

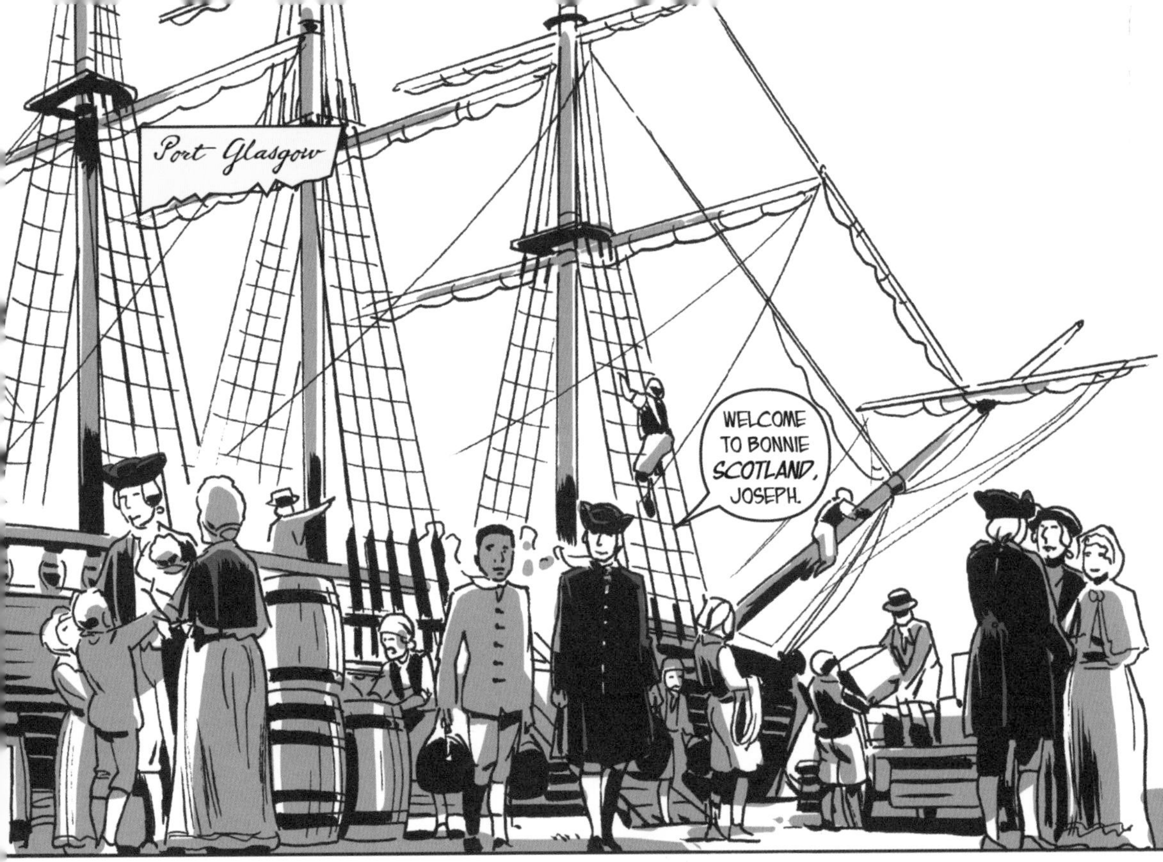
Port Glasgow
WELCOME TO BONNIE SCOTLAND, JOSEPH.

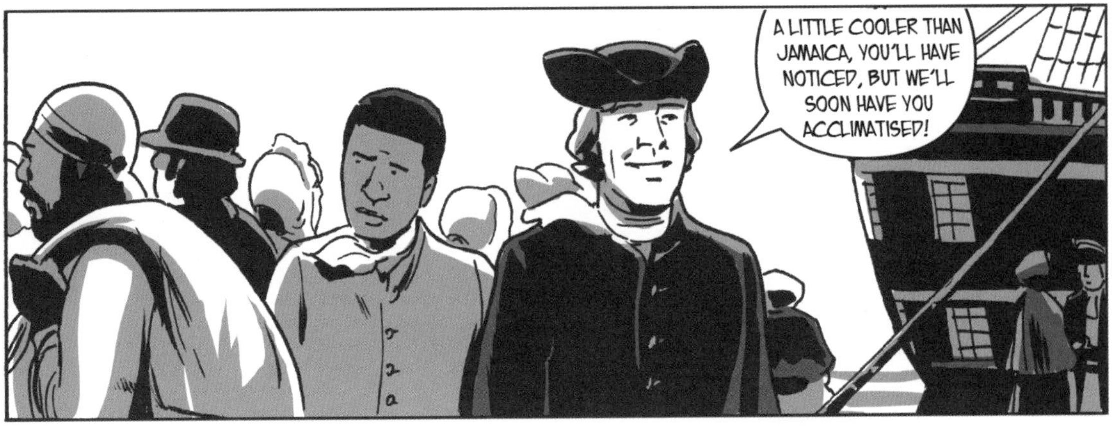
A LITTLE COOLER THAN JAMAICA, YOU'LL HAVE NOTICED, BUT WE'LL SOON HAVE YOU ACCLIMATISED!

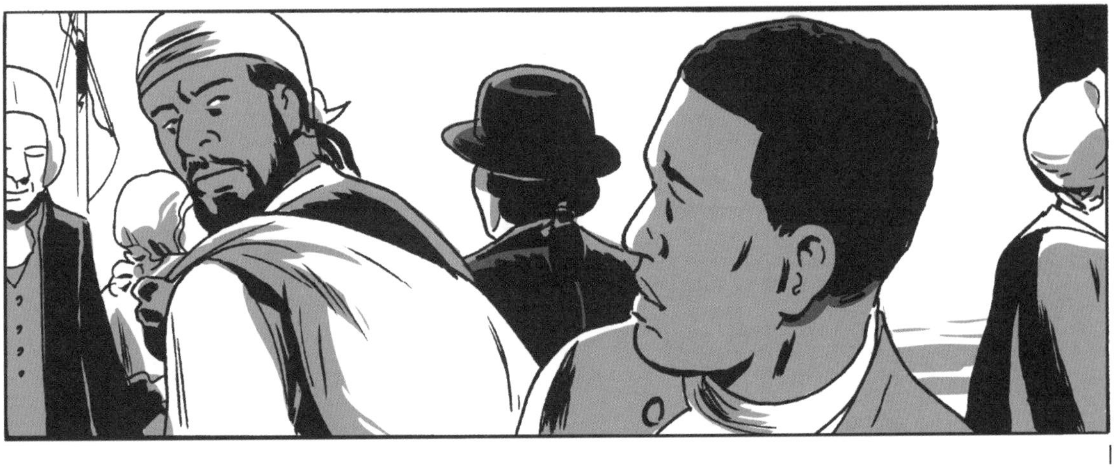

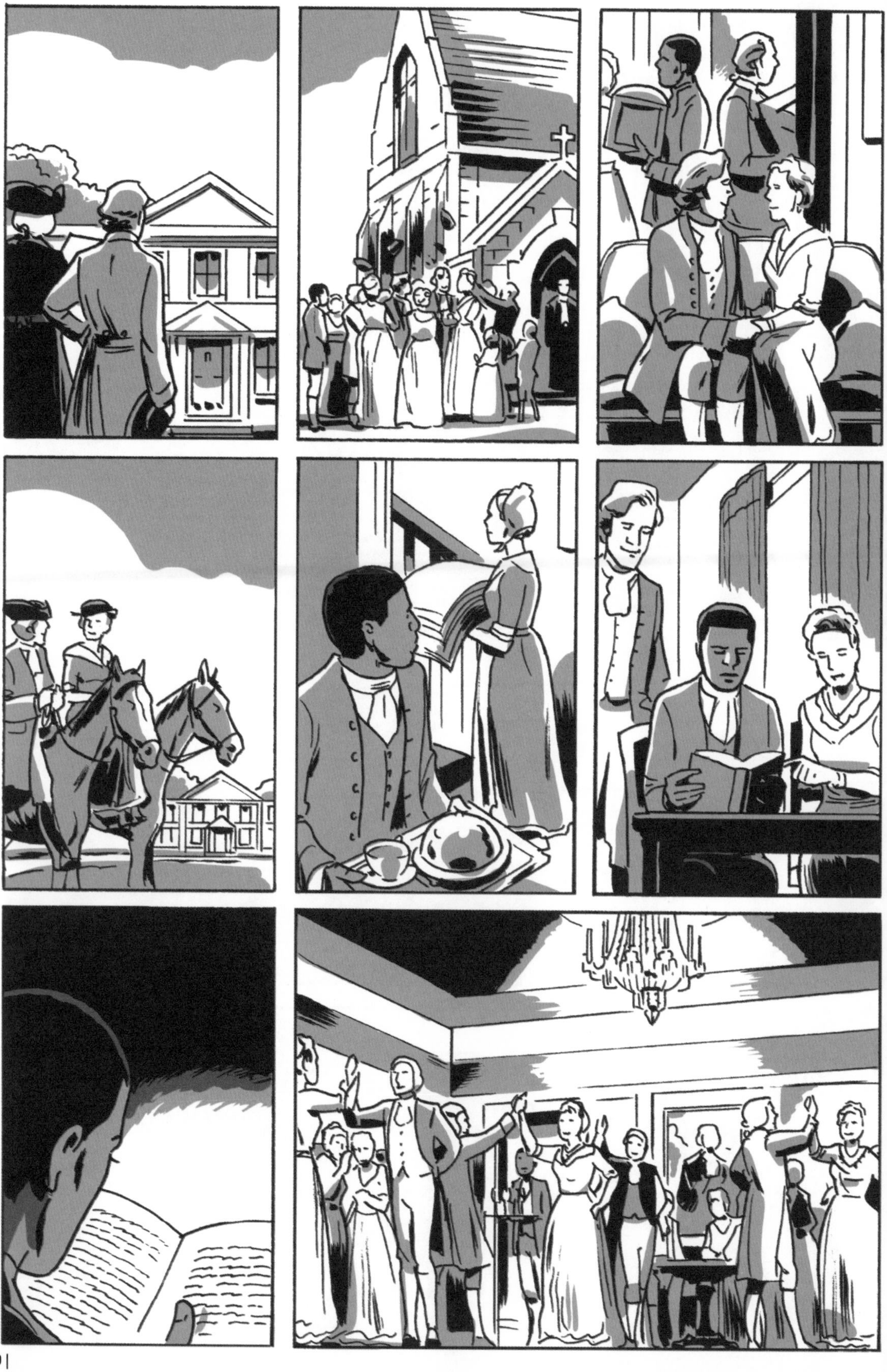

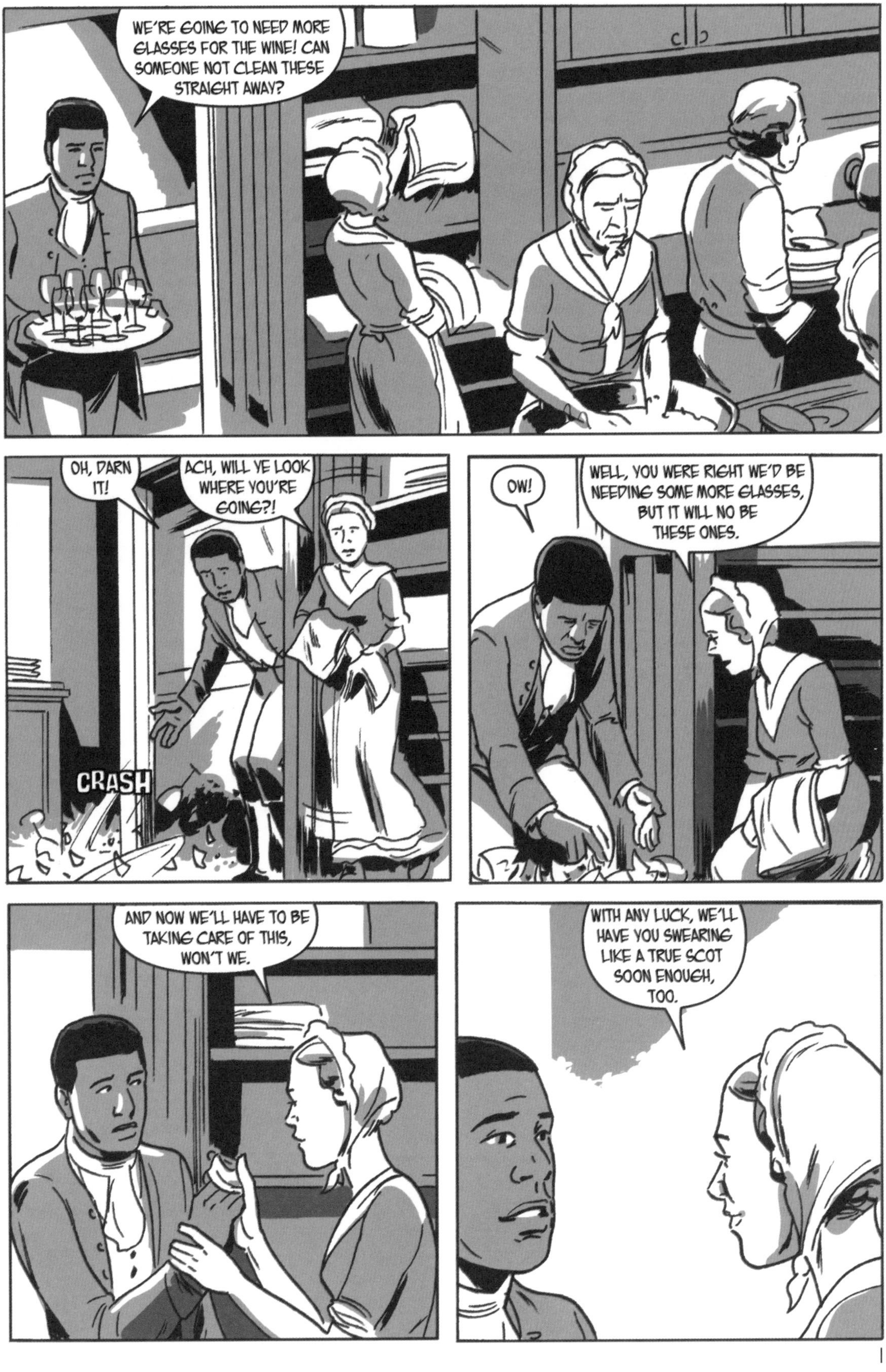
WE'RE GOING TO NEED MORE GLASSES FOR THE WINE! CAN SOMEONE NOT CLEAN THESE STRAIGHT AWAY?
OH, DARN IT!
ACH, WILL YE LOOK WHERE YOU'RE GOING?!
CRASH
OW!
WELL, YOU WERE RIGHT WE'D BE NEEDING SOME MORE GLASSES, BUT IT WILL NO BE THESE ONES.
AND NOW WE'LL HAVE TO BE TAKING CARE OF THIS, WON'T WE.
WITH ANY LUCK, WE'LL HAVE YOU SWEARING LIKE A TRUE SCOT SOON ENOUGH, TOO.

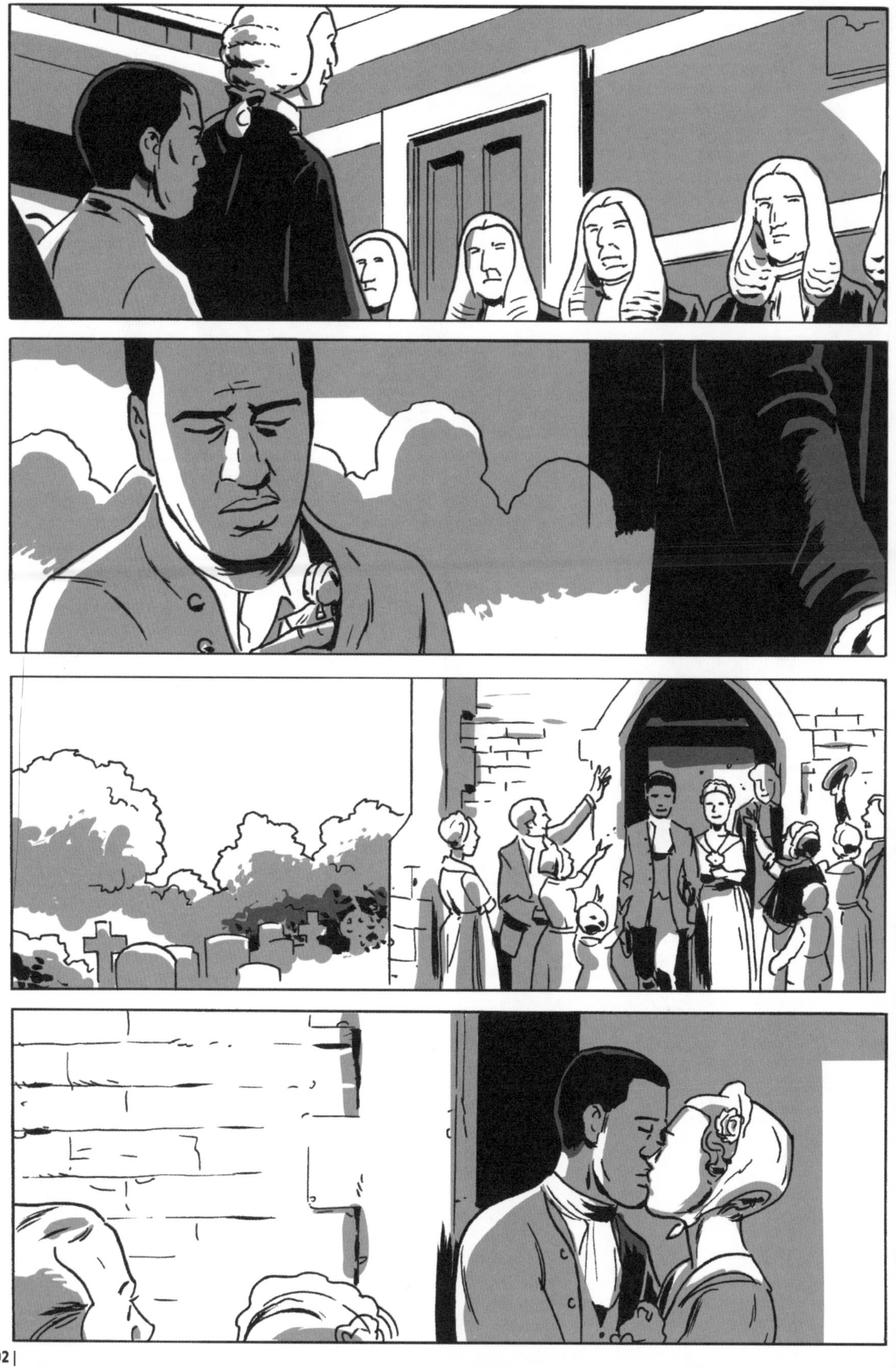

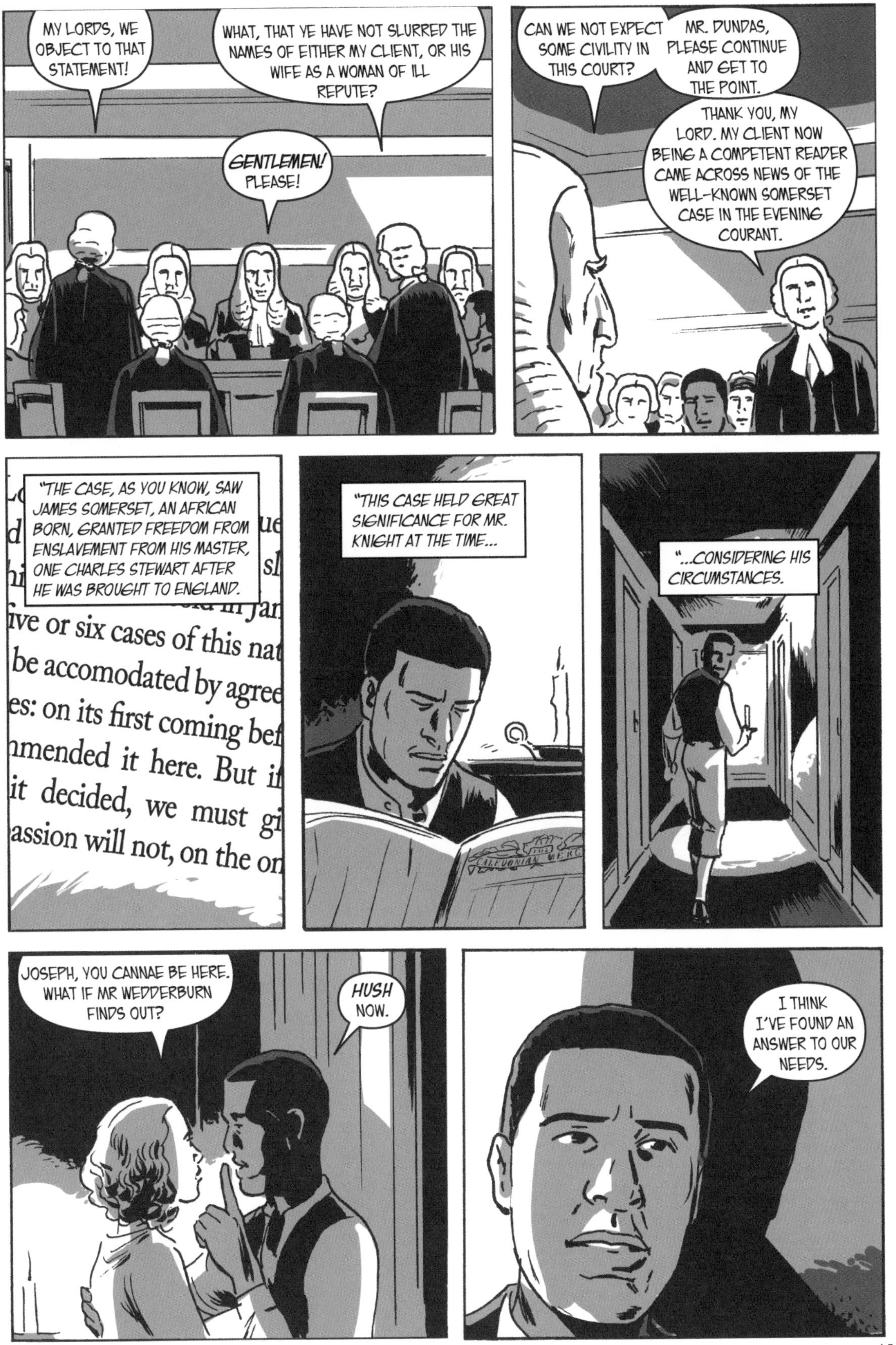
MY LORDS, WE OBJECT TO THAT STATEMENT!
WHAT, THAT YE HAVE NOT SLURRED THE NAMES OF EITHER MY CLIENT, OR HIS WIFE AS A WOMAN OF ILL REPUTE?
GENTLEMEN! PLEASE!
CAN WE NOT EXPECT SOME CIVILITY IN THIS COURT?
MR. DUNDAS, PLEASE CONTINUE AND GET TO THE POINT.
THANK YOU, MY LORD. MY CLIENT NOW BEING A COMPETENT READER CAME ACROSS NEWS OF THE WELL-KNOWN SOMERSET CASE IN THE EVENING COURANT.
"THE CASE, AS YOU KNOW, SAW JAMES SOMERSET, AN AFRICAN BORN, GRANTED FREEDOM FROM ENSLAVEMENT FROM HIS MASTER, ONE CHARLES STEWART AFTER HE WAS BROUGHT TO ENGLAND.
"THIS CASE HELD GREAT SIGNIFICANCE FOR MR. KNIGHT AT THE TIME...
"...CONSIDERING HIS CIRCUMSTANCES.
JOSEPH, YOU CANNAE BE HERE. WHAT IF MR WEDDERBURN FINDS OUT?
HUSH NOW.
I THINK I'VE FOUND AN ANSWER TO OUR NEEDS.

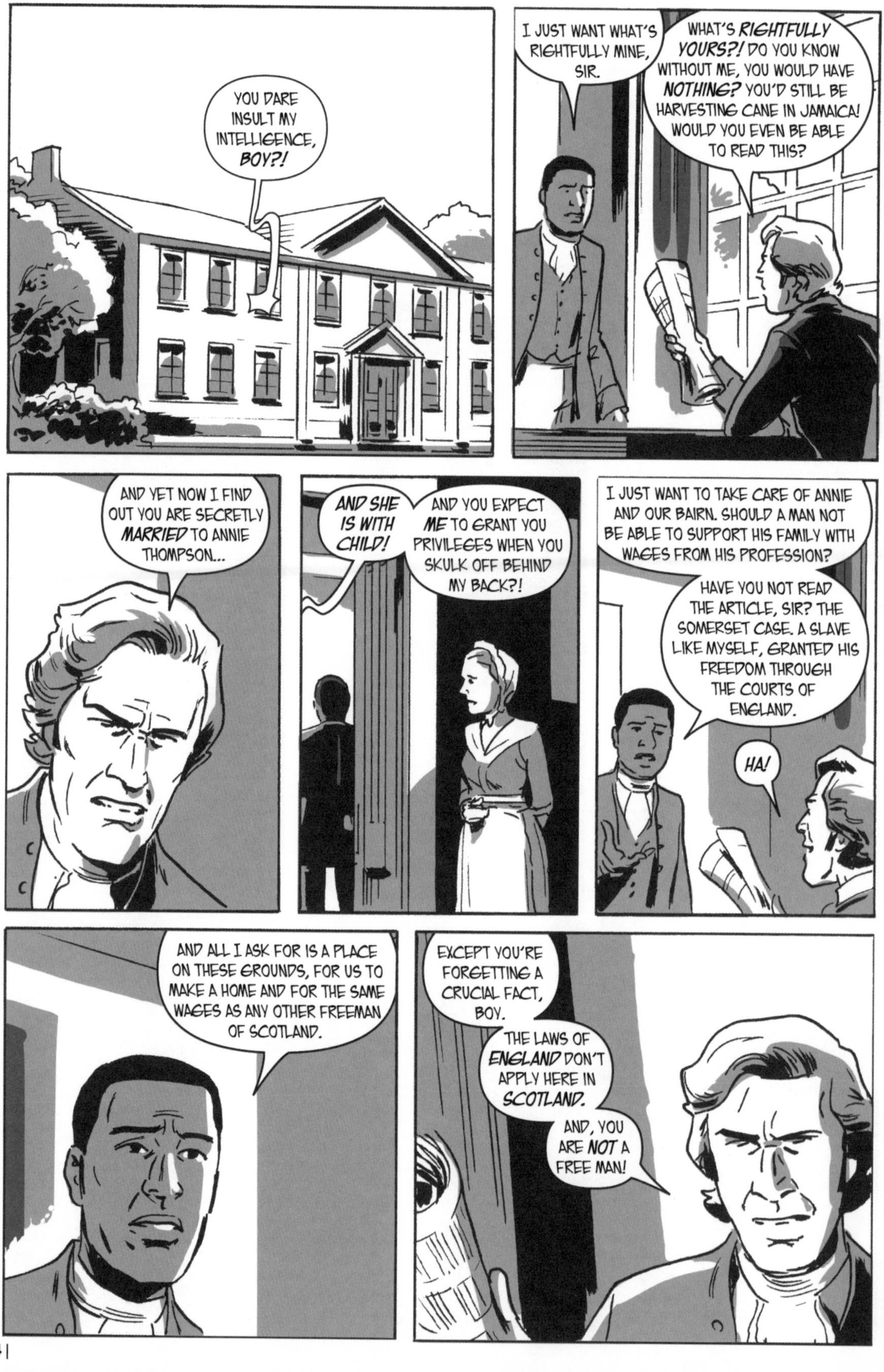
YOU DARE INSULT MY INTELLIGENCE, BOY?!
I JUST WANT WHAT'S RIGHTFULLY MINE, SIR.
WHAT'S RIGHTFULLY YOURS?! DO YOU KNOW WITHOUT ME, YOU WOULD HAVE NOTHING? YOU'D STILL BE HARVESTING CANE IN JAMAICA! WOULD YOU EVEN BE ABLE TO READ THIS?
AND YET NOW I FIND OUT YOU ARE SECRETLY MARRIED TO ANNIE THOMPSON...
AND SHE IS WITH CHILD!
AND YOU EXPECT ME TO GRANT YOU PRIVILEGES WHEN YOU SKULK OFF BEHIND MY BACK?!
I JUST WANT TO TAKE CARE OF ANNIE AND OUR BAIRN. SHOULD A MAN NOT BE ABLE TO SUPPORT HIS FAMILY WITH WAGES FROM HIS PROFESSION?
HAVE YOU NOT READ THE ARTICLE, SIR? THE SOMERSET CASE. A SLAVE LIKE MYSELF, GRANTED HIS FREEDOM THROUGH THE COURTS OF ENGLAND.
HA!
AND ALL I ASK FOR IS A PLACE ON THESE GROUNDS, FOR US TO MAKE A HOME AND FOR THE SAME WAGES AS ANY OTHER FREEMAN OF SCOTLAND.
EXCEPT YOU'RE FORGETTING A CRUCIAL FACT, BOY.
THE LAWS OF ENGLAND DON'T APPLY HERE IN SCOTLAND.
AND, YOU ARE NOT A FREE MAN!

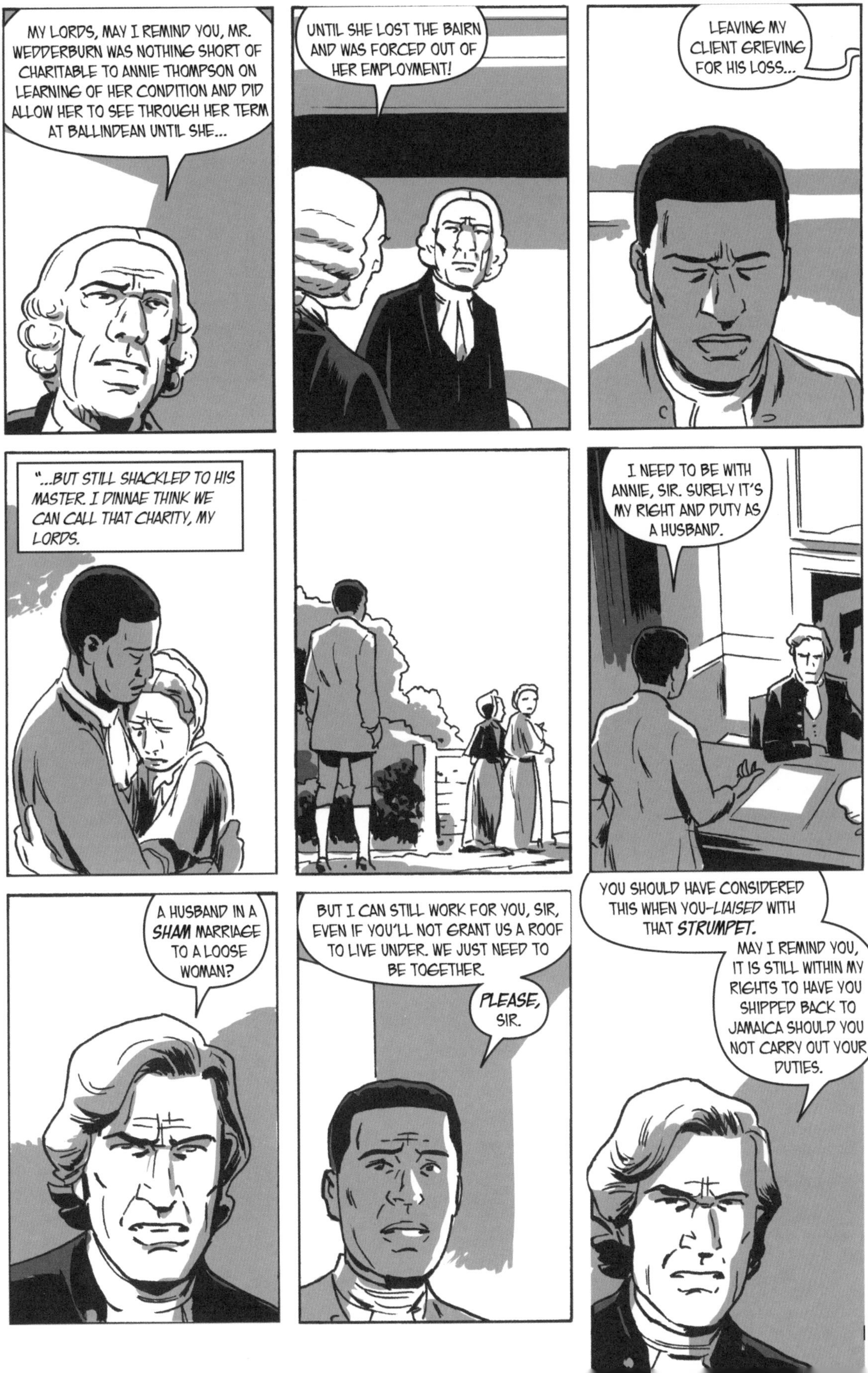
MY LORDS, MAY I REMIND YOU, MR. WEDDERBURN WAS NOTHING SHORT OF CHARITABLE TO ANNIE THOMPSON ON LEARNING OF HER CONDITION AND DID ALLOW HER TO SEE THROUGH HER TERM AT BALLINDEAN UNTIL SHE...
UNTIL SHE LOST THE BAIRN AND WAS FORCED OUT OF HER EMPLOYMENT!
LEAVING MY CLIENT GRIEVING FOR HIS LOSS...
"...BUT STILL SHACKLED TO HIS MASTER. I DINNAE THINK WE CAN CALL THAT CHARITY, MY LORDS.
I NEED TO BE WITH ANNIE, SIR. SURELY IT'S MY RIGHT AND DUTY AS A HUSBAND.
A HUSBAND IN A SHAM MARRIAGE TO A LOOSE WOMAN?
BUT I CAN STILL WORK FOR YOU, SIR, EVEN IF YOU'LL NOT GRANT US A ROOF TO LIVE UNDER. WE JUST NEED TO BE TOGETHER.
PLEASE, SIR.
YOU SHOULD HAVE CONSIDERED THIS WHEN YOU–LIAISED WITH THAT STRUMPET.
MAY I REMIND YOU, IT IS STILL WITHIN MY RIGHTS TO HAVE YOU SHIPPED BACK TO JAMAICA SHOULD YOU NOT CARRY OUT YOUR DUTIES.

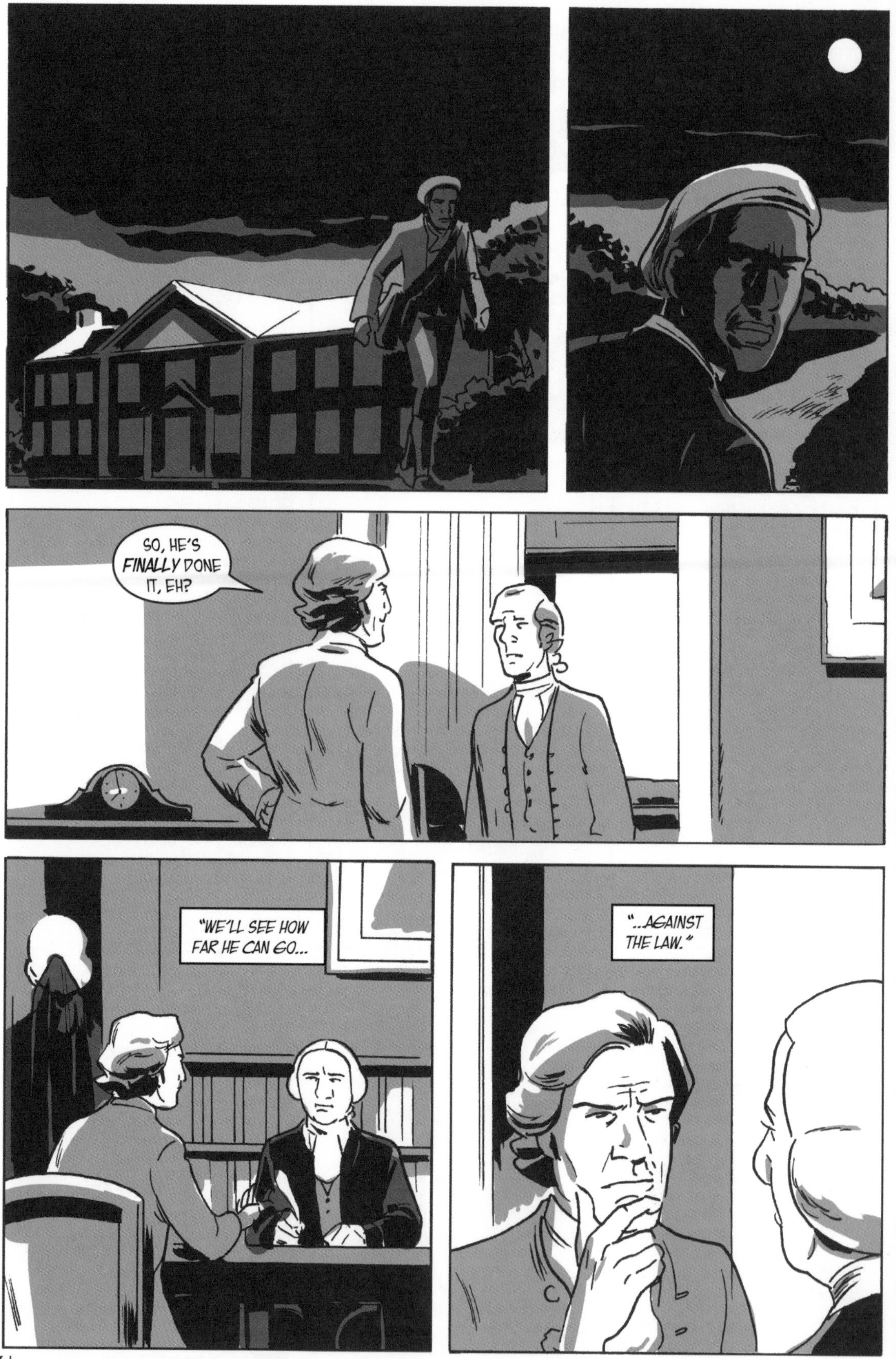
SO, HE'S FINALLY DONE IT, EH?
"WE'LL SEE HOW FAR HE CAN GO...
"...AGAINST THE LAW."

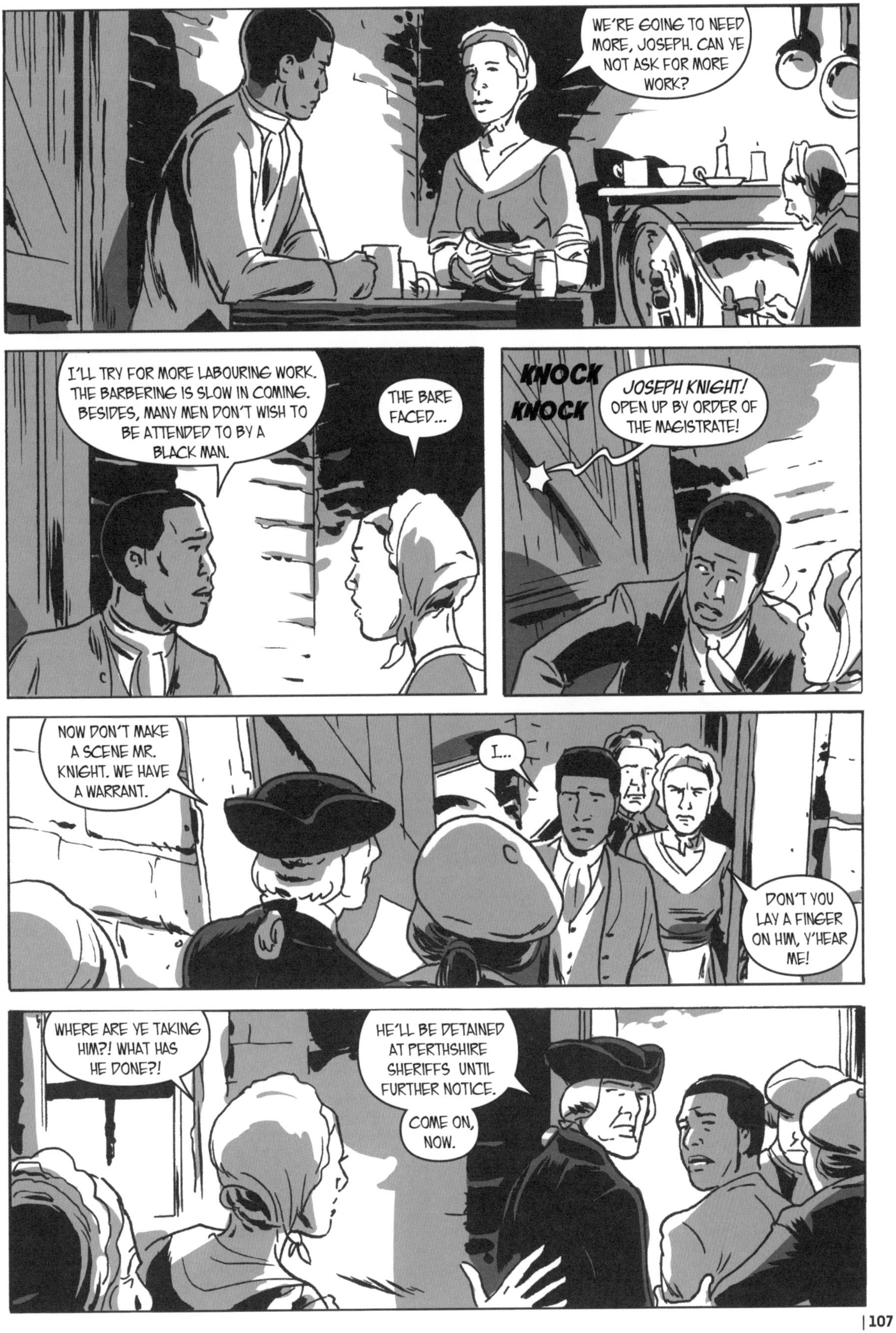
WE'RE GOING TO NEED MORE, JOSEPH. CAN YE NOT ASK FOR MORE WORK?
I'LL TRY FOR MORE LABOURING WORK. THE BARBERING IS SLOW IN COMING. BESIDES, MANY MEN DON'T WISH TO BE ATTENDED TO BY A BLACK MAN.
THE BARE FACED...
KNOCK KNOCK
JOSEPH KNIGHT! OPEN UP BY ORDER OF THE MAGISTRATE!
NOW DON'T MAKE A SCENE MR. KNIGHT. WE HAVE A WARRANT.
I...
DON'T YOU LAY A FINGER ON HIM, Y'HEAR ME!
WHERE ARE YE TAKING HIM?! WHAT HAS HE DONE?!
HE'LL BE DETAINED AT PERTHSHIRE SHERIFFS UNTIL FURTHER NOTICE.
COME ON, NOW.

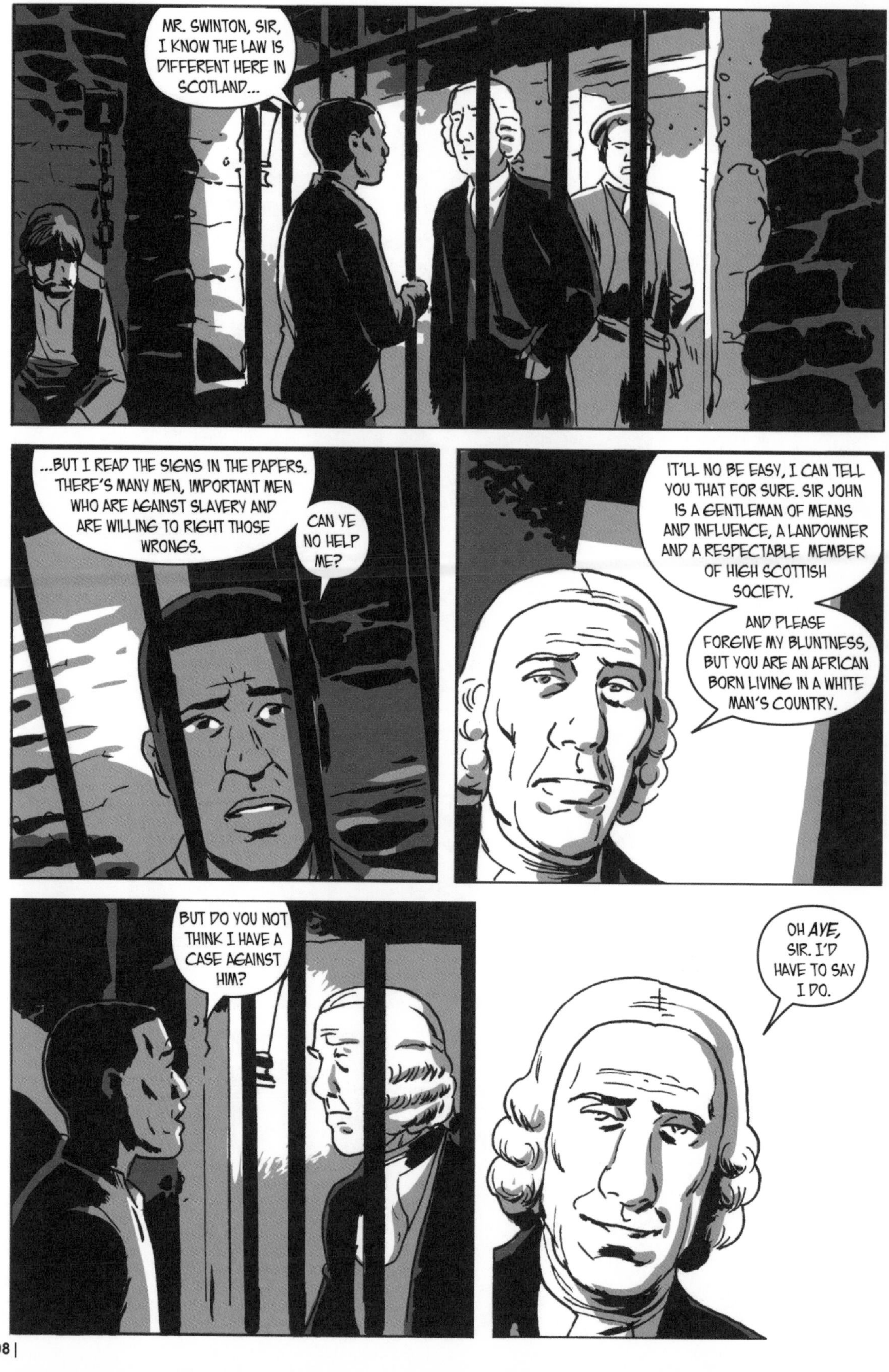
MR. SWINTON, SIR, I KNOW THE LAW IS DIFFERENT HERE IN SCOTLAND...
...BUT I READ THE SIGNS IN THE PAPERS. THERE'S MANY MEN, IMPORTANT MEN WHO ARE AGAINST SLAVERY AND ARE WILLING TO RIGHT THOSE WRONGS.
CAN YE NO HELP ME?
IT'LL NO BE EASY, I CAN TELL YOU THAT FOR SURE. SIR JOHN IS A GENTLEMAN OF MEANS AND INFLUENCE, A LANDOWNER AND A RESPECTABLE MEMBER OF HIGH SCOTTISH SOCIETY.
AND PLEASE FORGIVE MY BLUNTNESS, BUT YOU ARE AN AFRICAN BORN LIVING IN A WHITE MAN'S COUNTRY.
BUT DO YOU NOT THINK I HAVE A CASE AGAINST HIM?
OH ***AYE***, SIR. I'D HAVE TO SAY I DO.

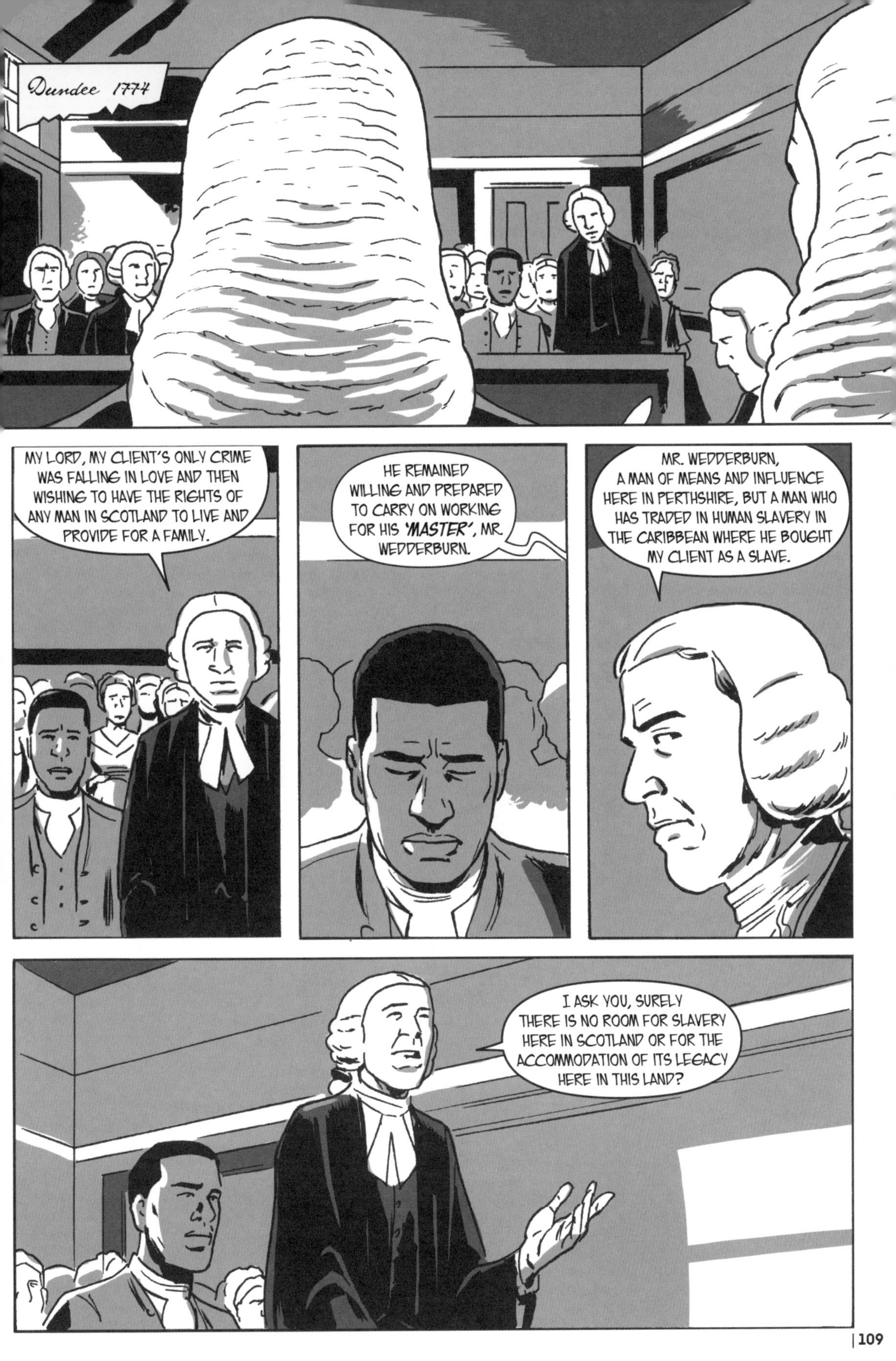
Dundee 1774
MY LORD, MY CLIENT'S ONLY CRIME WAS FALLING IN LOVE AND THEN WISHING TO HAVE THE RIGHTS OF ANY MAN IN SCOTLAND TO LIVE AND PROVIDE FOR A FAMILY.
HE REMAINED WILLING AND PREPARED TO CARRY ON WORKING FOR HIS **'MASTER'**, MR. WEDDERBURN.
MR. WEDDERBURN, A MAN OF MEANS AND INFLUENCE HERE IN PERTHSHIRE, BUT A MAN WHO HAS TRADED IN HUMAN SLAVERY IN THE CARIBBEAN WHERE HE BOUGHT MY CLIENT AS A SLAVE.
I ASK YOU, SURELY THERE IS NO ROOM FOR SLAVERY HERE IN SCOTLAND OR FOR THE ACCOMMODATION OF ITS LEGACY HERE IN THIS LAND?

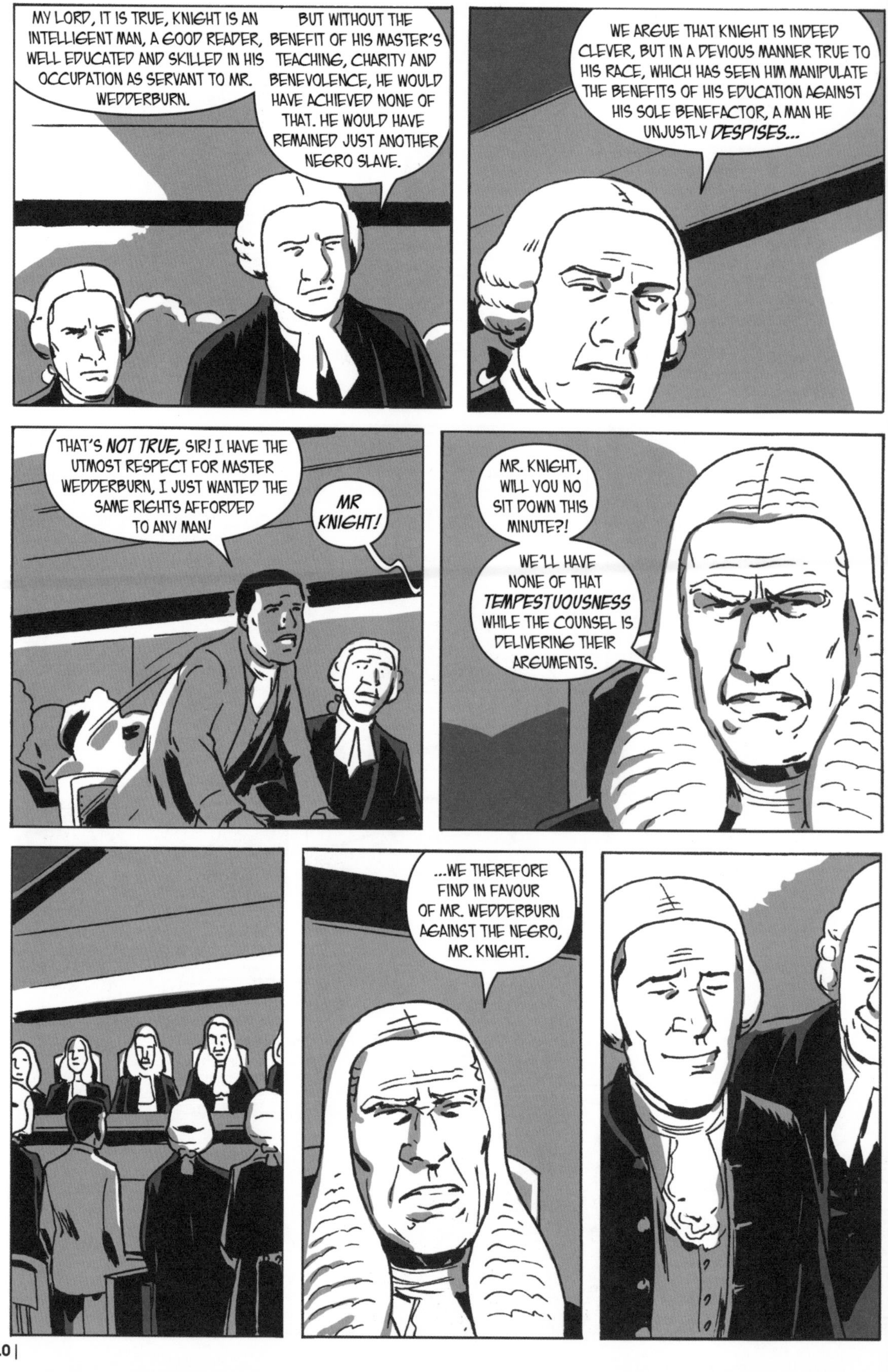
MY LORD, IT IS TRUE, KNIGHT IS AN INTELLIGENT MAN, A GOOD READER, WELL EDUCATED AND SKILLED IN HIS OCCUPATION AS SERVANT TO MR. WEDDERBURN.
BUT WITHOUT THE BENEFIT OF HIS MASTER'S TEACHING, CHARITY AND BENEVOLENCE, HE WOULD HAVE ACHIEVED NONE OF THAT. HE WOULD HAVE REMAINED JUST ANOTHER NEGRO SLAVE.
WE ARGUE THAT KNIGHT IS INDEED CLEVER, BUT IN A DEVIOUS MANNER TRUE TO HIS RACE, WHICH HAS SEEN HIM MANIPULATE THE BENEFITS OF HIS EDUCATION AGAINST HIS SOLE BENEFACTOR, A MAN HE UNJUSTLY *DESPISES...*
THAT'S *NOT TRUE,* SIR! I HAVE THE UTMOST RESPECT FOR MASTER WEDDERBURN, I JUST WANTED THE SAME RIGHTS AFFORDED TO ANY MAN!
*MR KNIGHT!*
MR. KNIGHT, WILL YOU NO SIT DOWN THIS MINUTE?!
WE'LL HAVE NONE OF THAT *TEMPESTUOUSNESS* WHILE THE COUNSEL IS DELIVERING THEIR ARGUMENTS.
...WE THEREFORE FIND IN FAVOUR OF MR. WEDDERBURN AGAINST THE NEGRO, MR. KNIGHT.

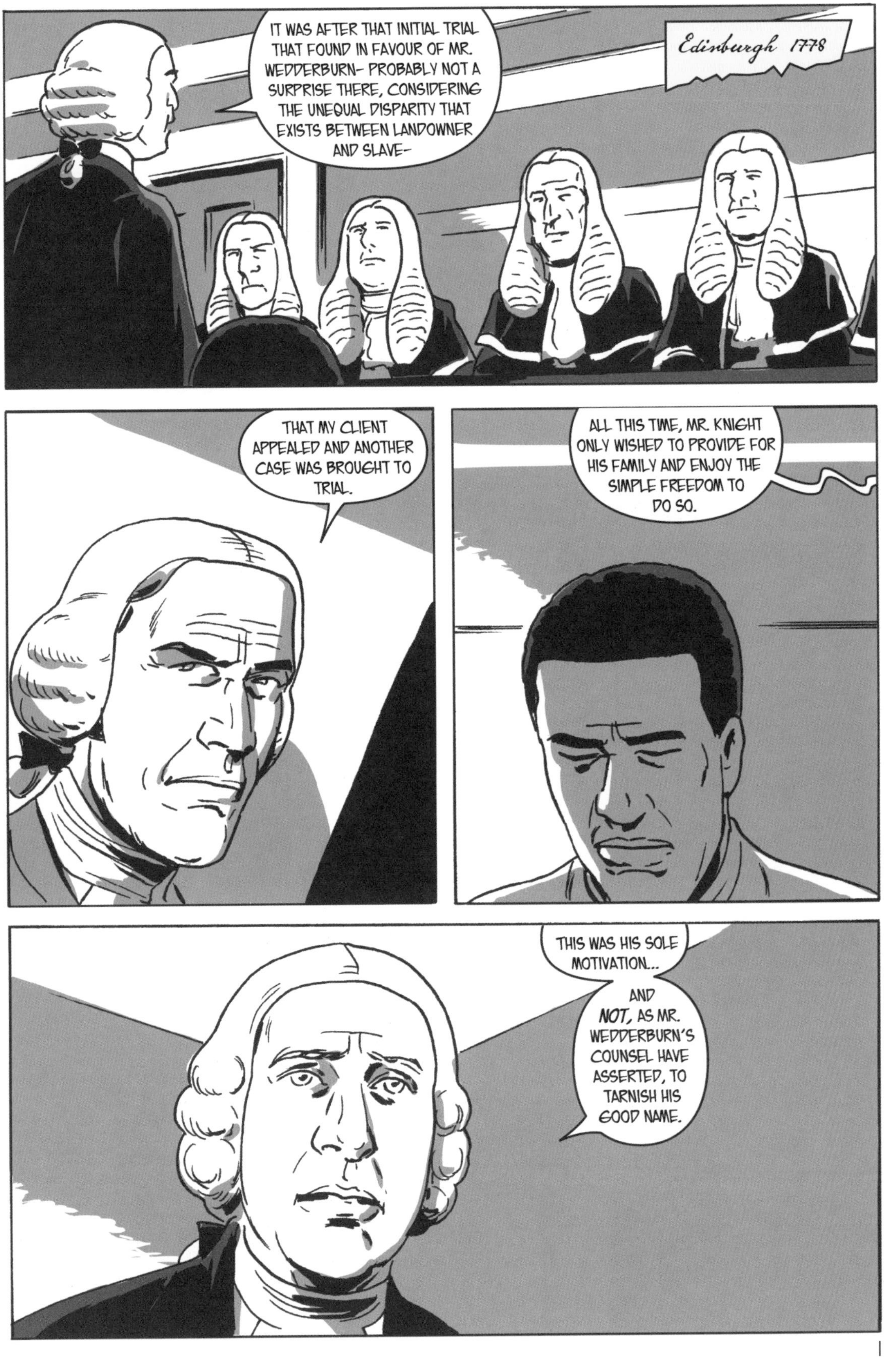
IT WAS AFTER THAT INITIAL TRIAL THAT FOUND IN FAVOUR OF MR. WEDDERBURN- PROBABLY NOT A SURPRISE THERE, CONSIDERING THE UNEQUAL DISPARITY THAT EXISTS BETWEEN LANDOWNER AND SLAVE-
Edinburgh 1778
THAT MY CLIENT APPEALED AND ANOTHER CASE WAS BROUGHT TO TRIAL.
ALL THIS TIME, MR. KNIGHT ONLY WISHED TO PROVIDE FOR HIS FAMILY AND ENJOY THE SIMPLE FREEDOM TO DO SO.
THIS WAS HIS SOLE MOTIVATION...
AND *NOT,* AS MR. WEDDERBURN'S COUNSEL HAVE ASSERTED, TO TARNISH HIS GOOD NAME.

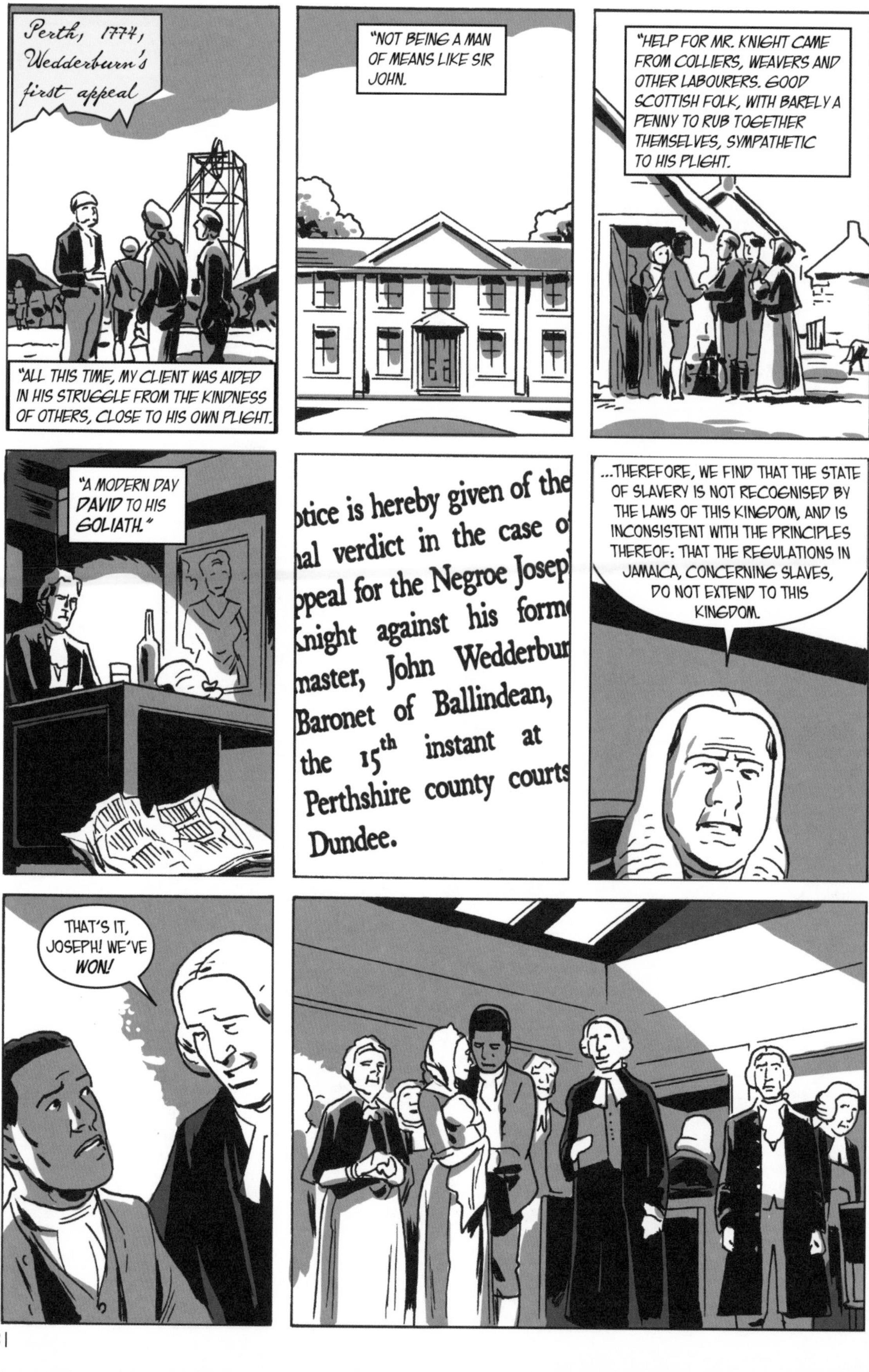
Perth, 1774, Wedderburn's first appeal
"ALL THIS TIME, MY CLIENT WAS AIDED IN HIS STRUGGLE FROM THE KINDNESS OF OTHERS, CLOSE TO HIS OWN PLIGHT.
"NOT BEING A MAN OF MEANS LIKE SIR JOHN.
"HELP FOR MR. KNIGHT CAME FROM COLLIERS, WEAVERS AND OTHER LABOURERS. GOOD SCOTTISH FOLK, WITH BARELY A PENNY TO RUB TOGETHER THEMSELVES, SYMPATHETIC TO HIS PLIGHT.
"A MODERN DAY DAVID TO HIS GOLIATH."
otice is hereby given of the
al verdict in the case of
ppeal for the Negroe Josep
Knight against his form
master, John Wedderbur
Baronet of Ballindean,
the 15th instant at
Perthshire county courts
Dundee.
...THEREFORE, WE FIND THAT THE STATE OF SLAVERY IS NOT RECOGNISED BY THE LAWS OF THIS KINGDOM, AND IS INCONSISTENT WITH THE PRINCIPLES THEREOF: THAT THE REGULATIONS IN JAMAICA, CONCERNING SLAVES, DO NOT EXTEND TO THIS KINGDOM.
THAT'S IT, JOSEPH! WE'VE WON!

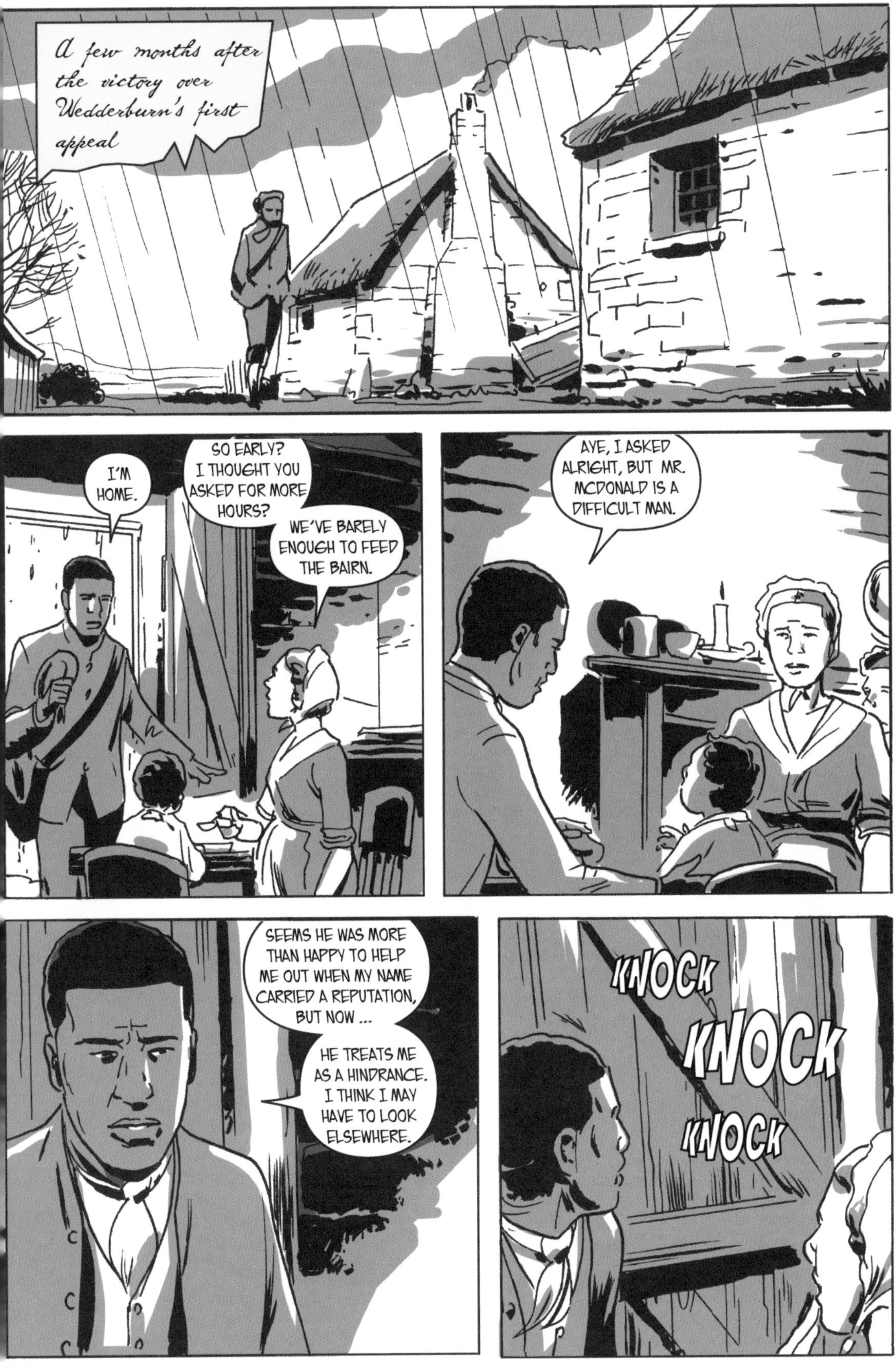
A few months after the victory over Wedderburn's first appeal
I'M HOME.
SO EARLY? I THOUGHT YOU ASKED FOR MORE HOURS?
WE'VE BARELY ENOUGH TO FEED THE BAIRN.
AYE, I ASKED ALRIGHT, BUT MR. MCDONALD IS A DIFFICULT MAN.
SEEMS HE WAS MORE THAN HAPPY TO HELP ME OUT WHEN MY NAME CARRIED A REPUTATION, BUT NOW ...
HE TREATS ME AS A HINDRANCE. I THINK I MAY HAVE TO LOOK ELSEWHERE.
KNOCK
KNOCK
KNOCK

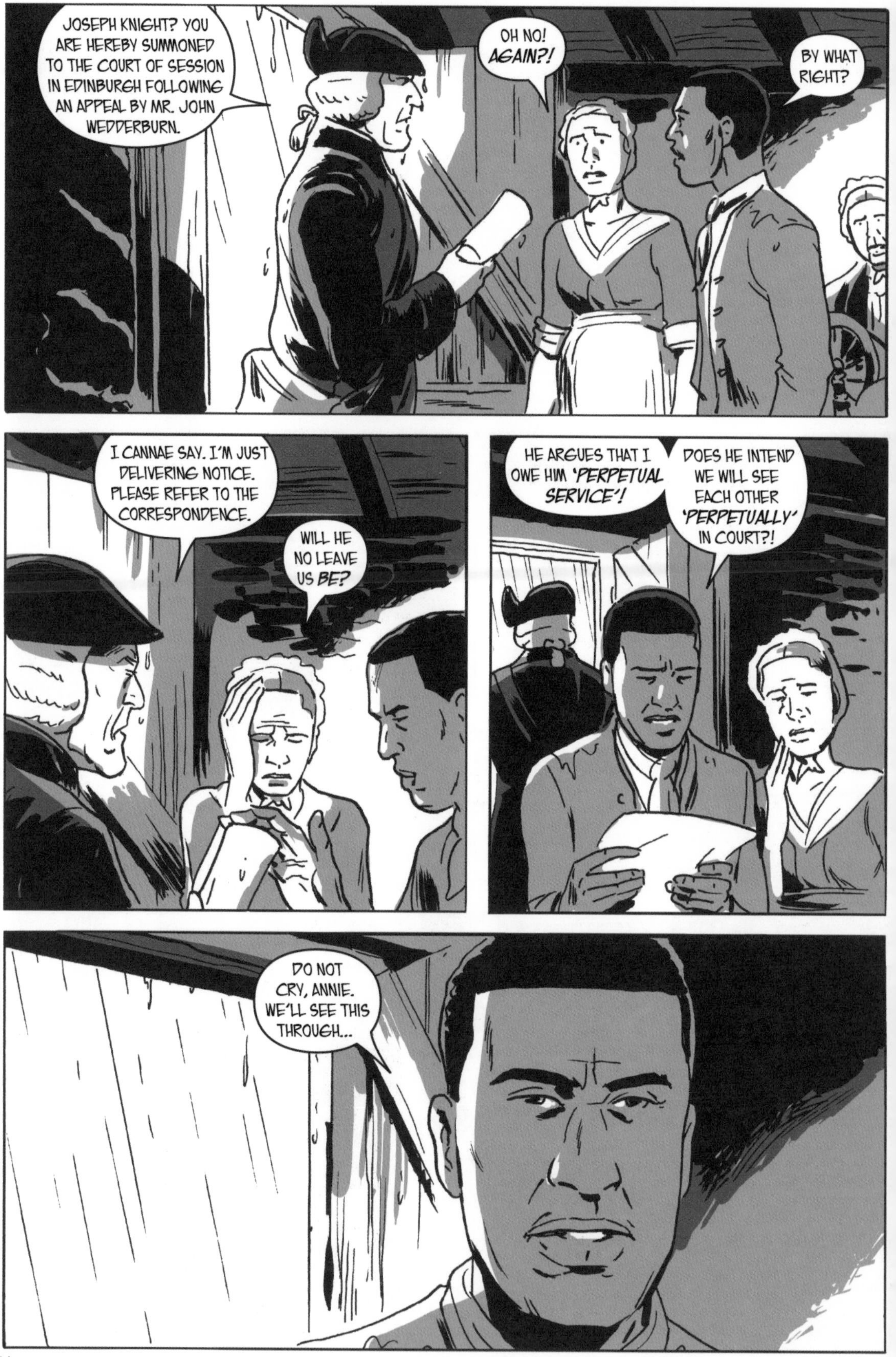
JOSEPH KNIGHT? YOU ARE HEREBY SUMMONED TO THE COURT OF SESSION IN EDINBURGH FOLLOWING AN APPEAL BY MR. JOHN WEDDERBURN.
OH NO! *AGAIN?!*
BY WHAT RIGHT?
I CANNAE SAY. I'M JUST DELIVERING NOTICE. PLEASE REFER TO THE CORRESPONDENCE.
WILL HE NO LEAVE US *BE?*
HE ARGUES THAT I OWE HIM *'PERPETUAL SERVICE'!*
DOES HE INTEND WE WILL SEE EACH OTHER *'PERPETUALLY'* IN COURT?!
DO NOT CRY, ANNIE. WE'LL SEE THIS THROUGH...

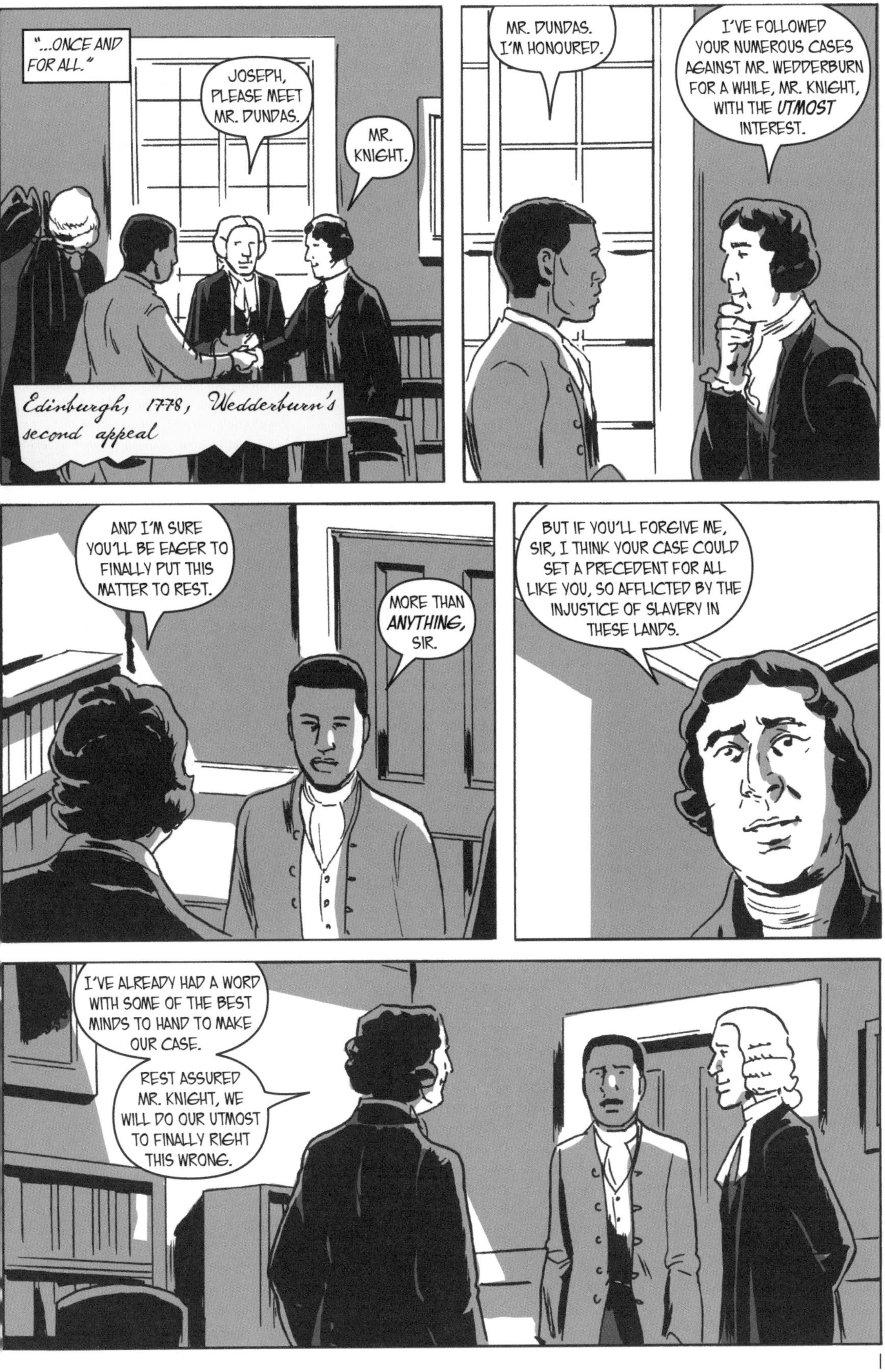
"...ONCE AND FOR ALL."
JOSEPH, PLEASE MEET MR. DUNDAS.
MR. KNIGHT.
Edinburgh, 1778, Wedderburn's second appeal
MR. DUNDAS. I'M HONOURED.
I'VE FOLLOWED YOUR NUMEROUS CASES AGAINST MR. WEDDERBURN FOR A WHILE, MR. KNIGHT, WITH THE *UTMOST* INTEREST.
AND I'M SURE YOU'LL BE EAGER TO FINALLY PUT THIS MATTER TO REST.
MORE THAN *ANYTHING,* SIR.
BUT IF YOU'LL FORGIVE ME, SIR, I THINK YOUR CASE COULD SET A PRECEDENT FOR ALL LIKE YOU, SO AFFLICTED BY THE INJUSTICE OF SLAVERY IN THESE LANDS.
I'VE ALREADY HAD A WORD WITH SOME OF THE BEST MINDS TO HAND TO MAKE OUR CASE.
REST ASSURED MR. KNIGHT, WE WILL DO OUR UTMOST TO FINALLY RIGHT THIS WRONG.

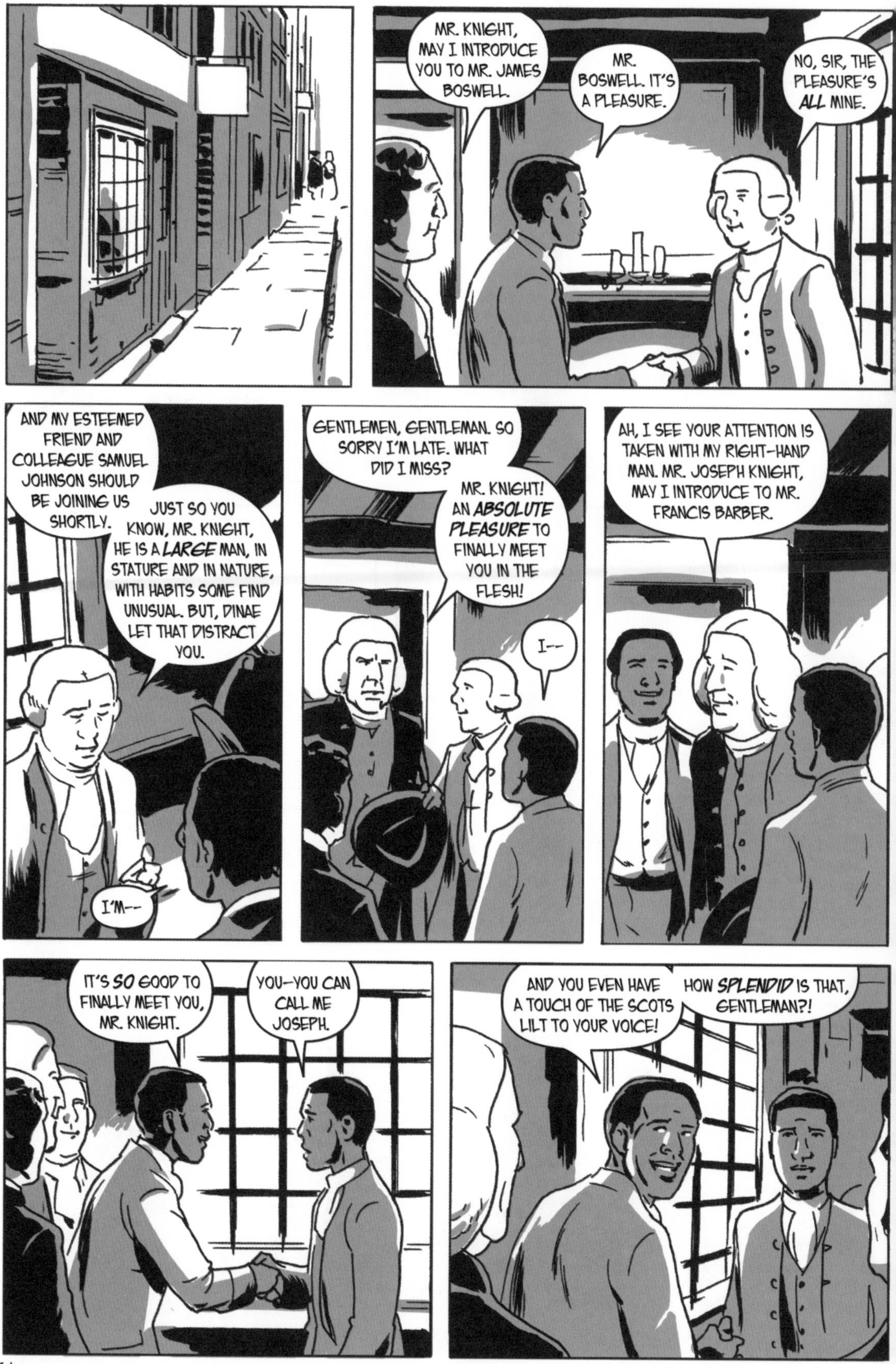
MR. KNIGHT, MAY I INTRODUCE YOU TO MR. JAMES BOSWELL.
MR. BOSWELL. IT'S A PLEASURE.
NO, SIR, THE PLEASURE'S ALL MINE.
AND MY ESTEEMED FRIEND AND COLLEAGUE SAMUEL JOHNSON SHOULD BE JOINING US SHORTLY.
JUST SO YOU KNOW, MR. KNIGHT, HE IS A LARGE MAN, IN STATURE AND IN NATURE, WITH HABITS SOME FIND UNUSUAL. BUT, DINAE LET THAT DISTRACT YOU.
I'M--
GENTLEMEN, GENTLEMAN. SO SORRY I'M LATE. WHAT DID I MISS?
MR. KNIGHT! AN ABSOLUTE PLEASURE TO FINALLY MEET YOU IN THE FLESH!
I--
AH, I SEE YOUR ATTENTION IS TAKEN WITH MY RIGHT-HAND MAN. MR. JOSEPH KNIGHT, MAY I INTRODUCE TO MR. FRANCIS BARBER.
IT'S SO GOOD TO FINALLY MEET YOU, MR. KNIGHT.
YOU—YOU CAN CALL ME JOSEPH.
AND YOU EVEN HAVE A TOUCH OF THE SCOTS LILT TO YOUR VOICE!
HOW SPLENDID IS THAT, GENTLEMAN?!

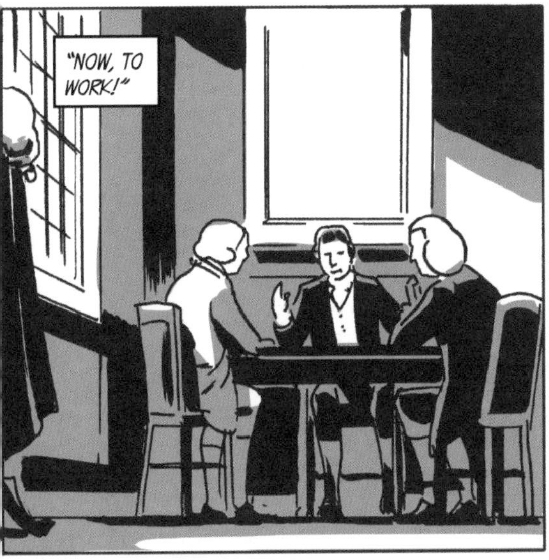
"NOW, TO WORK!"

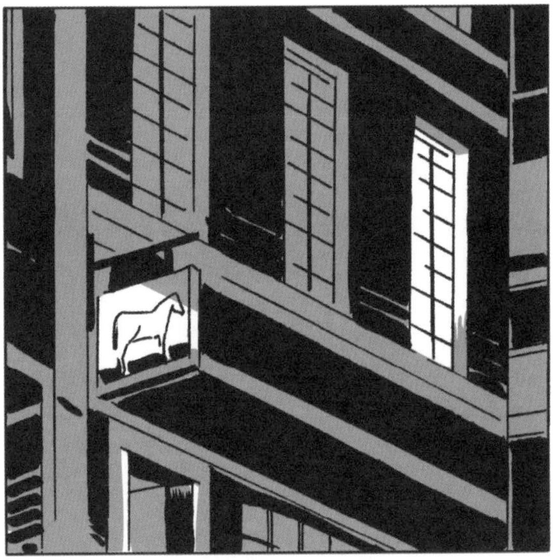

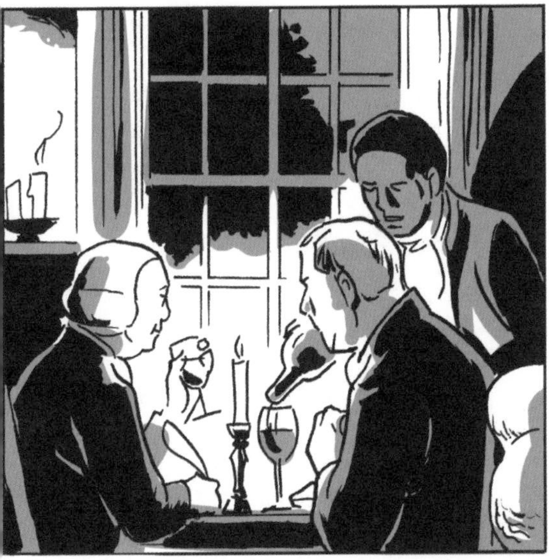

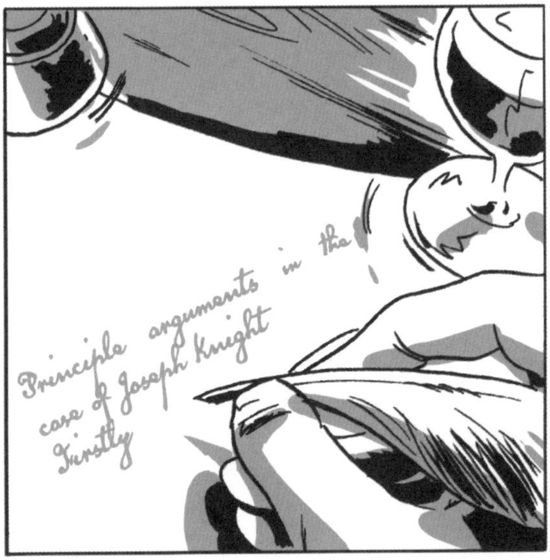
Principle arguments in the
case of Joseph Knight
Firstly

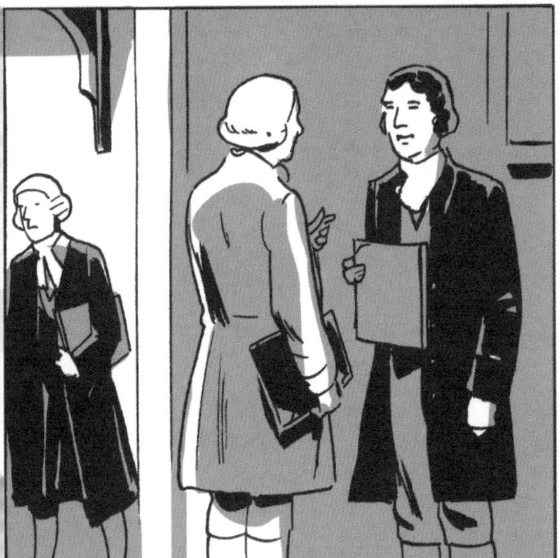

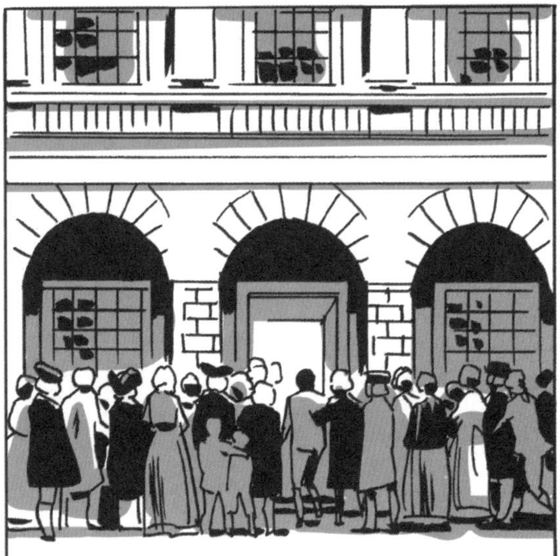

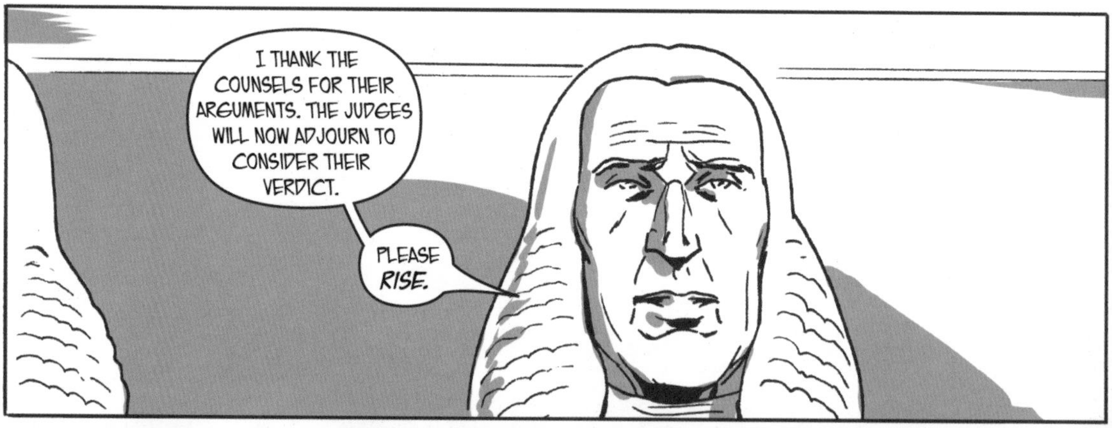
I THANK THE COUNSELS FOR THEIR ARGUMENTS. THE JUDGES WILL NOW ADJOURN TO CONSIDER THEIR VERDICT.
PLEASE *RISE.*

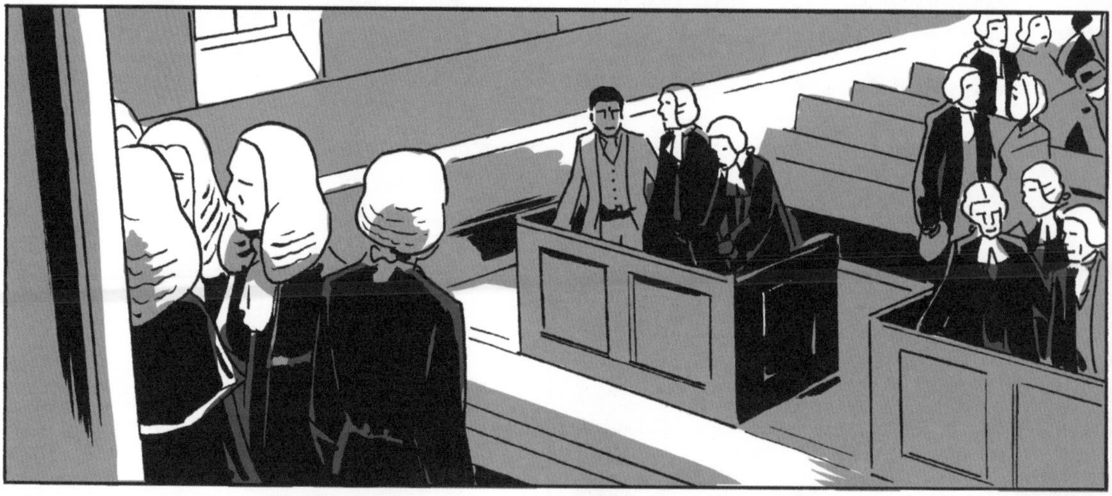

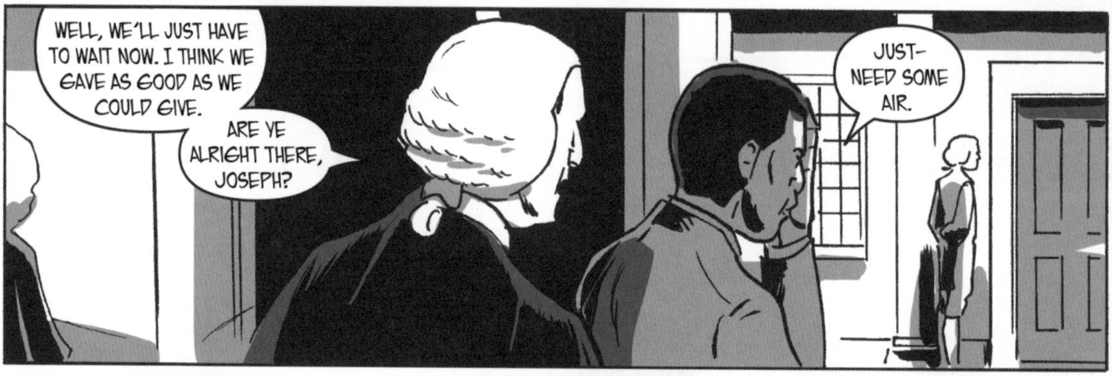
WELL, WE'LL JUST HAVE TO WAIT NOW. I THINK WE GAVE AS GOOD AS WE COULD GIVE.
ARE YE ALRIGHT THERE, JOSEPH?
JUST- NEED SOME AIR.

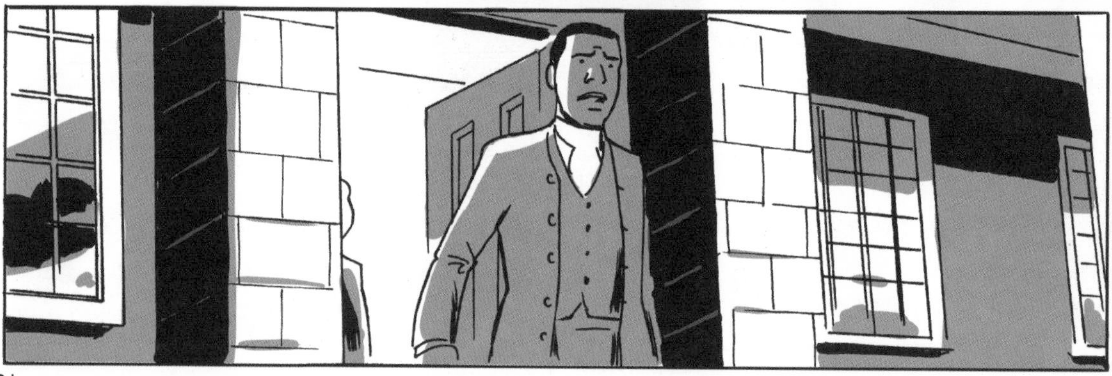

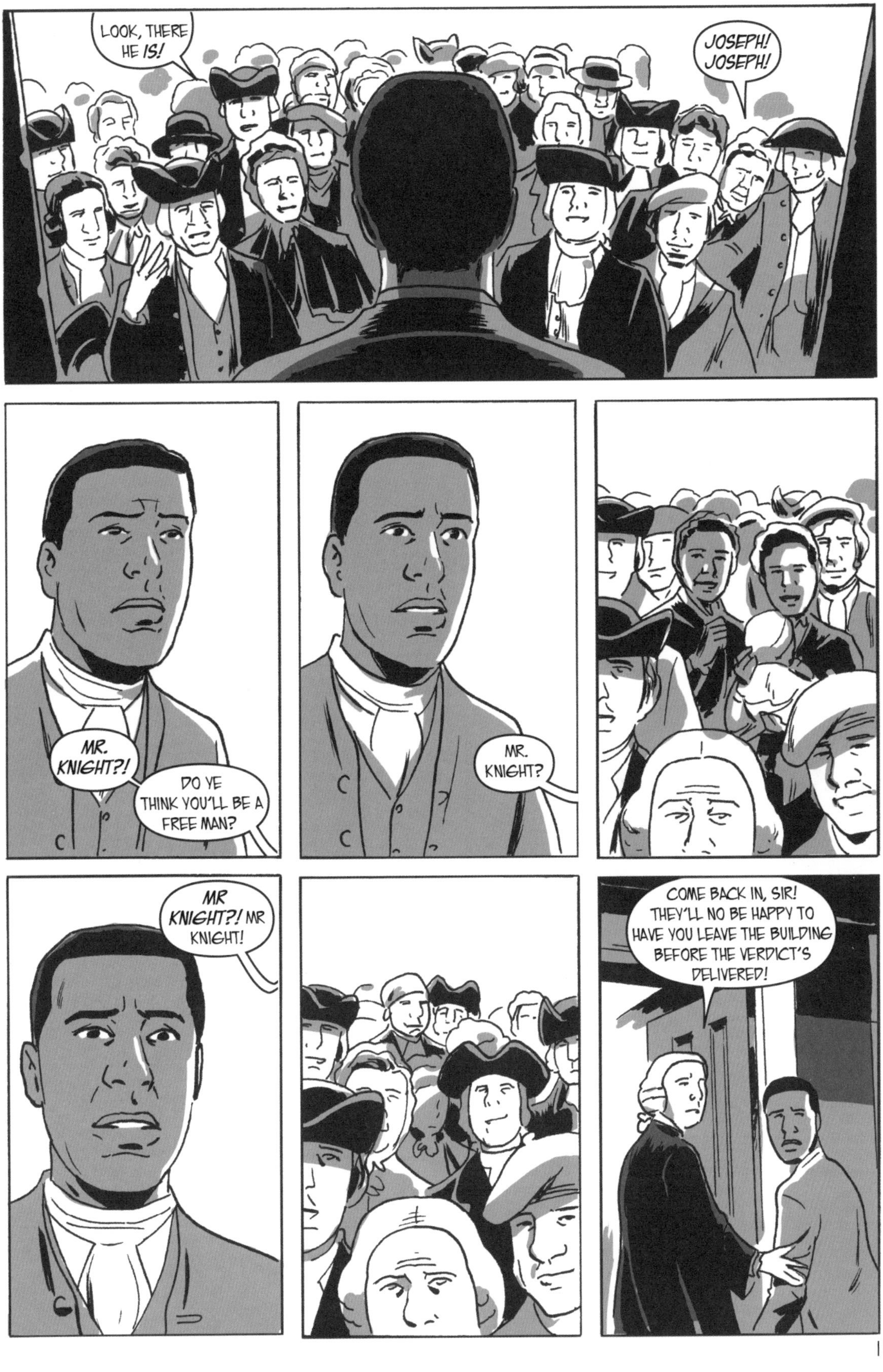

LOOK, THERE HE *IS*!
JOSEPH! JOSEPH!
MR. KNIGHT?!
DO YE THINK YOU'LL BE A FREE MAN?
MR. KNIGHT?
MR KNIGHT?! MR KNIGHT!
COME BACK IN, SIR! THEY'LL NO BE HAPPY TO HAVE YOU LEAVE THE BUILDING BEFORE THE VERDICT'S DELIVERED!

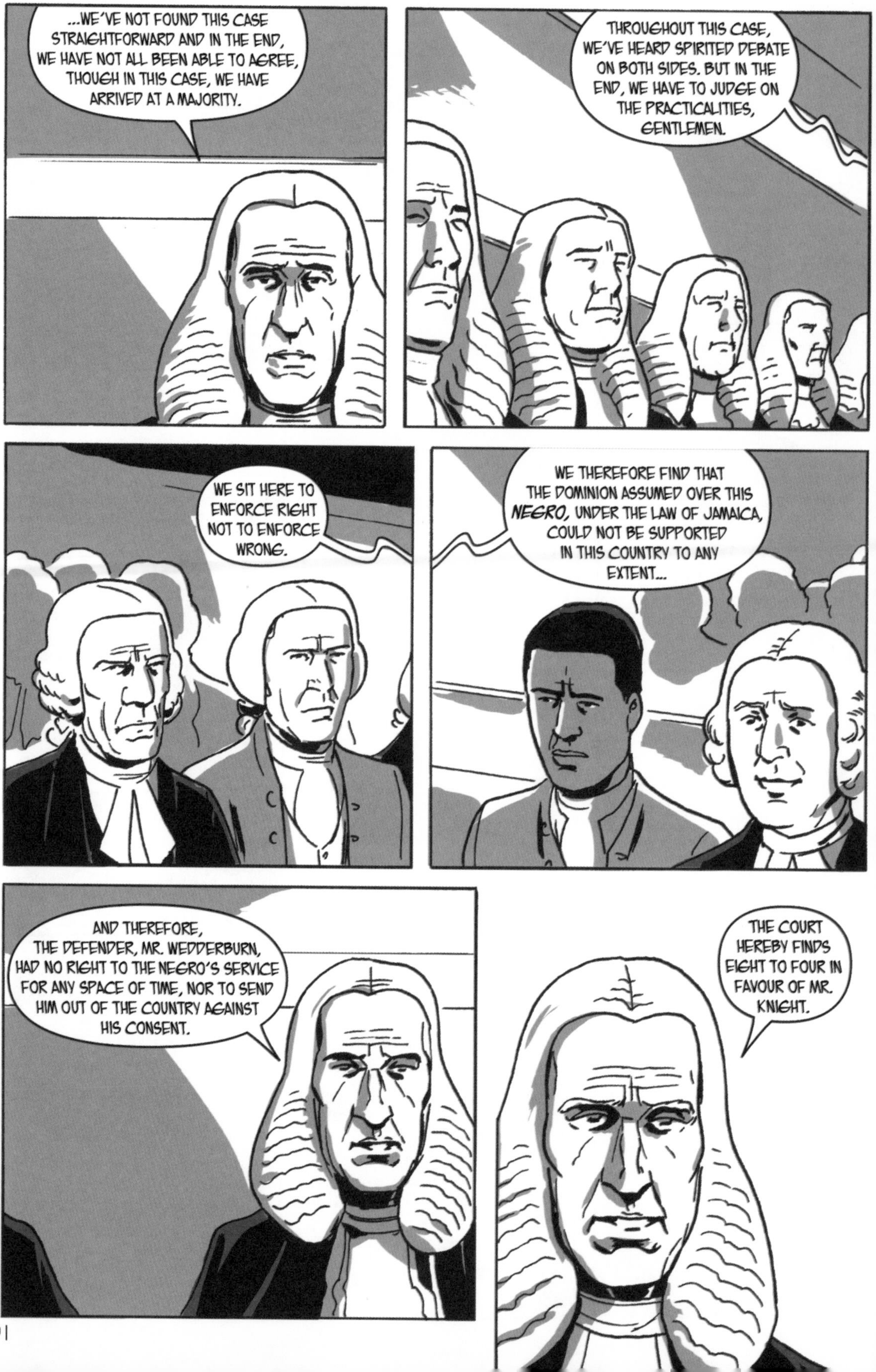
...WE'VE NOT FOUND THIS CASE STRAIGHTFORWARD AND IN THE END, WE HAVE NOT ALL BEEN ABLE TO AGREE, THOUGH IN THIS CASE, WE HAVE ARRIVED AT A MAJORITY.
THROUGHOUT THIS CASE, WE'VE HEARD SPIRITED DEBATE ON BOTH SIDES. BUT IN THE END, WE HAVE TO JUDGE ON THE PRACTICALITIES, GENTLEMEN.
WE SIT HERE TO ENFORCE RIGHT NOT TO ENFORCE WRONG.
WE THEREFORE FIND THAT THE DOMINION ASSUMED OVER THIS *NEGRO*, UNDER THE LAW OF JAMAICA, COULD NOT BE SUPPORTED IN THIS COUNTRY TO ANY EXTENT...
AND THEREFORE, THE DEFENDER, MR. WEDDERBURN, HAD NO RIGHT TO THE NEGRO'S SERVICE FOR ANY SPACE OF TIME, NOR TO SEND HIM OUT OF THE COUNTRY AGAINST HIS CONSENT.
THE COURT HEREBY FINDS EIGHT TO FOUR IN FAVOUR OF MR. KNIGHT.

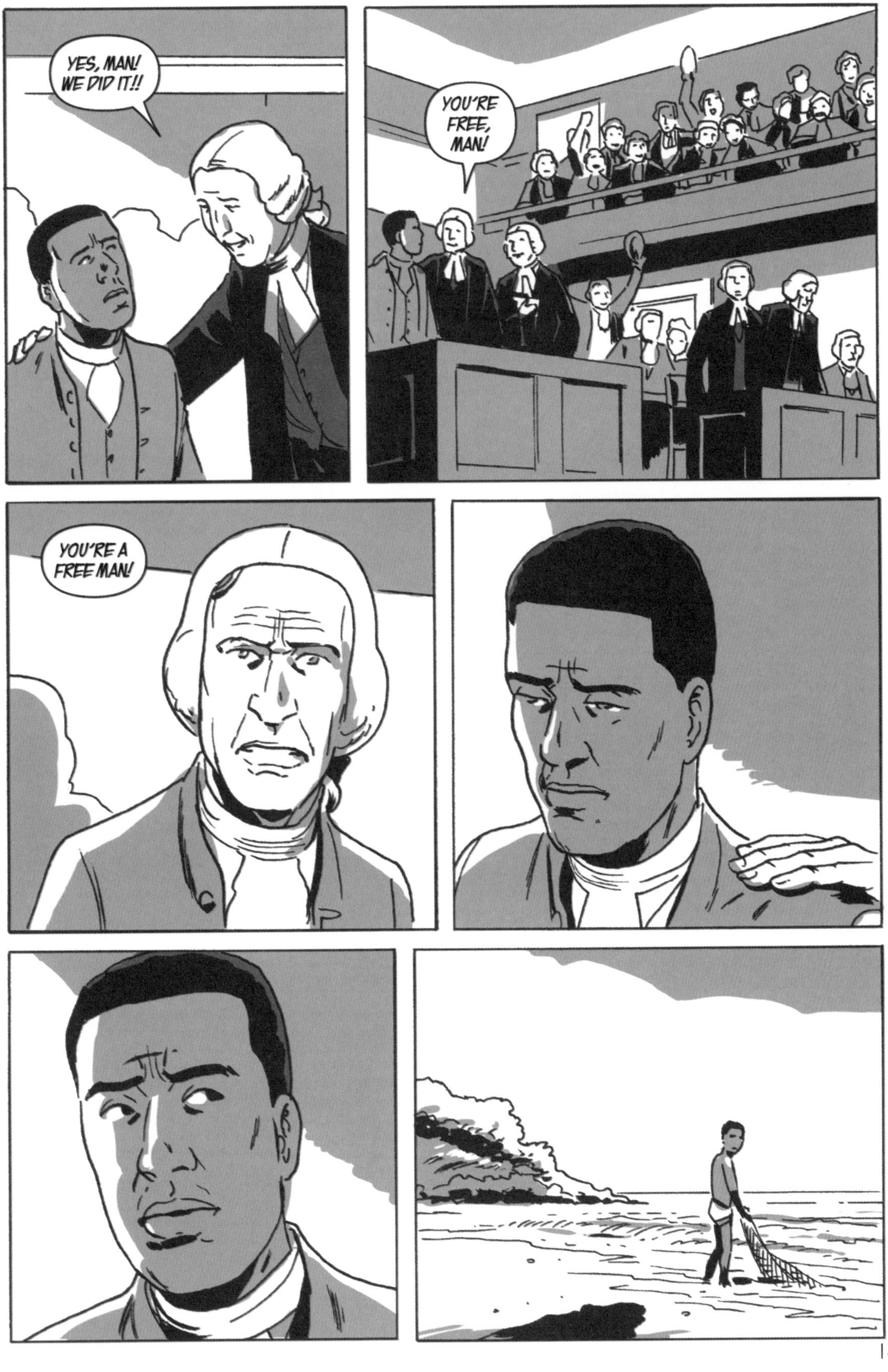
YES, MAN! WE DID IT!!
YOU'RE FREE, MAN!
YOU'RE A FREE MAN!

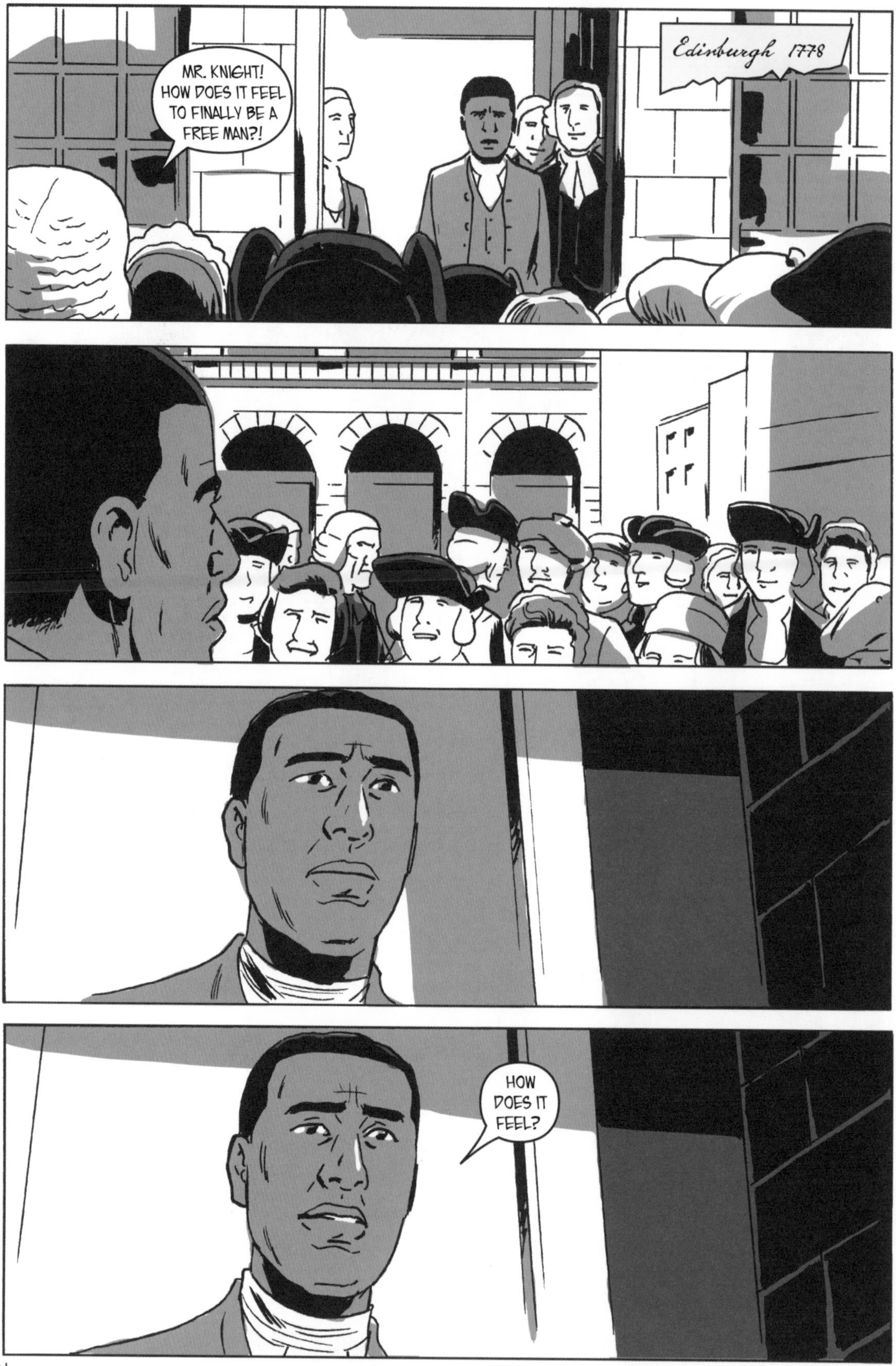
MR. KNIGHT! HOW DOES IT FEEL TO FINALLY BE A FREE MAN?!
Edinburgh 1778
HOW DOES IT FEEL?

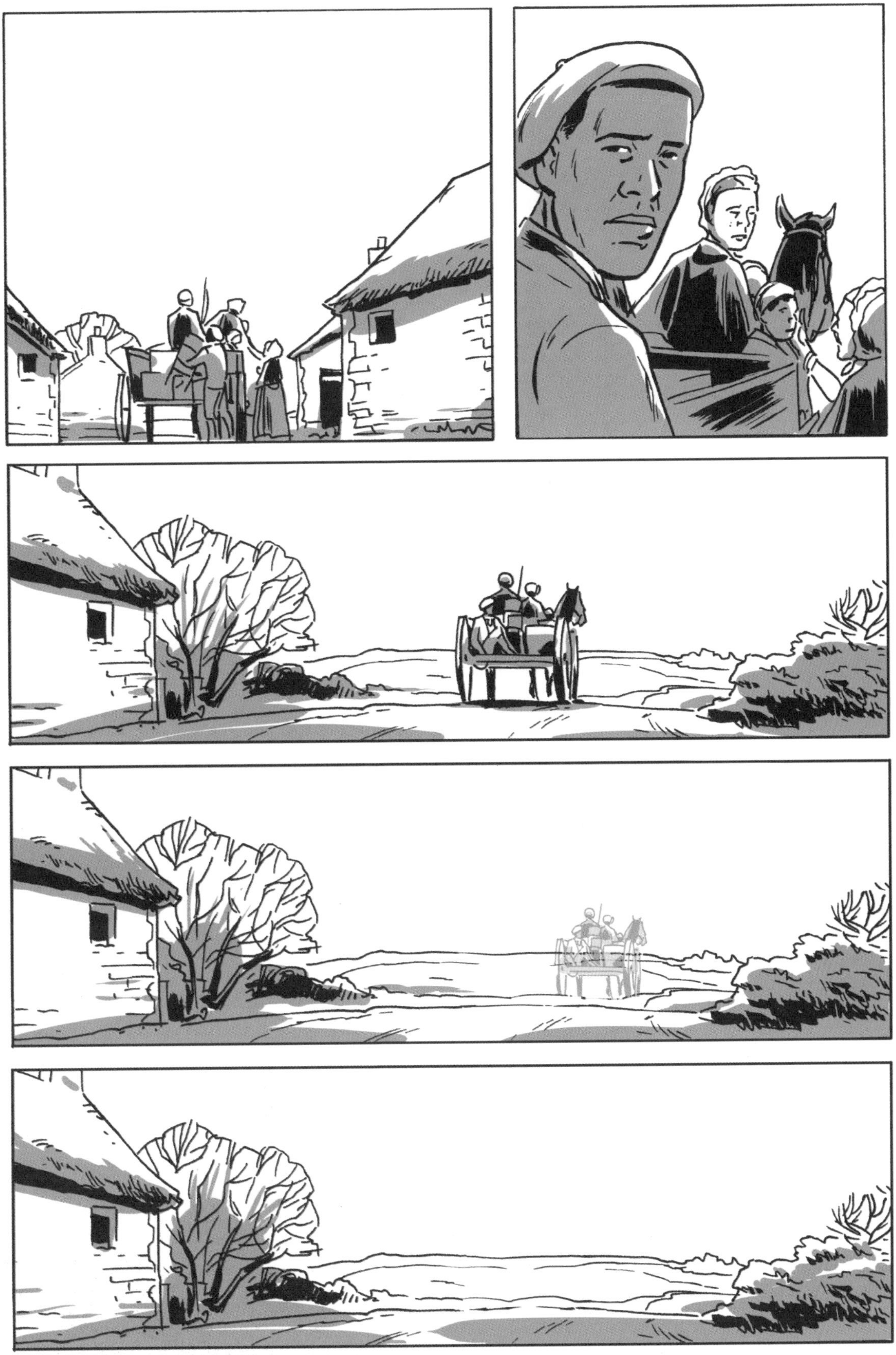

## Additional Materials

Additional information about
Ann (Chapter 1)............................**124**

Additional information about
Jamie Montgomery (Chapter 2).........**126**

Additional information about
Joseph Knight (Chapter 3)..................**130**

Map of locations in Scotland.............**133**

Examples of runaway slave
advertisements...............................**134**

Examples of advertisements
for the sale of enslaved people..........**135**

The Transatlantic Slave Trade...........**136**

Racial slavery ...............................**137**

The legacy of runaways
on British soil................................**139**

Further reading and resources .........**140**

# Ann

We do not know anything about Ann and her life before or after she ran away from Dr. Gustavus Brown. Was her escape successful, and if so what kind of life did she have? Or was she recaptured and forced to return with Brown to his Maryland tobacco plantation? The first story in this book imagines one possibility.

Gustavus Brown had been born in Dalkeith in 1689 and was trained as a doctor at the University of Edinburgh. After emigrating to Maryland Brown established a successful medical practice and in 1711 married Frances Fowke, the daughter of a wealthy Maryland tobacco planter. They lived together at Brown's tobacco plantation at Rich Hill in Maryland, which was worked by enslaved men, women and children owned by Gustavus Brown. We do not know why Brown returned to Scotland in 1726-7, but it may have been to visit family, take care of business matters, and to show off his new-found wealth. It is unlikely that his wife Frances accompanied him, as she was pregnant and had two children under the age of five.

In North America and the Caribbean enslaved people were sometimes forced to wear iron collars and chains, often as punishment or to stop them from escaping. In Scotland and England these were unusual, but some masters fitted silver or brass collars to enslaved people in order to mark them as property, to make it difficult for them to escape, and to flaunt the master's wealth. Sir John Baptiste de Medina's portrait of the Jacobite *James Drummond, 2nd Titular Duke of Perth* (1700), which is on display in Scotland's National Portrait Gallery in Edinburgh, depicts an enslaved boy who is wearing a silver collar standing beside the Duke.

When Gustavus Brown died in 1762 an inventory of his property showed that the doctor was a wealthy man, owning property in Maryland and in Scotland. Included alongside the lists of his land, buildings, and livestock were the names of the forty-five enslaved people owned by Brown, and how much money each one was judged to be worth. A quite elderly woman named Nan was recorded as being worth only £35 (about half the value of a healthy young adult). Nan was a common nickname for women named Ann, so could this have been the Ann who Brown had taken to Scotland thirty-five years earlier? We can never know.

Run away on the 7th Instant from Dr Gustavus Brown's Lodgings in Glasgow, a Negro Woman, named Ann, being about 18 years of Age, with a Green Gown and a Brass Collar around her Neck, on which are engraved these Words ["Gustavus Brown in Dalkieth his Negro, 1726."] Whoever apprehends her, so as she may be recovered, shall have Two Guineas Reward, and necessary Charges, allowed by Laurance Dinwiddie Junior Merchant in Glasgow, or by James Mitchellson, Jeweller in Edinburgh.

*Edinburgh Evening Courant*
13 February 1727, p.4.

## Sources


Hayden, Horace Edwin. *Virginia Genealogies. A Genealogy of the Glassell Family of Scotland and Virginia* (1891), (Baltimore, Maryland: Clearfield, 2004), 147-8, 151-2.

Conway, Moncure Daniel. *Autobiography, Memories and Experiences of Moncure Daniel Conway* (Boston: Houghton, Mifflin and Company, 1904), I, 1-5.

Toner, J.M. Toner. 'A Sketch of the Life of Gustavus Richard Brown,' *Sons of the Revolution in State of Virginia Quarterly Magazine*, 2 (January 1923), 12.

Inventory of Gustavus Brown's possessions, taken 29 May 1762, recorded 20 July 1768, Charles County Inventories 1766-1773, Maryland, CR 39,592-1 CM 386-5, pages 203-9. Center for History and New Media, George Mason University, http://chnm.gmu.edu/probateinventory/pdfs/brown62.pdf (accessed 4 March 2018).

Sir John Baptiste de Medina, *James Drummond, 2nd Titular Duke of Perth* (1700), National Portrait Gallery, Edinburgh, https://www.nationalgalleries.org/art-and-artists/3473/james-drummond-2nd-titular-duke-perth-1673-1720-jacobite (accessed 4 March 2018).

# Jamie Montgomery

We know more about Jamie Montgomery thanks to detailed records from the court case following his recapture in Edinburgh. The court sought to determine whether Montgomery should be freed or returned to his master Robert Sheddan, and the story uses these records and stays close to Montgomery's own account of his life and experiences.

Jamie's parents may have been born in Africa and then sold to British slave traders and transported across the Atlantic on slave ships to Virginia, and it is probable that Jamie was born and spent some of his childhood working on a tobacco plantation. The Edinburgh court records include a bill of sale (dated 9 March 1750) which details the business transaction that saw 'One Negro Boy named Jamie' sold by Virginia planter Joseph Hawkins to Robert Sheddan for fifty-six pounds twelve shillings and five pence. Sheddan, from Beith in Ayrshire, was one of many West of Scotland merchants who were trading slave-grown tobacco between North America and Glasgow, and this trade brought great wealth to these merchants and the city.

In 1752 Jamie was taken from his family and community in Virginia and sent to the home of Sheddan's sister Elizabeth and her husband Robert Morrice, who was a skilled 'wright' (carpenter) in Beith. For a couple of years Jamie lived and worked with the Morrice family as an apprentice joiner, learning carpentry skills. He accompanied the family to church, and was baptised by the Rev. John Witherspoon, who would later move to America and become a leading revolutionary and a signer of the Declaration of Independence. Witherspoon's wife Elizabeth's maiden name was Montgomery, a fairly common name in Ayrshire, and perhaps

Fredricksburgh
March the 9 1750

Know all men by these present that I Joseph Hawkins of Spotselvenia County for & in Consideration of the Sum of Fifty Six pound twelve shillings & six pence Virginia Curr[en]cy to me in hand payd by Robert Shedden Merch[an]t in Fred[ricksburgh] the Rece[i]pt whereof I acknowledge Have bargain[e]d Sold & deliv[e]red & by these presents do bargain sell & deliver unto the said Robert Shedden One Negroe Boy Named Jamie, To have & to hold the said Negroe unto the said Robert Shedden his Executors administrators for Ever, And I the said Joseph Hawkins for my self my Executors & admin[istrato]rs shall & will warant & forever defend against all Persons whatsum Ever In witness whereof I have herunto sett my hand & seal this Ninth day of March One thousand seven hundred & fifty

Signed Seal[e]d & Deli[e]red Joseph Hawkins

Ja[mes] Hilldrop

Jo[h]n Stewart

The original Bill of Sale recording Robert Shedden's purchase of Jamie (National Records of Scotland, CS234/S/3/12).

she inspired Jamie to adopt this as his own surname: like most enslaved people in America he had not had a last name.

By 1753 Robert Sheddan had become a wealthy merchant, and he decided to move back to Scotland and purchase an Ayrshire estate named Morrishill. It seems likely that Sheddan was unhappy that Jamie was growing to manhood with a strong sense of his own identity and even his rights, having chosen a surname and joined a local church. The court records contain Sheddan's angry complaint that Jamie had 'got it into his Head, that by being baptized he would become free.' To Sheddan Jamie was a slave and his property, and he did not like the young man's 'Fancies of Freedom.' So Sheddan took Jamie away from his training with Robert Morrice, and instead of employing him as a trained carpenter Sheddan used Jamie for hard, unskilled labour. The court records include Jamie's complaint that Sheddan employed him 'in the most slavish and servile business', suggesting that Jamie had begun to recognise himself as having certain skills and rights. Sheddan even refused to recognise the name 'Jamie Montgomery', and renamed the young man 'Shanker'.

The court records show that Jamie and Sheddan disagreed about what happened next. Robert Sheddan's brother Matthew was returning to Virginia, and the two of them decided to send Jamie back there and sell him as a skilled, and therefore valuable, enslaved carpenter. Sheddan promised Jamie that he would be reunited with his family and friends, and later he told the court that Jamie willingly went to join the ship at Port Glasgow. However, Jamie testified that he had been forcibly taken from his bed, tethered to a horse and dragged to Port Glasgow under cover, 'not upon the King's high way, but thro' muirs or lonely places, and other by-roads'. While waiting for the ship to Virginia, Jamie escaped and made his way to Edinburgh, a journey of almost seventy miles. To run away was a momentous decision for the

RUN away from the Subscriber, living near Beith, Shire of Ayr, **ONE NEGROE MAN**, aged about 22 Years, five Feet and a half high or thereby. He is a Virginia born Slave, speaks pretty good English; he has been five Years in this Country, and has served sometime with a Joiner; he has a deep Scare above one of his Eyes, occasioned by a Stroke from a Horse; he has also got with him a Certificate, which calls him James Montgomerie, signed, John Witherspoone Minister. Whoever takes up the said Run-away, and brings him home, or secures him, and gets Notice to his Master, shall have two Guineas Reward, besides all other Charges paid, by me

ROB. SHEDDEN.

Morrishill, April 26th 1756.

N.B. The Negroe run away the 21st Inst.

*Glasgow Journal*, 3 May 1756, p.3.

*May 13th 1756*

*Then received from David Murray Stabler in Edin.*
*The sum two pounds two shillings Sterling Money for apprehending one Negro Black who [is] named James Montgomerie according to the advertisement in the newspapers and also received from the said David Murray six shillings sterling for maintaining and other payments laid out for the said Black by*

*John Braidwood*

Written at the bottom of the Bill of Sale, in different handwriting, is the receipt for the reward paid to John Braidwood for capturing Jamie Montgomery young man, because by escaping he likely knew that he would never return to see his family and friends in Virginia. But Jamie had grown to manhood in Scotland: he had acquired a profession and joined a church, and apparently saw a future for himself. Not long after arriving in Edinburgh, he appears to have found work with another carpenter, Peter Wright.

Unfortunately for Jamie, John Braidwood (an officer of the Baillie Court in Edinburgh) found the young man and imprisoned him in the Edinburgh tolbooth (jail). Braidwood them claimed Sheddan's offer of two guineas reward 'for apprehending one Negro Black boy named James Montgomerie'. Jamie was incarcerated for the duration of the court case, but the tolbooth was an unhealthy place and he died before the judges reached a verdict. However, a note on some of the court documents recorded that 'it seemed to be the Opinion of the Lords, that he [the enslaved man Jamie Montgomery] ought to go back to his Master', and thus it appears probable that had Jamie survived he would have been returned to Sheddan, who would then surely have sent him back to a life of slavery in Virginia.

" As the Respondent had the Prospect, at that Time, of going to Scotland; it was, at the Time of the Sale, agreed betwixt Captain Hawkins and him, that if the Memorialist would get him bred to the Business of a Joiner, Mr Hawkins would afterwards take him back from the Memorialist, repeat the Price, repay the Charges, and besides give a 1000 Pound Weight of Tobacco to the Memorialist...

Some Time ago the Negroe got it into his Head, that by being baptized he would become free; and for that Reason was very pressing for the Ceremony of Baptism, which the Memorialist all along opposed, not so much from any Fear of the Civil Effects thereof, as for the Fancies of Freedom which it might instill into his Slave. However, at the pressing Instances of the Negroe, he was baptized by the Minister of Beith; but was over and over again told by him, that his Baptism by no means freed him from his Servitude...

## Sources

Bill of Sale, dated Fredricksburgh, 9 March 1750, National Records of Scotland, CS234/S/3/12. The receipt for payment of the reward for recapturing Jamie Montgomery is also written on this document. See http://webarchive.nrscotland.gov.uk/20170106021747/http://www.nas.gov.uk/about/070823.asp (accessed 4 March 2018).

*Memorial for James Montgomery – Sheddan [sic]; against Robert Sheddan* (23 July 1756), Advocates Library, Session Papers, Campbell's Collection.

*Memorial for Robert Sheddan of Morrice Hill, Late Merchant in Glasgow* (9 July 1756), Session Papers, Campbell's Collection, Advocates Library, Edinburgh. The note suggesting that Shedden might have been about to win his case is written on this document.

Cairns, John W. 'Enforced Sojourners: Enslaved Apprentices in Eighteenth-Century Scotland,' in *Ad Fontes: Liber Amicorum prof. Beatrix van Erp-Jacobs*, ed. E.J.M.F.C. Broers, et al (Oisterwijk: Wolf Legal Publishers, 2014), 67-81.

_____. 'Slavery without a *Code Noir*: Scotland 1700-78,' in Felix M. Larkin and N.M. Dawson, eds., *Lawyers, the law and history* (Dublin: Four Courts Press, 2013) 148-78.

Newman, Simon P. 'Rethinking Runaways in the British Atlantic World: Britain, the Caribbean, West Africa and North America.' *Slavery & Abolition*, 38, 1 (2017), 49-75.

Men may talk of abstract Rights or Wrongs as they please; but what Mankind in general concur in, is generally right: And therefore, according to these Principles, we find that Slavery has at one Time or other been adopted by almost every Nation under the Sun...

And indeed as every other Nation who have Settlements in these Parts the Americas] cultivate them by Slaves, we are necessituated to do the same; the Want of Slavery would be attended with the Want of our Colonies and Trade in those Parts...

it would be absurd, that a Man by crossing a Mountain or a River should be in a certain Condition one Day, and in another the next; or that a Negroe who is a Slave in America should by the Chance of being driven into Europe in a Storm, or by running away from his Master and escaping into Europe, become thereby in a Moment a Freeman..."

Memorial for Robert Sheddan of Morrice-hill (Advocates' Library, Session Papers, Campbell's Collection, V)

"it seemed to be the Opinion of the Lords, that he [Jamie Montgomery] ought to go back to his Master"

Hand-written note added to Memorial for Robert Sheddan, page 1 (Signet Library, Collection of Session Papers, Edinburgh)

"However, the defender found time and leisure upon holy-days, and particularly on the Sabbaths, to be instructed in the principles of our holy religion; and after satisfying and convincing proofs both of his conversion and of his sincerity, by a well ordered life and conversation, was publicly baptized, by order and injunction of the presbytery, about two years ago...

But... the pursuer and his associates seized the defender, living under the protection, and in the pursuer's own house, in the parish of Beith, and ordered him to be bound and fettered with ropes, and in the dead hour of the night the pursuer, together with Matthew Sheddan, and James his brother, Morris and Gavin Montgomery of Barogan, and others, having got on horseback, inhumanly and barbarously drove and dragged the defender from the pursuer's house, to New-Port-Glasgow, being about ten miles distance, not upon the king's highway, but thro' muirs or lonely places, and other by-roads, and imprisoned him in the house of Robert Hunter butcher there; from whence, in the same night, they carried him a-ship-board: but as he could not be so well secured and confined there, he was brought back in a few hours to the said Hunter's house, where the pursuer and his associates watched and kept a guard on him all night, and next day, the 13th of April... when the pursuer was prevailed upon to allow him liberty for a walk down the key, which was necessary for the recovery of his health, after such barbarous and unheard of treatment. The defender is not ashamed to acknowledge that he made a different use of the short interval of liberty; for not chusing to court the violence and oppression of the pursuer... he attempted, and happily made his escape to Edinburgh, where he enjoyed for a short time his personal liberty, and the protection of the laws; but upon an advertisement in the news papers he was apprehended a second time, and committed prisoner to the city-guard...

The defender is sorry to observe, that a question has been made of the most valuable and inestimable rights of mankind, and that in Scotland it has become a doubt if the subjects are free men: nay, the point is carried so far, that slavery is asserted and chained upon the subjects; the defender put out of the protection of his majesty, of his laws, and magistrates...

And as he apprehends it to be the law that by setting foot in Scotland he became free, as also by the subsequent baptism publicly administered in the church..."

Memorial for James Montgomery-Sheddan (Advocates' Library, Session Papers, Campbell's Collection, V)

# Joseph Knight

The Knight v. Wedderburn court case in 1778 which determined that Joseph was not the enslaved property of John Wedderburn has left many records telling us about this young man and his life. Our story is based on what we know of Joseph's life, with some imagined additions to fill the gaps in the records.

Joseph was born in about 1753 in West Africa, although we do not know his original African name. It is possible that he was aboard the *Phoenix*, a slave ship which took nearly 300 enslaved people from the Gold Coast to Montego Bay, Jamaica where they arrived in April 1765. The ship was captained by John Knight who may have owned the young boy and given him the name Joseph Knight: often ship captains and officers were allowed to buy several slaves in Africa and sell them on their own account. Knight sold the boy, then aged around thirteen, to John Wedderburn, a Scottish planter who owned the profitable Glen Islay sugar plantation.

Wedderburn was the son of Sir John Wedderburn, a Scottish nobleman who had been executed after the failure of the 'Forty-Five' Jacobite uprising. Following the loss of his father's title and the confiscation of the family's property, the young John Wedderburn had gone to Jamaica where he became very wealthy. Wedderburn appears to have become fond of Joseph, training him to be a personal servant rather than requiring him to work in the fields planting and harvesting sugar cane. Knight was dressed in the better clothing of a domestic servant rather than the rough garments of field slaves, and he had better food and living conditions. Wedderburn even began teaching Knight how to read and write.

Having made his fortune Wedderburn returned to Scotland in 1768. About 40 years old

Sir John Wedderburn, Deposition before the Sheriff of Perth, 15 November 1774 (National Records of Scotland, CS235/2/2)

[John Wedderburn] has the best reason to believe [Joseph Knight] thought himself fully as happy as any Servant in Great Britain But having fallen under the dominian of one of the Fair Sex [Annie Thompson] not very famous for her virtues he has been thereby induced to desire to leave the complainers service Because he would not agree to all her extrivagant fancies.

[Joseph Knight] first cohabited with [Annie Thompson] as his Mistress when she was a servant in [John Wedderburn's] house unknown to any person till at last her being with child made the discovery upon which she was discharged from her service.

Joseph and Annie had tried to hide their relationship from John Wedderburn and his wife, until Annie became noticeably pregnant, upon which Wedderburn sacked her.

Memorial for John Wedderburn against Joseph Knight, a Negro, 1775 (National Records of Scotland, CS235/2/2)

That by the practice and Laws of England, and after the Union of Great Britain, that the point is intirely fixed and Established that the practice of furnishing America and the West India colonies with slaves from Africa is considered as perfectly legal and supported by various grants from the Crown and Acts of Parliament.

Baptism does not alter the Condition of a Negro– there is a fancy which sometimes enters into the heads of the Negro themselves when brought to this Country that Baptism gives them a title to their freedom.

Some enslaved black men and women believed that by becoming Christian and being baptised they would become free and equal with white people.

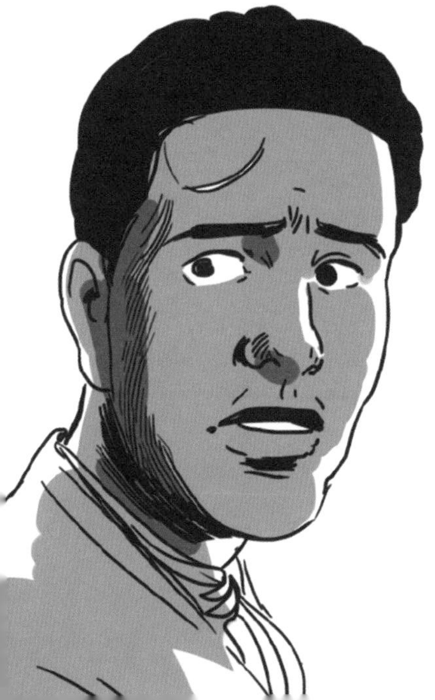

and a very wealthy man, he married Margaret Ogilvy (the daughter of the 6th Early of Airlie), and set about restoring his family's ancestral lands and titles. Wedderburn brought Knight back to his Ballindean estate in Perthshire to live with and serve him as his personal manservant.

Knight was one of many servants in and around Ballindean and at some point the young man fell in love with another servant named Ann Thomson, who subsequently became pregnant. Wedderburn refused Knight's request for a salary, nor would he give Knight and Ann permission to marry and live on a small house on the estate. Instead, Wedderburn fired Ann and he expected Knight to have nothing further to do with her, and to continue his work as a manservant. However, Joseph Knight ignored his master and married Ann on 9 March 1773.

During the months that followed Knight continued working in Wedderburn's house, although relations between the two men were not good. At about this time Knight happened to read a short article in the *Edinburgh Advertiser* newspaper about Lord Mansfield's decision in the Somerset v. Stewart case in England, which had resulted in the enslaved man James Somerset being freed. Knight assumed that the decision applied to him too (not realising that England and Scotland had quite different legal systems), and he promptly ran away from Ballindean to live with Ann in Dundee. Feeling angry and betrayed Wedderburn began court proceedings to confirm his ownership of Knight and his right to command Knight's labour, but late in 1774 the Sheriff of Perthshire ruled 'That the State of Slavery is not recognised by the Laws of this Kingdom, and is inconsistent with the principles thereof and Found that the Regulations in Jamaica concerning slaves do not extend to this Kingdom and repelled the Defender's Claim to perpetual Service.' Wedderburn was unhappy with the decision and appealed the decision to the Court of Sessions in Edinburgh, but four years later they too ruled that Wedderburn did not have the right to send Knight back to slavery in Jamaica. Moreover, although the court was divided (with some of the twelve judges believing that Wedderburn was entitled to the perpetual service of Knight) the majority confirmed the ruling of the lower court: Knight was entitled to his freedom. Unfortunately, at this point that Joseph Knight disappears from the records, and we know nothing of the life that he, Ann and their family then enjoyed.

## Sources

*Joseph Knight v Sir John Wedderburn: Question of right of property in a Negro slave.* Extract process, CS 235/K/2/2. Information for Joseph Knight (1775), additional information (1776), information for John Wedderburn (1775), additional information (1777). National Records of Scotland. For details see http://catalogue.nrscotland.gov.uk/nrsonlinecatalogue/details.aspx?reference=CS235%2fK52f2%2f2&st=1&tc=y&tl=n&tn=n&tp=n&k=&ko=a&r=CS235%2fK%2f2%2f2&ro=s&df=&dt=&di=y

Cairns, John W. 'After Somerset: The Scottish Experience,' *The Journal of Legal History*, 33, 3 (2012), 291-312.

————. 'Knight, Joseph (b. c. 1753).' In *Oxford Dictionary of National Biography*, online ed. Oxford and New York: Oxford University Press, 2009. http://www.oxforddnb.com.ezproxy.lib.gla.ac.uk/view/10.1093/ref:odnb/9780198614128.001.0001/odnb-9780198614128-e-93749?rskey=UIeT8g&result=1 (accessed 4 March 2018).

————. 'Knight v. Wedderburn', in David Dabydeen, John Gilmore and Cecily Jones, eds., *The Oxford Companion to Black British History* (Oxford: Oxford University Press, 2007), 244-6.

Robertson, James. *Joseph Knight* (London: Harper Collins, 2003). (A fictional account).

Memorial for Joseph Knight late servant to Sir John Wedderburn of Ballindean Baronet (National Records of Scotland, CS235/2/2)

He observed in Summer 1772 an article in the newspapers mentioning the noted decision of the Court of Kings bench in England in favour of Sommerset the Negro, and he judged from thence that he also was entitled to be free. At the same time as he felt gratitude to his Master for his good usage of him, he remained quietly in his service till after his marriage with a girl who had been a maidservant also in the family. It was then very natural for him to wish to procure some place of residence for his wife in the Neighbourhood where he lived he accordingly apply'd to Sir John for a house for his wife to live in but this Sir John absolutely refused, so he had no other alternative but to quit his service or live separate from his wife.

The free & haughty spirit of the Scots never stooped to a foreign Yoke, and it cannot be supposed that a nation of Aborigines would stoop to a more humbling domestic one... but where is there a shadow of ground to believe that ever a Scotsman considered himself as the property as the chattel as the slave of his Brother?

In the case Somerset v Stewart (1772) Lord Mansfield ruled that under Common Law slavery was not allowed in England and Wales: the decision did not apply to Scotland, which had a different legal system, but Joseph Knight did not realise this.

Knight and his lawyers sought out ways of arguing that Scottish law, like English law, did not allow slavery on home soil.

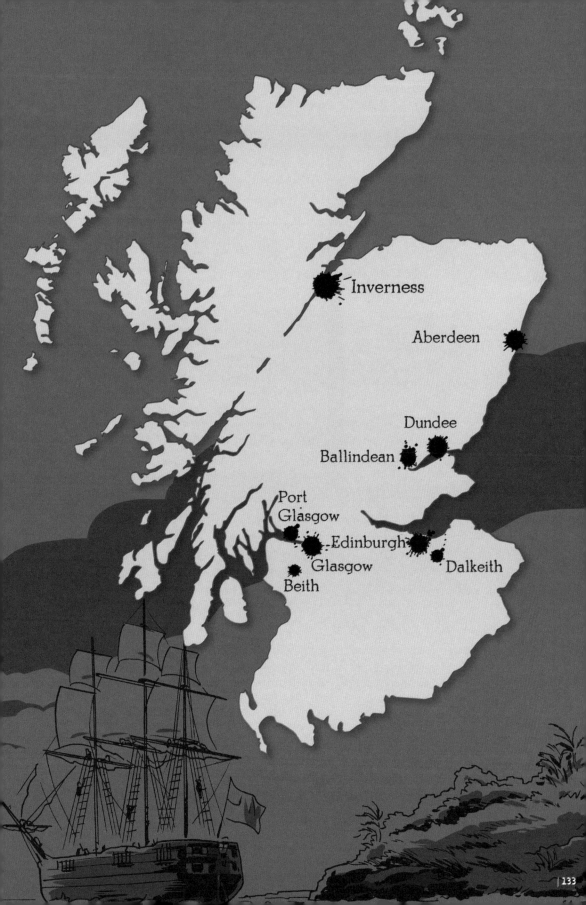

Inverness

Aberdeen

Dundee

Ballindean

Port
Glasgow

Edinburgh

Glasgow

Dalkeith

Beith

# Examples of runaway slave advertisements

Glasgow Journal (Glasgow),
26 July 1770, p.4.

## RUNAWAY.

FROM the Subscriber in Glasgow, an African Negro Boy named Boyd, about 16 years of age, well made, has a small scar (or Country mark) on one side of his face, and speaks rather broken English, wore a brown coat and waist coat, blue breeches and a bonnet, when he went off, He was seen at Greenock on the 11th Instant, but has not been heard of since.

Whoever shall secure said boy, so as his master may have him again shall be handsomely rewarded.

JAMES KIPPEN.

Daily Post (London), 11 January 1724, p.2.

A Negroe Slave, going by the Name of Beatrix, aged about 15 Years, tall of her Age, with a flat Nose, and Scars on each of her Temples, from bleeding, and very thick Lips; who is also bound Apprentice; went from her Service in Devonshire-street, near Queen Square, Holborn, on Tuesday last about 8 a-Clock in the Evening, taking several Things of her Mistresses. She is used to go with a coloured or white Handkerchief about her Wooly Head, wearing a Stuff Crimson and White strip'd Jacket, with a brown and white strip'd Sattin Petticoat, or a blue and white chequer'd Holland one; sometimes a strip'd white Dimmity Gown and Petticoat: She is supposed to be deluded away. Whoever gives Notice where she may be found, to Mrs. Smith, Stationer in Boswell-Court, or to Mrs. Church, a Glover, next the Fountain Tavern in the Strand, shall have a Guinea Reward.

Daily Post (London), 28 October 1732, p.2.

WHEREAS Christopher Corydon, a Negro, Servant to Mr. Arthur Vaughan, of Red-Lion-street, Holbourn, did on Friday the 15th of September last run away from his Master's Service, and has not been heard of since; this is to caution all Persons whatever not to harbour or entertain the said Black, unless they have an Inclination to be prosecuted for the same; and if any Person will secure the said Black, and bring him to Capt. Pritchard, at Mr. Samuel Brookes's in Seething-lane near Tower-street, shall have Two Guineas Reward; but if the said Christopher Corydon will (of his own accord) return home, his Master absolutely promises him Forgiveness, and declares, that no Consideration shall induce him to send the said Corydon beyond the Sea, the Fear of which ('tis believ'd) occasion'd his leaving his Service; but that upon making a due Submission for his Fault, he may be assur'd he shall be kindly receiv'd.

N.B. He is a young Lad of 17 Years of Age, not five Feet high, has a good Countenance, a well-turn'd Body, a Scar on his right Eyebrow, and bow Legs; he speaks good English, and had on, when he went away, a blue Cloth Coat, the Sleeves turn'd up with red, and Brass Buttons.

Caledonian Mercury (Edinburgh), 12 January 1774, p.3.

There is now in the Prison at Glasgow a MULATTO or INDIAN BOY, who calls himself Essex Peter, and who has Indented for a certain Term of Years as a Servant to Jamaica: Any Persons who have Pretensions to hinder the said Boy, are desired to apply to James Denniston Merchant in Glasgow; otherwise he will be accordingly transported the Beginning of February next.

# Examples of advertisements for the sale of enslaved people

*Liverpool General Advertiser*, or *Commercial Register* (Liverpool), Friday 15th October 1779, p.3.

TO BE SOLD by Auction,
At George Dunbar's office, on Thursday next, the 21st instant, at one o'clock,

A Black **BOY** about 14 years old, and a large Mountain Tyger **CAT**.

*Daily Advertiser* (London), 12 March 1741, p.2.

TO BE SOLD
A Very clever Negro Boy, about nineteen Years of Age, has had the Small-Pox, if any Gentleman or Lady has a Mind to see him, by directing a Letter to Mr. Kemp, in West-Smithfield, where to come, they will be waited on.

Note, a House at Highgate, having a very pleasant Prospect, to be let [sic]. Enquire at the Castle at Highgate, or at the above Mr. Kemp's.

*Gazetteer* and *Daily Advertiser* (London), 25 May 1765.

TO be disposed of, a Creole Negro Girl, about twelve years of age; has been in England a year in an English family, during which time she has had the small-pox, can speak English very well, and is very tractable in household affairs. Please to direct or enquire at the Cherry-garden coffee-house in Cherry-garden-street, Rotherhithe, where the principal and the girl may be seen.

*Evening Post* (London), 20 November 1716, p.3.

TO be dispos'd of a likely young Negro Man, about nineteen Years of Age, that speaks English and Shaves well, being fit for a Footman, or to wait on a Gentleman. Also a light plain Serviceable Chariot lin'd with grey Cloth (with or without a pair of Harness) fit for Town or Country. Inquire of Mr. Syddall at George Alehouse in New North-street, near Red Lyon-Square.

*Edinburgh Evening Courant* (Edinburgh), 18 April 1768, p.3.

A BLACK BOY to sell.
TO be sold a **BLACK BOY**, with long hair, stout made, and well limb'd, is good tempered, can dress hair and take care of a horse indifferently. He has been in Britain near three years.

Any person that inclines to purchase him, may have him for 40 l. He belongs to Captain Abercrombie at Broughton.

This advertisement not to be repeated.

*Daily Post* (London), 26 May 1725, p.1.

A beautiful Negro Boy about eight Years of Age, lately come from Barbadoes, to be dispos'd off, any Person that pleases may see the Boy at Mrs Eades, at the Cabinet on Ludgate Hill near Fleet Bridge; who likewise sells Right Barbadoes Citron Water, and true French Hungary Water.

# The Transatlantic Slave Trade

The shipment of enslaved people across the Atlantic Ocean from Africa to the Americas was the largest forced migration in human history. Between 1500 and 1875 approximately 12.5 million African men, women and children were transported across the ocean to be worked as slaves. Roughly 65% were men, about 15% were women, and a shocking 20% were children.

The enslaved people's journey across the Atlantic is known as the Middle Passage. In order to cut costs and maximise the profits they could make in selling slaves, ship owners crammed as many people as possible into specially designed spaces below deck. These were horribly cramped: people were chained together lying down, without enough space to sit or stand. The voyage could take as long as three months, and poor sanitation and insufficient food and water meant that many people fell ill or contracted diseases. Approximately 12% of the enslaved Africans loaded on to these ships died before they reached the Americas. The slave ship crews threw the bodies of dead slaves overboard, and many were immediately consumed by sharks which regularly followed the slave ships across the ocean.

Olaudah Equiano was enslaved as a young boy but eventually secured his freedom and became an abolitionist in Britain. He wrote and published an autobiography describing his and other Africans' experiences of the Middle Passage.

The first object which saluted my eyes when I arrived on the coast was the sea, and a slave ship, which was then riding at anchor, and waiting for its cargo... I was soon put down under the decks, and there I received such a salutation in my nostrils as I had never experienced in my life: so that, with the loathsomeness of the stench, and crying together, I became so sick and low that I was not able to eat, nor had I the least desire to taste anything.

The stench of the hold while we were on the coast was so intolerably loathsome, that it was dangerous to remain there for any time... The closeness of the place, and the heat of the climate, added to the number in the ship, which was so crowded that each had scarcely room to turn himself, almost suffocated us. This produced copious perspirations, so that the air soon became unfit for respiration, from a variety of loathsome smells, and brought on a sickness among the slaves, of which many died... The shrieks of the women, and the groans of the dying, rendered the whole a scene of horror almost inconceivable.

Olaudah Equiano, *The Interesting Narrative of the Life of Olaudah Equiano* (London, 1789)

# Racial slavery

The major question about slavery in Britain's colonies is did it develop because of white people's belief in their own racial superiority, or was it the result of an 'unthinking decision' to employ slave labour? When English colonists arrived in North America and the Caribbean in the early seventeenth century their greatest need was for labour, and at first the plantations growing tobacco, then sugar and other crops used white labour from England, Scotland and Ireland, forcing convicts, vagrants and prisoners of war to work for fixed periods of as long as seven to ten years. At first many died, but as more and more survived and were freed, planters began looking for alternative sources of labour. From the mid-1600s onwards ships began arriving from Africa offering enslaved Africans for sale, and planters began purchasing them, as well as enslaved indigenous Americans.

For a brief period the labour system was quite fluid, and white and black plantation workers sometimes worked side-by-side, and the differences between them were not yet fixed in law. This soon changed as planters began buying more and more enslaved Africans who did not have to be freed, guaranteeing their owners a long-term source of labour. The legislative assemblies of American and Caribbean colonies developed 'slave codes', sets of laws that restricted the rights of enslaved Africans, differentiating them from white people. Slave codes helped develop a white belief in the inherent inferiority of Africans. This racism helped whites to justify their enslavement of black people, and their use of violence to force black people to work for them.

A great many enslaved Africans worked on plantations, often large-scale agricultural enterprises growing and processing crops such as sugar, tobacco, rice, cotton, coffee and indigo. These crops often required large labour forces working long hours, with overseers and slave drivers using whips and physical violence to force the enslaved people to work. Living in small and cramped shacks, often with more than one family in a small, single room dwelling, the enslaved were often poorly fed and clothed, and the hard work and poor diet meant that many were weak and susceptible to disease and illness. For much of the period between the 1650s and 1800 it was often financially attractive to planters to work enslaved people so hard that they quickly died, and then buy more enslaved people to replace them.

Over the course of the 17th and 18th centuries British conceptions of racial difference hardened into a particularly extreme form of racism, backed up by law. British people came to regard Africans and their descendants as uncivilized, savage and heathen, and racism and slavery became mutually reinforcing. Although some white servants and labourers had been worked with unusual brutality early in the colonial period, this never compared with the extremes of racial slavery, and while whites had been forced to work for fixed periods enslaved Africans (and some indigenous Americans) were enslaved for life, and their children inherited this condition.

Almost all enslaved Africans and indigenous Americans owned by Britons lived and worked in the American and Caribbean colonies, mostly on plantations, but also on farms and a few as household servants. Some were urban workers and even sailors. On rare occasions masters decided to take enslaved people with them when they went to Britain, and over the course of the 1600s and 1700s thousands of enslaved people came to Britain, but these were only ever a tiny minority of the enslaved people in the British colonies. At the same time Britons who spent time in South Asia occasionally brought servants from India to Britain, and some of these were enslaved.

# The legacy of runaways on British soil

## By May Sumbwanyambe

Looking at runaway slave advertisements, an argument can be put forward that black history and British history are one and the same thing.

This vital information, is a powerful antidote to what I consider to be mainstream and frankly poisonous notions that exist in this society saying exactly the opposite. In most recent times these mainstream ideas have shaped the history of black identity and how it relates to Britain in the rhetoric of the political right wing. We are all familiar with common refrain that people "want their country back", that they want to go back to a time, perhaps, before the Windrush passengers from the Caribbean arrived on British shores 70 years ago, when everyone in Britain was white.

This ignorance about the depth of British history that black people were factually part of is not unique to white Britons. Exploring eighteenth-century runaway slave advertisements (https://www.runaways.gla.ac.uk/) during my research for my radio play, stage play and screenplay about the Slave Joseph Knight, challenged my preconceptions in invaluable ways, as a black Briton wanting to know more about his history and also as a playwright trying to shape a new narrative about the slave Joseph Knight. For example, whilst I knew that there were many slaves in Britain during the 18th century, I didn't know that there were 30,000 black people living in London at a time when London had 6.1 million in total population.

This runaway slave advertisements helped me join the dots and begin to form an understanding of what Joseph Knight would have experienced. It helped me dramatize the possibility that like many other runaway slaves of that time he would have seriously considered travelling to East London as it was something of a safe haven - a place and a community in which runaway slaves could hide.

And simply as a Black Scot these advertisements and their stories are invaluable. Seeing evidence that there were at least 60 black runaways (of a much larger black Scottish population) reported in newspapers of the day demonstrated that no matter which part of the British Isles you call home, black people have a history to look towards and draw from.

These sources, and the people whose stories they tell, have already challenged my preconceptions in a profound way. They articulate how from the creation of the Union of England and Scotland (1707) Britain has never truly been an island nation of one race and challenge the dangerous myths that black people have only been part of this country's history for a very short time.

May Sumbwanyambe was born in Scotland and grew up in England, and proudly describes himself as Black British. He is an award-winning playwright, and has recently completed a play about Joseph Knight for the National Theatre of Scotland and the BBC.

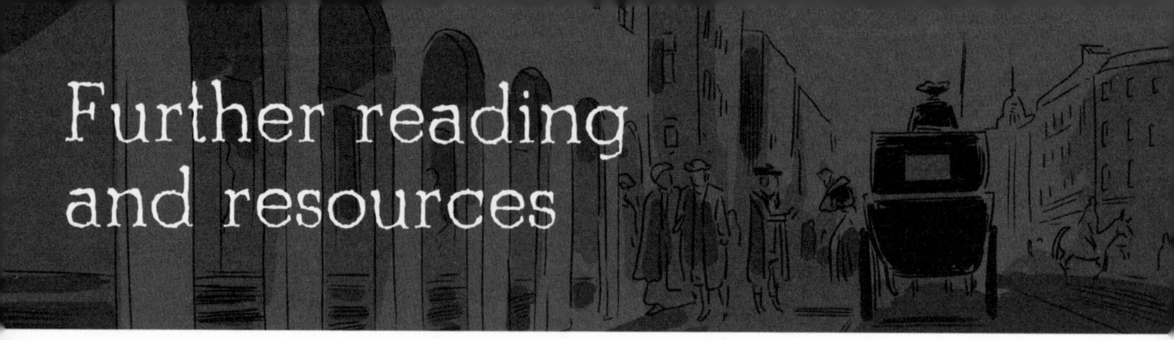

# Further reading and resources

## Primary sources


Olaudah Equiano, *The interesting narrative and other writings*, ed. Vincent Carretta (2003)

Ignatius Sancho, *Letters of the Late Ignatius Sancho: An African*, ed. Vincent Carretta (2015)

Granville Sharp, *A Representation of the Injustice of Tolerating Slavery in England* (1769)


## Race and slavery in eighteenth-century Britain


Stephen Ahern, ed., *Affect and Abolition in the Anglo-Atlantic: 1770–1830* (2013)

Anthony J. Barker, *The African Link: British Attitudes to the Negro in the Era of the Atlantic Slave Trade, 1550-1807* (1978)

George Boulukos, *The grateful slave: The emergence of race in eighteenth-century British and American culture* (2011)

Stephen J. Braidwood, *Black Poor and White Philanthropists* (1994)

John W. Cairns, 'Slavery without a *Code Noir*: Scotland 1700-78,' in Felix M. Larkin and N.M. Dawson, eds., *Lawyers, the law and history* (2013)

Brycchan Carey, *British Abolitionism and the Rhetoric of Sensibility: Writing, Sentiment and Slavery*, 1760– 1807 (2005)

Kathleen Chater, 'Black People in England, 1660-1807,' *Parliamentary History*, 26 (2007), 68-72

________, *Untold Histories: Black people in England and Wales during the period of the British slave trade*, c.1660-1807 (2009)

Linda Colley, Britons: *Forging the Nation, 1707–1837* (1992) (2005)

Ray Costello, *Black Salt: Seafarers of African Descent on British Ships* (2014)

David Dabydeen, *Hogarth's Blacks: Images of Blacks in Eighteenth Century English Art* (1987)

Audrey Dewjee, 'Runaways,' *Black and Asian Studies Association*, 60, 61 (2011) 20-22

T.M. Devine, ed., *Recovering Scotland's slavery past: The Caribbean connection* (2015)

Seymour Drescher, 'Manumission in a society without slave law: Eighteenth century England', *Slavery and Abolition*, 10:3 (1989), 85-101

Madge Dresser and Andrew Hahn, *Slavery and the British Country House* (2013) http://content.historicengland.org.uk/images-books/publications/slavery-and-british-country-house/slavery-british-country-house-web.pdf/

Paul Edwards and David Dabydeen, eds., *Black Writers in Britain* 1760-1890 (1991)

C. Eickelmann and D. Small, *Pero: the Life of a Slave in Eighteenth-Century Bristol*, (2004)

Peter Fryer, *Black People in the British Empire* (1988)

________, *Staying Power: The History of Black People in Britain* (1984)

Jagdish S. Gundara and Ian Duffield, *Essays on the History of Blacks in Britain: From Roman Times to the Mid-twentieth Century* (1992)

J.J. Hecht, 'Continental and Colonial Servants in 18th Century England', *Smith College Studies in History*, Vol. 60 (1954), 33-49

Gretchen Holbrook Gerzina, *Black London: Life Before Emancipation* (1995), https://www.dartmouth.edu/~library/digital/publishing/books/gerzina1995/

Douglas A. Lorimer, 'Black slaves and English liberty: A re-examination of racial slavery in England', *Immigrants & Minorities*, 3:2 (1984), 121-150

Catherine Molineux, 'Hogarth's fashionable slaves:

moral corruption in eighteenth-century London,' *English Literary History* 72, 2 (2005), 495-520

Norma Myers, 'The black presence through criminal records, 1780–1830', *Immigrants & Minorities*, 7:3 (1988), 292-307

_____, *Reconstructing the Black Past: Blacks in Britain, 1780-1830* (1996)

David Olusoga, *Black and British: An untold story* (2016)

David Paisley, 'Black English in Britain in the Eighteenth Century,' *Electronic British Library Journal* (2015) https://www.bl.uk/eblj/2015articles/pdf/ebljarticle122015.pdf

Nicholas Phillipson and Rosalind Mitchison, eds. *Scotland in the Age of Improvement: Essays in Scottish History in the Eighteenth Century* (1970)

Folarin O. Shyllon, *Black Slaves in Britain* (1974)

_____, *Black People in Britain 1555-1833* (1977)

James Walvin, *Black Ivory: A History of British Slavery* (1992)

_____, *The Black Presence: A Documentary History of the Negro in England* (1971)

_____, *Black and white: The negro and English society*, 1555-1945 (1973)

Roxann Wheeler, *The Complexion of Race: Categories of Difference in Eighteenth-Century British Culture* (2000)

Iain Whyte, *Scotland and the Abolition of Black Slavery, 1756-1838* (2006)

Helena Woodward, *African-British Writings in the Eighteenth Century* (1999)

Rozina Visram, *Asians in Britain: 400 Years of History* (2002)

Rozina Visram, *Ayahs, Lascars, and Princes: Indians in Britain, 1700-1947* (1986)

# Runaway slaves

Antonio T. Bly, 'A Prince among Pretending Free Men: Runaway Slaves in Colonial New England Revisited,' *Massachusetts Historical Review*, 14 (2012), 87-118

Tom Costa, 'What Can We Learn From A Digital Database Of Runaway Slave Advertisements?' *International Social Science Review*, 76, 1/2 (2001), 36-43

Mary J. Gallant, 'Slave Runaways in Colonial Virginia: Accounts and Status Passage as Collective Process,' *Symbolic Interaction*, Vol. 15, No. 4 (1992), 389-412

Robert Hay, '"And Ten Dollars Extra, for Every Hundred Lashes Any Person Will Give Him, to the Amount of Three Hundred": A Note on Andrew Jackson's Runaway Slave Ad of 1804 and on the Historian's Use of Evidence,' *Tennessee Historical Quarterly*, 36, 4 (1977), 468-478

Gad Heuman, ed., *Out of the House of Bondage: Runaways, Resistance and Marronage in Africa and the New World* (1986)

Graham R. Hodges and Edward B. Alan, *"Pretends to Be Free": Runaway Slave Advertisements from Colonial and Revolutionary New York and New Jersey* (1994)

Michael P. Johnson, 'Runaway Slaves and the Slave Communities in South Carolina, 1799 to 1830.' *William and Mary Quarterly*, 3d. ser., 38 (1981), 418-41

Marvin L. Michael Kay and Lorin Lee Cary, 'Slave Runaways in Colonial North Carolina, 1748-1775,' *The North Carolina Historical Review*, 63, 1 (1986), 1-39

Daniel E. Meaders, 'South Carolina Fugitives as Viewed Through Local Colonial Newspapers with Emphasis on Runaway Notices, 1732-1801,' *Journal of Negro History*, 60 (1975), 288-319

Philip Morgan, 'Colonial South Carolina Runaways: Their Significance for Slave Culture,' *Slavery and Abolition* 6, 3 (1985), 57-78

Stephen Mullen, Nelson Mundell and Simon P. Newman, 'Black Runaways in Eighteenth-Century Britain' in *Britain's Black Past*, ed. Gretchen Gerzina (forthcoming)

Gerald W. Mullin, *Flight and Rebellion: Slave Resistance in Eighteenth-Century Virginia* (1972)

Simon P. Newman, 'Escaping Enslavement in Eighteenth Century Scotland.' Forthcoming in *Negotiating Status and Scope of Action: Interrelations between Slavery and Other Forms of Dependency in Early Modern Europe*, ed. Rebekka von Mallinckrodt (forthcoming)

_____, 'Hidden in Plain Sight: escaped slaves in late-18th and early-19th century Jamaica' in late-18th and early-19th century Jamaica,' *The William and Mary Quarterly* (2018)

_____, 'Rethinking Runaways in the British Atlantic World: Britain, the Caribbean, West Africa and North America.' *Slavery & Abolition*, 38, 1 (2017), 49-75

Robert M. Owens, 'Law and Disorder North of the Ohio: Runaways and the Patriarchy of Print Culture, 1793-1815,' *Indiana Magazine of History*, 103, 3 (2007), 265-289

Richard Price, ed., *Maroon Societies: Rebel Slave Communities in the Americas* (1979)

Jonathan Prude, "'To Look Upon the Lower Sort': *Runaway Ads and the Appearance of Unfree Laborers in America*, 1750-1800,' The Journal of American History, 78 no.1 (1991)

Cassandra Pybus, 'From Epic Journeys of Freedom Runaway Slaves of the American Revolution and Their Global Quest for Liberty,' *Callaloo*, 29, 1 (2006), 114-130

Karin Sennefelt, 'A Discerning Eye,' *Cultural and Social History*, 12:2, 179-195 (2015)

Billy G. Smith and Richard Wojtowicz, *Blacks Who Stole Themselves: Advertisements for Runaways in the Pennsylvania Gazette, 1728-1790* (1989)

Mitsuhiro Wada, 'Running from Bondage: An Analysis of the Newspaper Advertisements of Runaway Slaves in Colonial Maryland and Georgia,' *JSL*, 2, (2006), 11-21

David Waldstreicher, 'Reading the Runaways: Self-Fashioning, Print Culture, and Confidence in Slavery in the Eighteenth-Century Mid-Atlantic,' *The William and Mary Quarterly*, Third Series, 56, 2, African and American Atlantic Worlds (1999), 243-272

David Waldstreicher, *Runaway America: Benjamin Franklin, Slavery and the American Revolution* (2004)

Lathan A. Windley, A *Profile of Runaway Slaves in Virginia and South Carolina from 1730 through 1787* (1995)

# Web-resources

Africa's Sons Under Arms: https://warwick.ac.uk/fac/arts/history/research/projects/asua/

Legacies of British Slave-Ownership: https://www.ucl.ac.uk/lbs/

Voyages: The Trans-Atlantic Slave Trade Database: http://www.slavevoyages.org/

The Geography of Slavery in Virginia: Runaway Slaves: http://www2.vcdh.virginia.edu/gos/

Freedom on the Move: http://freedomonthemove.org/

North Carolina Runaway Slave Advertisements: http://libcdm1.uncg.edu/cdm/landingpage/collection/RAS

Runaway Slave Advertisements, Baltimore County, Maryland: http://www.afrigeneas.com/library/runaway_ads/balt-intro.html

Beacons of Freedom: Slave Refugees in North American 1800-1860: https://www.universiteitleiden.nl/en/research/research-projects/humanities/beacons-of-freedom-slave-refugees-in-north-america-1800-1860

Marronage in Saint-Domingue (Haiti): http://www.marronnage.info/en/accueil.php

Slavery Adverts 250: https://twitter.com/SlaveAdverts250

Black Presence: Asian and Black History in Britain, 1500-1850: http://www.nationalarchives.gov.uk/pathways/blackhistory/about.htm

The Black Presence in Britain: https://blackpresence.co.uk/

The Black Presence in Bristol: http://www.discoveringbristol.org.uk/slavery/

International Slavery Museum: http://www.liverpoolmuseums.org.uk/ism/

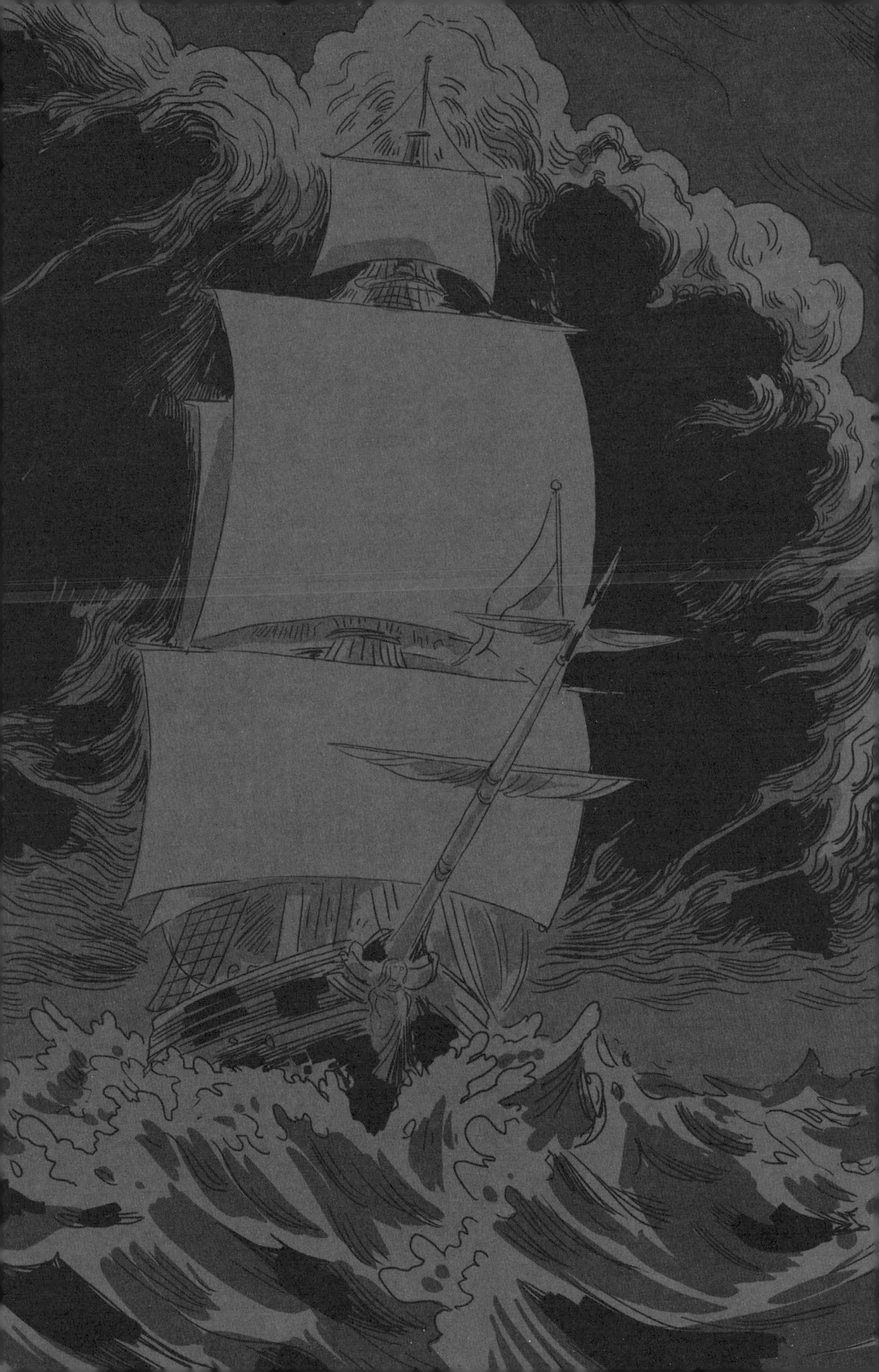